Instructor's Manual

for Comer's

Abnormal Psychology

Second Edition

Janet A. Simons
University of Iowa
School of Social Work

Ronald J. Comer
Princeton University

W. H. Freeman and Company
New York

ISBN 0-7167-2690-4

Printed in the United States of America

1 2 3 4 5 6 7 8 9 0 RRD 0 9 8 7 6 5 4

CONTENTS

PREFACE

It is my pleasure to revise the *Instructor's Manual* that accompanies the second edition of Ronald J. Comer's *Abnormal Psychology.* As with the first edition, I have tried to make this manual instructor friendly, simple, practical, and useful.

Each chapter is outlined to help instructors prepare appropriate lecture material. A list of appropriate learning objectives is provided in each chapter that not only help to focus lecture needs, but can be adapted to essay questions. Each chapter provides several suggestions for classroom instruction, many of them adaptable to large lecture sections. Many of these suggestions are new to this edition.

Some general suggestions for conducting a successful abnormal psychology course are included in the section "Especially for New Teachers." These suggestions are based on twelve years of teaching abnormal psychology at Des Moines Area Community College, two years of teaching at Upper Iowa University, and four years of teaching personality and psychopathology at the University of Iowa School of Social Work. After all these years of experience, I still review this list when I put a semester's syllabus together.

The sections "Book Resources for Instructors" and "General Resources: Media List" have been updated for this edition.

I hope you find this manual to be a worthwhile assistant in your abnormal psychology course.

Janet A. Simons, Ph.D.
University of Iowa School of Social Work
Des Moines Extension

About the Supplements Package

In addition to this *Instructor's Manual*, a notable set of supplements has been assembled to accompany *Abnormal Psychology*, Second Edition. They offer a variety of ways to facilitate your job of teaching, and will also make your course more stimulating, enjoyable, and ultimately more rewarding for your students. They are designed to appeal to first-time and veteran instructors alike. Additional supplements are:

Video Segments for Abnormal Psychology by Ronald J. Comer (ISBN 0-7167-2719-6)

For many years, Dr. Comer has had great success in supplementing his lectures with brief video clips that highlight and bring to life certain aspects of abnormal psychology in a way that just isn't possible on the printed page. Dr. Comer has now compiled the best of these clips into a series that correlates directly to his textbook coverage. There are approximately 50 segments, which average 2–3 minutes each. They vividly illustrate clinical topics, pathologies, treatments, historical footage, laboratory experiments, clinical dilemmas, and other useful subjects. Among the many benefits of this package is that you don't have to search through hours of film to find the right footage for your lecture. Dr. Comer has also prepared a *Video Guide* (ISBN 0-7167-2742-0) that describes ways of getting the best use out of each segment.

Test Bank by Melvyn B. King, Debra E. Clark, and Ronald J. Comer (printed version ISBN 0-7167-2691-2, computerized Macintosh version ISBN 0-7167-2693-9), (computerized IBM version ISBN 0-7167-2692-0)

This collection of approximately 2100 multiple-choice and 450 fill-in questions has been completely revised and bolstered for the new edition of the text. Each question comes with an answer, a page reference, a difficulty rating, and a type designation (factual or applied). They have been thoroughly checked to make sure they meet the highest standards of test-question construction, insuring that they are as error-free and unambiguous as possible. The computerized versions provides testing software that makes generating tests and quizzes quite simple. The software also affords you the opportunity to edit questions or to add your own.

And new to this edition for your students:

Student Workbook by Katherine M. Nicolai (ISBN: 0-7167-2695-5)
This all new supplement offers students at all levels a stimulating way to add to their understanding of the concepts and ideas presented in the textbook. Taking a "hands-on" approach, the *Student Workbook* offers hundreds of carefully-crafted exercises that not only draw upon the students' knowledge of the concepts, but also call upon them to apply the information in a way that demonstrates a deeper understanding of the material. The *Student Workbook* combines a variety of questioning approaches, including sample cases, flow charts, and tables. This variety will keep students engaged as they study, as will the thought-provoking exercises that call upon them to answer questions by putting themselves in the place of clinicians of a particular theoretical perspective. Also included are 15 multiple-choice questions for each chapter that are meant to serve as a final review and "warm-up" for students before they take tests. The *Student Workbook* will help students to leave the course with an enhanced understanding of the concepts and the dynamics of abnormal psychology.

W. H. Freeman and Company is interested in any suggestions, comments, or questions you have about any of the supplements in the Comer package. All comments and suggestions will be taken into consideration during the planning for future editions. Please address them to:

W. H. Freeman and Company
Supplements Editor
41 Madison Avenue
New York, New York 10010

CHAPTER

1

ABNORMAL PSYCHOLOGY: PAST AND PRESENT

■

TOPIC OVERVIEW

This chapter begins by defining psychological abnormality in terms of deviance, distress, dysfunction, and danger. Next, the chapter provides a historical perspective on defining and treating abnormality. Finally, the chapter introduces the current state of the field of abnormal psychology.

LECTURE OUTLINE

I.   Defining Psychological Abnormality

    A. Deviance
       1. Behavior diverges from the standard of appropriate and normal functioning.
       2. Behavior violates social norms.
       3. Behavior judged deviant varies from culture to culture.

    B. Distress
       1. Some theorists believe one's way of functioning must cause distress in addition to being unusual to qualify as deviant.
       2. Although unusual kinds of behavior can bring enjoyment, some unusual behavior is clearly abnormal whether or not distress is experienced.
       3. Indeed, euphoria and an unrealistic sense of well-being can enter into the diagnosis.

C. Dysfunction
   1. Dysfunctional behavior is abnormal behavior that interferes with daily living.
   2. Culture plays a role because it defines effective daily living.
   3. Some dysfunctional behaviors do not indicate psychological abnormality; e.g., the self-sacrifice of a hero.

D. Danger
   1. A behavior pattern of carelessness, poor judgment, hostility, or misinterpretation may result in danger to oneself or others.
   2. Most people struggling with anxiety and depression pose no immediate danger to themselves or anyone else.

E. Difficulties in defining psychological abnormality
   1. The definition is culturally relative, very selective, and subjectively interpreted.
   2. Thomas Szasz was a vocal critic of the label "mental illness" and preferred the term "problems in living.

II. Past Views and Treatment

A. Ancient views and treatments
   1. Although 20% of people currently have mental disturbances, mental illness is not a product of modern life.
   2. Early beliefs about the causes of mental illness focused on magic and evil spirits.
   3. Stone Age people practiced a crude operation called trephination, perhaps to release evil spirits.
   4. Early literate cultures (e.g., Egypt, China, Israel) all wrote about demonic causes of mental illness.
   5. One early treatment was exorcism, which consisted of a variety of methods for coaxing evil spirits from the body.

B. Greek and Roman views and treatments
   1. The Greeks described and named mental disorders, including melancholia, mania, dementia, and hysteria.
   2. Striking symptoms, such as delusions and hallucinations, were named and described.
   3. Hippocrates attributed mental disorders to brain pathology caused by an imbalance of bodily fluids called humors.
   4. Well-known philosophers and physicians also believed in treating mental illness by healing the underlying physical problems.

5. Treatments in these civilizations included a supportive atmosphere, music, massage, exercise, baths, sobriety, a vegetarian diet, bleeding, and restraints.

C. Europe in the Middle Ages: demonology returns
1. The collapse of the Roman Empire was also a collapse of scientific reasoning.
2. Plagues, wars, and urban uprisings undermined science and fostered belief in evil spirits.
3. Tarantism and lycanthropy were forms of mass madness in which many persons simultaneously shared the same symptoms, which were thought to be caused by demonic possession.
4. The clergy engaged in mild to severe forms of exorcism for treatment.
5. Toward the end of this period, hospitals and the medical view began to reappear.

D. The Renaissance and the rise of asylums
1. Johann Weyer was the first medical practitioner to specialize in mental illness.
2. Treatment focused on home care and pilgrimages to holy shrines.
3. Some hospitals and monasteries were converted into asylums, which over time became filthy and degrading in their treatment of patients.
4. England's "Bedlam" and Vienna's "Lunatics' Tower" are two examples of deplorable conditions endured by mental patients during this period.
5. Some treatments intended to help patients, such as Benjamin Rush's drawing of blood from patients, were based on wrong ideas and were cruel rather than therapeutic.

E. The nineteenth century: reform and moral treatment
1. Reform in this period is attributable to influential individuals who made dramatic changes in treatment.
2. Philippe Pinel and Jean-Baptiste Pussin led significant reforms in France.
3. William Tuke led humane changes in Europe.
4. Pinel's and Tuke's methods became known as moral treatment.
5. Moral treatment in the United States was first embraced by Benjamin Rush, who adopted this strategy over his earlier harsh methods.

6. Dorothea Dix campaigned for and succeeded in getting better mental hospitals in the United States.
7. The decline of moral treatment was due to money and staffing shortages; the inadequate number of professionals lowered recovery rates.
8. As recoveries dwindled, prejudice grew and people viewed the mentally ill as strange and dangerous.
9. Moral treatment worked with many patients, but others needed medicines and counseling techniques that had not yet been developed.
10. Clifford Beers's book *A Mind That Found Itself* informed many people about hospital conditions and the experience of mental illness.
11. The somatogenic perspective was advanced by Emil Kraepelin's classification system and by Richard von Krafft-Ebing's discovery that untreated syphilis caused the mental illness of general paresis.
12. Early medical treatments included hydrotherapy, insulin coma shock, lobotomies, tonsillectomies, and teeth extraction.
13. The roots of the psychogenic perspective are hypnotism and Freud's psychoanalysis.

III. Current Trends

A. New treatments for the severely disturbed
1. Psychotropic medications alleviate symptoms by their actions on the brain.
2. Under the deinstitutionalization policy, the number of mental patients hospitalized in the United States has dropped from 600,000 in 1955 to under 125,000 now.
3. Emphasis has shifted to the community mental health approach.

B. New treatment settings for less severe psychological problems
1. Most patients receive outpatient care.
2. Mental health treatment is increasingly included in medical health insurance programs.

C. Today's practitioners—psychiatrists, clinical psychologists, counseling psychologists, educational psychologists, psychiatric nurses, psychiatric social workers

D. Emerging perspectives
   1. Emphasis on psychoanalytic therapy has declined.
   2. More numerous, often competing types of counseling have been developed.
   3. More effective biological treatments have been developed.

E. The emphasis on research
   1. Understanding of the need for research has grown since World War II.
   2. Research findings have altered ideas about abnormal psychological functioning.

IV. Organization of the Text

A. Basic perspectives and tools of scientists and practitioners

B. Major categories of psychological abnormality and treatments for each

C. Social issues and interactions with the legal and social realms

LEARNING OBJECTIVES

1. Define abnormal psychology and know the goals of this area of psychology.
2. List the general characteristics of abnormal patterns of psychological functioning.
3. Describe the early historical views of abnormal psychology, including those of Stone Age cultures and the societies of ancient Greece and Rome.
4. Know the popular view of mental illness during the Middle Ages and how this belief affected society.
5. Contrast the treatments of the mentally ill during the Renaissance and during the sixteenth century.
6. Discuss the improvements in the case of the mentally ill during the nineteenth century and specifically know the contributions of Philippe Pinel, William Tuke, Benjamin Rush, and Dorothea Dix in these reforms.
7. Describe how both the somatogenic perspective and the psychogenic perspective emerged in the late nineteenth century.
8. Explain the relationship between the development of psychotropic drugs and the policy of deinstitutionalization.

9. Distinguish among the specialties of professionals who work with people who have psychological problems: psychiatrists, clinical psychologists, psychiatric social workers, counseling psychologists, educational psychologists, and psychiatric nurses.
10. Describe the major characteristics of current psychological perspectives: psychoanalytic, behavioral, cognitive, humanistic-existential, and sociocultural.

INSTRUCTION SUGGESTIONS

1. *Class discussion.* Use the people listed in Box 1-1 to generate a variety of discussion topics. You might ask students for other names to add to the list (e.g., Jane Fonda, eating disorder; Pete Rose, compulsive gambling). Discuss the variety of outcomes for these individuals. For example, Patty Duke was successfully treated for her bipolar disorder but Freddie Prinze and Ernest Hemingway committed suicide. Discuss the books that some of these people have written about their problems (e.g., Patty Duke's *Call Me Anna* and Mark Vonnegut's *The Eden Express*). You can launch a discussion of the stigma attached to mental illness by talking about Thomas Eagleton's withdrawal as a vice presidential candidate in 1972 because of public reaction to the disclosure that he had once been treated for depression.

2. *Class discussion and outside assignment.* Have students find newspaper articles, magazine articles, talk show guests, television programs, and/or films that deal with mental illness issues. Have them explore the quality of the coverage, the accuracy or inaccuracy of the images presented, the assumptions made about mental illness, and the usefulness of the coverage. You can adapt this discussion to a written assignment.

3. *Class discussion and outside assignment.* Ask students to visit local bookstores or public libraries to look at self-help books (you might assign specific problem areas to different students). Have them evaluate the quantity and the quality of such books. Ask them to bring in examples of books that seem to be fairly useful. You can adapt this assignment to a written assignment.

4. *Class project and discussion.* Have students, working in small groups of no more than six, write a list of words used to label normal persons

and a second list of words used to label abnormal persons. After several minutes, collate the lists into two master lists. You should find that more words are listed for abnormal persons than for normal ones. Ask the class to explain the difference in length. Ask them to evaluate the positive and negative aspects of the list. You may wish to point out the origins of some of the terms used for the abnormal (e.g., "lunatic" is derived from the old belief that the moon influenced behavior).

5. *Classroom demonstration.* Start and maintain a file of newspaper clippings that depict the four criteria of abnormality (distress, dysfunction, danger, deviance). You can use this file each semester, both in connection with this first chapter and then again for each appropriate diagnosis. Develop your file so that it includes both well-publicized cases and less notorious local cases (you may wish to remove the names of the individuals involved).

6. *Class discussion.* Introduce students to the ideal that it is not only individuals that can be dysfunctional—families, workplaces, neighborhoods, and whole cultures can be dysfunctional. You might ask if any students have worked in a dysfunctional workplace (a "crazy-making job"). If so, you can ask them to describe the features that were dysfunctional (e.g., vindictive personnel, chaotic management, rules that kept changing, confusion, blaming, unethical practices).

7. *Minilecture: The Biblical Tradition*
   You can add to the text's material on the early Greek and Roman cultures by introducing students to early Judeo-Christian views on mental illness, or the biblical view. Here are some points you may include.
   *Both the Old Testament and the New Testament refer to evil spirits as the cause of mental illness. In the Old Testament, for example, King Saul's evil spirits are soothed when David plays his harp. In the New Testament, Jesus coaxes the evil spirits from a man and transfers them to swine.
   *The Judeo-Christian tradition also is a source of some people's belief that homosexuality is a mental illness. This belief is based on the interpretation of the book of Leviticus, which lists several prohibitions (e.g., do not eat shellfish, do not wear clothing made of mixed fibers), and on the words of St. Paul (who seems to

suggest that celibacy is preferred to heterosexuality too).
Opponents of this interpretation suggest that the Bible's guidelines
were prompted by the Hebrews' felt need for a high birth rate
rather than for any other reason. Our rich Judeo-Christian tradition
is a major reason why homosexuality was considered a mental
illness until 1974. Since that year, homosexuality has not been a
diagnosed mental illness. The debate over whether homosexuality
is an acceptable lifestyle or a sin continues in church circles.

*Because the Hebrews had viewed mental illness as a punishment
from God, the early Jews did not develop mental treatments as the
Greeks and Romans did. To do so would have been to go against
God's wishes.

*The Talmud, or authoritative body of Jewish tradition, also
viewed epilepsy as a punishment from God. Cruel stereotypes of
epileptics were common well into the twentieth century, and
religious belief was one reason for the misunderstanding of this
disorder.

*The Talmud also stated that abnormal and sinful sexual behaviors
led to mental illness in oneself or in any resulting offspring.
Wrongful sexual behaviors included having sex during a woman's
menstrual period or before she had undergone purification, sex
before a kindled lamp (not in the dark), sex in front of a mirror, and
sex on the floor. The belief that sex and mental illness are
connected has had a long history. As recently as the 1930s,
physicians believed that masturbation could cause mental illness
(there was even a diagnosis of masturbatory insanity).

*The Bible was also cited as a reason for the torture, prosecution,
and death of hundreds of mentally ill persons who were accused of
being witches in the Middle Ages. The pope ordered harsh
treatment for accused witches because of a passage in Exodus that
read: "Suffer not a witch to live."

8. *Lecture additions.* When you discuss material on the Middle Ages,
    you might want to add that the phrase "rocks in your head" originated
    in this time period. Quacks used to perform pseudosurgery on city
    street corners. A person troubled by negative emotions or other
    symptoms of mental illness would go to the quack, who would make a
    minor incision on the head; an assistant would give the "surgeon" a
    few small stones, and the surgeon would pretend to have taken them
    from the patient's head. The stones, he claimed, were the cause of the
    person's problems and the patient was now "cured." This is an
    appropriate time to introduce students to the concept of the placebo

effect. Ask them if this procedure might sometimes have worked because of the patients' belief system. When you discuss the Ship of Fools (Box 1-2), you can add that putting someone on "a slow boat to China" is an equivalent notion.

9. *Class discussion.* Have your students debate whether the demonology model exists today, and if so, in what forms. Does evil exist? The devil? Is there a role for exorcism or spiritual healing in psychotherapy? You may wish to review parts of Karl Menninger's *Whatever Became of Sin?* or Scott Peck's *People of the Lie.* According to Peck, evil consists of denial and projection. Some parents refuse to see their own limitations and faults, and project them onto their children—thereby ensuring that the children will have serious problems. Peck views this pattern as the essence of evil. You can introduce students to some of the excellent examples in Peck's book and also have them discuss examples that they see in many realms—families, workplaces, churches, politics, and the world arena. This discussion can include the concept of accidie (Maslow writes about it in *Toward a Psychology of Being*) or the sin of not doing all that we know we can do—so often "sin" is discussed only in terms of things that are done that should not be done.

10. *Class discussion.* The text points out that early asylums grew so fast and were so underfunded and understaffed that they became filthy, degrading human warehouses. Tie this early poor treatment of the mentally ill to problems that exist today. Not nearly as many mentally ill persons are warehoused in large mental hospitals today due to the deinstitutionalization policy of the last four decades, and more well-trained professionals exist today, but many people still fall through the cracks; mental health care and research are still greatly underfunded. One result that you can discuss is that a significant minority of the homeless in America are mentally ill and are not getting the help they need. Another consequence is that in many states mentally ill persons are being housed in jails even though they have not committed crimes. In 1991 the National Association for the Mentally Ill (NAMI) prepared a series of articles and press releases about the number of mentally ill who are spending time in jail rather than in treatment facilities.

11. *Minilecture: Clifford Beers's Mental Illness*
Try to get a copy of Clifford Beers's *A Mind That Found Itself,* which was published in 1908. Share with your class some aspects of Beers's

treatment and especially his description of mental illness. Here are a few examples:

*Clifford Beers had a brother who died as a result of epileptic seizures, and part of Clifford's delusional system was that he became convinced that he was doomed to get epilepsy. When Beers had the flu, he became convinced it was the start of his epilepsy.

*In college Clifford Beers refused to recite in his classes because he believed that was the situation that would trigger his first epileptic seizure.

*When he mistakenly believed that he had severe epilepsy, he tried to kill himself by jumping out of a window in his house. He survived, but a broken leg kept him bedridden. While bedridden, a number of severe symptoms developed. He came to believe that his attempted suicide was a crime, and that he was to be tried for attempted murder and would be hanged. He believed that the people around him were detectives looking for evidence.

*He believed that the foods he ate would be taken as indications that he was confessing to various crimes. If he ate burned toast, he was confessing to arson. In addition, all food began to taste as though it were full of blood. He soon stopped eating.

*He heard voices, saw faces in the dark, and read handwriting on his bedsheets.

*He believed his nurses were detectives and his brother was an impostor—someone who looked like his brother but was someone else (Capgras syndrome).

*He misunderstood statements. When his brother tried to reassure him that he'd "soon be straightened out" (at a sanitarium), Clifford thought it meant he was going to be straightened out at the end of a hangman's rope.

12. **Classroom demonstration.** Find examples of symptoms and treatments in other autobiographical materials and share them at the start of the course or in the contexts of appropriate mental disorders. For example, Frances Farmer's autobiography, *Will There Really Be A Morning?* includes descriptions of hydrotherapy and insulin coma shock as well as generally appalling mental hospital conditions. Sylvia Plath's autobiographical novel, *The Bell Jar*, includes a description of electroconvulsive therapy. Joanne Greenberg's autobiographical novel, *I Never Promised You a Rose Garden*, includes descriptions of schizophrenia and hospital treatment.

13. **Classroom demonstration.** Consider having a hypnotherapist speak to your class and conduct a demonstration with volunteering students. You could also put a self-hypnosis tape on reserve at the library and allow students to try it and evaluate the process.

CHAPTER

2

MODELS OF PSYCHOLOGICAL ABNORMALITY

■

TOPIC OVERVIEW

This chapter describes the basic assumptions of the major models that have been developed to explain abnormal psychological functioning—the biological, psychodynamic, behavioral, cognitive, humanistic-existential, and sociocultural models—and explores relationships among them.

LECTURE OUTLINE

I. The Biological Model

    A. Origins of the biological model
        1. One of the earliest models attributed mental illness to physical causes.
        2. This model regained prominence with Kraepelin's somatogenic theory and linking of general paresis with syphilis in the late nineteenth century.
        3. The biological model has been strong since the 1950s because of the development of effective psychotropic drugs.

    B. Biological explanations of abnormal behavior
        1. Brain cells include neurons and their support cells, called glia.
        2. The brain is made up of the hindbrain (medulla, pons, and cerebellum), midbrain, and forebrain (cerebrum, thalamus, hypothalamus); the cerebrum is made up of the corpus callosum, basal ganglia, hippocampus, and amygdala.

      3. Organic mental disorders have clear physical causes; functional mental disorders do not.
      4. Such techniques as computerized axial tomography and magnetic resonance tomography help in the search for biological explanations.
      5. The neuron has dendrites and one axon; the synapse separates one neuron from another, and they communicate through neurotransmitters.
      6. GABA, dopamine, norepinephrine, and serotonin are neurotransmitters.
      7. Family-pedigree studies and risk studies explore the biological risk for various disorders.

  C. Assessing the biological model
      1. Psychotropic medications and research on them are gaining in importance.
      2. Psychological processes have biological causes.
      3. Research is progressing rapidly.
      4. Biological treatments are often helpful.

II. The Psychodynamic Model

  A. Origins of the psychodynamic model
      1. The psychodynamic model was first formulated by Freud at the beginning of the twentieth century, after he studied hypnosis under Charcot and Breuer.
      2. Breuer wrote about Anna O. in an 1890s book, *Studies in Hysteria*.
      3. Freud developed psychoanalysis over several decades and wrote 24 volumes about the theory and treatment of mental problems.

  B. Freudian explanations
      1. Libido is sexual energy, which fuels the id, ego, and superego.
      2. The id operates in accordance with the pleasure principle and uses primary process thinking (e.g., wish fulfillment).
      3. The ego operates in accordance with the reality principle and uses secondary process thinking.
      4. The ego develops defense mechanisms to control unacceptable id impulses and avoid or reduce anxiety.
      5. The basic defense mechanism is repression.

6. The superego grows from the ego and introjects our parents' values thorough its two components, the conscience and the ego ideal.
7. The psychosexual stages are oral, anal, phallic, latency, and genital.

C. Other psychodynamic explanations
   1. Ego psychologists (e.g., Erikson) believe the ego is more independent and powerful than Freud recognized.
   2. Object relations theorists (e.g., Klein, Mahler) view people as motivated primarily by the need to establish relationships with others; therefore they focus on such ideas as attachment and separation.
   3. Self theorists (Kohut) focus on the role of the unified personality in defining one's sense of identity and use such terms as "self objects," "mirroring," "idealize," and "fitting in."

D. Assessing the psychodynamic model
   1. The model has had a significant impact on the understanding and treatment of abnormal functioning.
   2. It has helped us understand that abnormal functioning may be rooted in the same processes that underlie normal functioning.
   3. It depends largely on case studies and has received little research support.
   4. Its explanations often fail to establish clear guidelines for predicting abnormality.

III. The Behavioral Model

A. Origins of the behavioral model
   1. The behavioral model was the first clinical perspective developed in a psychological laboratory.
   2. Efforts to modify abnormal behaviors by means of conditioning were made as early as the 1920s.
   3. The 1950s were a decade of growing use of behavioral techniques.

B. Classical conditioning
   1. Classical conditioning is a process of learning by temporal association.

2. Before conditioning, the unconditioned stimulus elicits the unconditioned response; during conditioning, a neutral stimulus becomes through association the conditioned stimulus, which elicits the conditioned response.

C. Operant conditioning
1. Operant conditioning is a process of learning through reinforcement.
2. The law of effect states that responses that have satisfying consequences are strengthened and are likely to be repeated.
3. Shaping is the use of rewards for successive approximations to the desired behavior.

D. Modeling
1. Modeling is a process of acquiring responses through observation and imitation.
2. Language, gestures, and food tastes are learned largely through modeling.

E. Assessing the behavioral model
1. The model is a powerful force in the clinical field.
2. It can be tested in the laboratory, but treatments are easier to study than causes.
3. Actual behavior does not always follow the basic principles of conditioning.
4. Emphasis on the cognitive behavioral models is growing.

IV. The Cognitive Model

A. Origins of the cognitive model
1. Social psychologists' interest in attributions in the 1950s sparked the interests of abnormal psychologists.
2. A movement toward a more cognitively oriented behaviorism gained strength, especially with the impact of Beck and Ellis in the early 1960s.
3. Cognitive processes are seen to be at the center of behavior, thought, and emotions.

B. Cognitive explanations
1. Maladaptive or basic irrational assumptions are guiding thoughts that lead one to act and react in ways that lower one's chances of happiness and success.

2. Specific upsetting thoughts, or automatic thoughts, can contribute to abnormal thinking.
3. Illogical thinking processes include selective perception, magnification, and overgeneralization.

C. Assessing the cognitive model
1. The model has broad appeal.
2. Cognitive theories can be tested and much research has been carried out.
3. The cognitive approach may not help with all disorders, but it has been shown to be effective with depression, anxiety, and sexual disorders.
4. The model has been criticized for narrowness of scope.

V. The Humanistic-Existential Model

A. Origins of the humanistic-existential model
1. Carl Rogers pioneered the humanistic approach with his client-centered therapy.
2. Rogers's perspective and the more recent theories of Maslow and Perls have much in common with the philosophies of Rousseau and William James.
3. The existential view was influenced by Kierkegaard and Sartre.
4. Binswanger developed daseinanalyse (existential analysis), which guided patients through the process of being.
5. Other existential clinicians were Boss, May, and Frankl.

B. Humanistic explanations of abnormal behavior
1. Unconditional positive regard leads to unconditional self-regard.
2. Conditions of worth are the standards by which people judge themselves, the standards to which they must conform if they are to be acceptable.
3. Conditions of worth lead to self-deception, which inhibits self-actualization.

C. Existential explanations of abnormal behavior
1. Dysfunctioning is caused by self-deception, hiding from life's responsibilities and choices.
2. Overwhelmed with pressures, one may look to authorities, conform excessively, or build resentment.

   3. Abdication of responsibility leads to emptiness and inauthenticity, with prevailing emotions of anxiety, frustration, alienation, and depression.

   D. Assessing the humanistic-existential model
      1. The model focuses on broad human issues.
      2. It is optimistic.
      3. Humanistic-existential therapists view patients as people whose special potential has yet to be fulfilled, and whose behavior can be influenced by their innate goodness.
      4. These theories are not very adaptable to research.

VI. The Sociocultural Model

   A. Origins of the Sociocultural Model
      1. The sociocultural model derives its basic assumptions from sociology and anthropology.
      2. Sociologists linked forms of abnormal behavior to social classes, and anthropologists found that patterns of abnormal behavior varied among cultures.
      3. Family therapists linked the disturbed individual to a disturbed family structure.
      4. Szasz attacked the concept of mental illness.

   B. Sociocultural explanations of abnormal behavior
      1. Family systems theory suggests that to affect one family member is to affect other family members.
      2. Double-bind communications involve contradictory messages.
      3. Epidemiological studies identify the prevalence and incidence of specific disorders.
      4. Societies undergoing major change usually show a rise in mental disorders.
      5. Rates of psychological abnormality are three times higher in the lower socioeconomic classes than in higher classes.
      6. Prejudice and discrimination based on race, sex, or age make physical and psychological health and life satisfaction harder to achieve.
      7. At least twice as many women as men are diagnosed with anxiety and depression.
      8. Once a label is assigned, a person may be viewed in stereotypical ways, as David Rosenhan's study of normal persons in mental hospitals demonstrates.

C. Assessing the sociocultural model
1. The model added an important dimension to our understanding of abnormal functioning.
2. Research used to support the model is sometimes inaccurate or difficult to interpret.
3. Studies have failed to support some of the model's key predictions.
4. The model cannot predict psychopathology in specific individuals.

VII. Relationships with the models

A. No model is consistently superior to the others.

B. All relevant factors—biological, psychological, and sociocultural—need to be appreciated.

C. Predisposing factors occur long before a disorder appears; precipitating factors trigger the disorder; maintaining factors keep it going.

D. Diathesis-stress explanations involve the interaction between one's predispositions and immediate stresses.

LEARNING OBJECTIVES

1. Summarize the origins of the behavioral model and assess its usefulness today.
2. Define and describe the basic biological terminology, including parts of neurons and the brain and kinds of neurotransmitters.
3. Distinguish between organic mental disorders and functional mental disorders.
4. Summarize the origins of the psychodynamic model and assess its usefulness today.
5. Describe Freud's id, ego, and superego, ego defense mechanisms and psychosexual stages.
6. Compare and contrast ego theory, object relations theory, and self theory.
7. Summarize the origins of the behavioral model and assess its usefulness today.
8. Describe the main features of classical conditioning and how it explains abnormal behavior.

9. Describe the main features of operant conditioning and how it explains abnormal behavior.
10. Describe the main features of modeling and how it explains abnormal behavior.
11. Summarize the origins of the cognitive model and assess its usefulness today.
12. Describe typical maladaptive assumptions, specific upsetting thoughts, and illogical thinking processes.
13. Summarize the origins of the humanistic-existential model and assess its usefulness today.
14. Describe the basic ideas of Rogers's humanistic psychology and define "unconditional positive regard," "unconditional self-regard," and "conditions of worth."
15. Summarize the basic assumptions of existential explanations of abnormal behavior.
16. Summarize the origins of the sociocultural model and assess its usefulness today.
17. Describe family structure and communication.
18. Discuss societal stress.
19. Explain the effects of societal labels and reactions.
20. Compare and contrast the various models.

INSTRUCTION SUGGESTIONS

1. *Classroom activity.* Write the names of the various models (biological, psychodynamic, behavioral, cognitive, humanistic-existential, sociocultural) across the blackboard. Then ask students to list words, ideas, and names that they associate with each of the models. This activity is a good way to reintroduce students to the models and helps them realize how much they already know about them. Of course, you can fill in some of the notable gaps. A real plus of this activity is that you can assess the knowledge of students near the beginning of the semester and use this information to provide lecture material at the needed level.

2. *Minilecture: The Brain-Blood Barrier (bbb)*
   You can make each perspective come alive by discussing some current topic from that perspective. For the biological perspective, you might want to present material about the brain-blood barrier (bbb). Both *Scientific American* and *Discover* magazines have recently done understandable and interesting articles on the bbb, so you can brush

up on the topic beforehand. Here are some ideas you can include in your lecture:

*The walls of blood vessels are different in the brain than in other parts of the body. As a result, fewer substances can get into the brain than can flow freely into other body organs.

*Usually this is a very good thing. For example, the bbb is effective in keeping the hallucinogen LSD out of the brain. Less than 1/10 of 1 percent gets into the brain. Can you imagine what the results would be if even more got past the barrier?

*However, some brain diseases are difficult to treat because the effectiveness of the bbb makes it hard to get needed medications into the brain. Scientists are developing ways to outwit the bbb.

*The capillaries in the brain make up only 5 percent of its volume but add up to 400 miles of vessels. The unique feature of these capillaries is that they have a continuous wall called the endothelium, which is surrounded by astrocytes, one type of glial cells. The endothelium is composed of lipid molecules; as a result, water-soluble molecules (e.g., albumin, sodium, penicillin) cannot cross this wall easily, but lipid-soluble molecules (e.g., nicotine, ethanol, heroin, caffeine, Valium, codeine) can cross the endothelium easily.

*One way to determine the addictiveness of an illicit drug is to see how easily it passes though the bbb. Nicotine and cocaine are the two such substances that pose the biggest problem. Both easily pass through the bbb and can quickly alter the brain. No wonder that cigarettes and crack are difficult for users to give up.

*The antiluminal membrane, or "metabolic" bbb, is a second barrier. Some substances (e.g., L-dopa) can cross the endothelium but not the antiluminal membrane.

*Heroin gets through the bbb more easily than morphine does. As a result, heroine is stronger and more addictive. Moreover, once heroin is in the brain, it changes back into morphine, making it difficult to pass through the antiluminal membrane and leaving the brain—a double-whammy effect. Methadone gets through the bbb even more easily than heroin and thus is more addictive than heroin, yet it is used in treating heroin addicts because it does not give as pleasurable an experience as heroin does.

*Some medications (e.g., the antibiotic chloramphenolcol) can enter the brain readily because they are lipid-soluble, but others (e.g., penicillin) are blocked from the brain because they are not lipid-soluble. Researchers are looking for ways to get around this blockage so that more medications can treat brain infections. Possible solutions? Injecting the carotid with a hyperosmotic sugar solution (e.g., mannitol), which temporarily lowers the bbb (however, other unwanted substances can then also enter). Or inject substances directly into the cerebrospinal fluid. Or modify the substance to get it through the bbb and then have it alter again so that it does not come back out (much as heroin operates).

3. *Class discussion.* Let students know that accurate genetic testing is now available for the genetic disorder of Huntington's disease. Family members can be tested before they make reproductive decisions to find out if they might pass this dominant-gene disease on to offspring. All individuals with the genetic marker develop this fatal degenerative disease in middle age; those who test free of the genetic marker never get this disease. Without testing, a person with a parent with Huntington's disease has a 50 percent chance of having the disease. Testing takes the odds to 100 percent or to 0 percent. If this disease were in your family, would you get the genetic test done and find out whether you (and your potential offspring) were destined for the disease or cleared of the possibility?

4. *Class demonstration.* Give your students this study aid developed by Don Irwin at Des Moines Area Community College to help them remember the neuron's parts: Have them look at their hands and think of the fingers as dendrites (a neuron can have several), the palm as the soma or cell body, and the thumb as the neuron's one axon. Tell them to visualize an impulse beginning at the fingers (dendrites), moving down the palm (soma) and the thumb (axon), where it then communicates to the fingers (dendrites) on the other hand (a second neuron).

5. *Minilecture: A Different Translation of Freud*
You can use material from Bruno Bettelheim's ***Freud and Man's Soul*** to give students a fresh view of Freud. Here are a few of Bettelheim's ideas:
    *Freud is poorly translated into English.
    *Freud chose the term "psychoanalysis" because it translated as "soul analysis," and Freud viewed therapy as a spiritual journey of self-discovery.
    *Freud can be interpreted as suggesting the need for a spontaneous sympathy of one's unconscious with that of others.
    *"Libido," which is translated as "sex drive," is better translated as

"sensual drive." Bettelheim says, "Although Freud is often quoted today in introductory psychology texts . . . his writings have only superficially influenced the work of the academic psychologists who quote him . . . American psychology has become all analysis—to the complete neglect of the psyche, or soul" (p. 19).
*A child may fall in love with a parent, but the child also wishes not to be able to fulfill this desire or to harm the parent.
*Destructive consequences occur from acting without knowing what one is doing.

6. *Class discussion.* After describing the penis envy of Freud's Electra complex, you can introduce Karen Horney's concept of womb envy. Basically, Horney suggested that males envy the female's ability to be pregnant and give birth, and deal with this envy by belittling motherhood, pregnancy, childbirth, and women's achievements. Have students evaluate the concepts of castration envy, penis envy, and womb envy. Do they have relevance in any or all cultures? It has been proposed that they are specific ways of expressing power envy. What do your students think about that idea?

7. *Classroom project.* If you did not do a demonstration of hypnosis with Chapter 1, you might want to assign a self-hypnosis option in relation to the origins of the psychodynamic model.

8. *Lecture additions.* It is good to include in your lectures several examples of interactions among the perspectives—both supportive and critical exchanges. You might want to include some biological research that provides tentative support for Freud's concept of the unconscious. You can find material in Milner's December 1986 article in *Psychology Today* or in Jonathan Winson's *Brain and Psyche: The Biology of the Unconscious*.
*Benjamin Libbit's research indicates that a sensation requires about half a second of processing to reach consciousness, yet the subjective experience is that one is aware of the sensation as it is occurring.
*Jonathan Winson suggests that this half-second is the neurophysical basis of repression.
*Howard Sherrin measures subliminal perception processing with evoked potential (EP) recordings and has found more EP in

connection with subliminal "meaningful" stimuli than with "less meaningful" stimuli. Also, repressors, or individuals who typically keep unpleasant feelings from conscious awareness, exhibit fewer EP in response to meaningful stimuli than do others.

9. *Minilecture: Freud and Seduction Theory*
You might want to address Freud's early seduction theory, in which he dealt with the problem of incest and suggested that it was a common experience. Before the turn of the century Freud proposed that many of his clients were dealing with the aftermath of early sexual abuse by a family member. When his theory was met with outrage from professional colleagues, Freud publicly rejected it and proposed instead his fantasy versions of parental seduction of Oedipus complex and the Electra complex. Privately he may have continued to believe in his original seduction theory. To develop a good lecture, become familiar with the writings of the psychoanalyst Alice Miller, who has nicely addressed the effects of incest from a psychoanalytic perspective. You can have the class discuss how society and treatment might be different if Freud had held to his original idea—would he have become an obscure theorist/doctor or would he still have become famous and been able to help generations of incest victims?

10. *Lecture additions.* A good addition to the section on classical conditioning is conditioned taste aversions. Students are interested in practical examples, so you can discuss taste aversions associated with chemotherapy and the flu. You can also relate Garcia's research on coyotes that avoided sheep after eating lithium-treated mutton. Students may have some other examples to provide.

11. *Class activity.* An excellent way to introduce cognitive theory and the idea or irrational ideas and cognitive errors is to generate a list of common cognitive mistakes that college students make, such as "An A is the only grade worth earning" or "The teachers are out to fail us." You can use the following list from Freeman and DeWolf's *Woulda, Coulda, Shoulda* to help students develop relevant examples of incorrect thinking.
    *All-or-nothing thinking; i.e., the world is all good or all bad, all gain or all loss.
    *Catastrophizing; i.e., exaggerating the negative aspects of an event.

*Comparing; i.e., judging by others rather than by one's own performance, feelings, and values.
*Emotion reasoning; i.e., letting emotions overwhelm common sense.
*Fortune-telling; i.e., being disappointed with oneself from not being able to predict the future.
*Mind reading; i.e., jumping to conclusions about what others think or what they think you are thinking.
*Overgeneralization; i.e., thinking that if something has happened once, it will always happen.
*Perfectionism; i.e., requiring oneself to perform flawlessly.
*Unquestioning acceptance of critics; i.e., letting others define one's self-worth.

12. *Class discussion.* Using Erich Fromm's book *To Have or to Be,* introduce students to the idea of a having mode and a being mode. Have them discuss the difference in self-definition and self-evaluation based on one's possessions, property, and ability to take and get things vs. self-definition and self-evaluation based on one's activity and being. How do values differ? Goals? Language? Mental health?

13. *Lecture additions.* Tell students about Murray Bowen's ideas about family triangles and how they distort family situations and hinder efforts to resolve family problems. In the wicked-stepparent triangle, there is open conflict between stepchild and stepparent, with the biological parent caught between them, trying to defend one or both. The perfect-stepparent triangle occurs when the stepparent is the rescuer who "straightens out" the child or "makes up" for the past. The ghost-of-the-former-spouse triangle occurs when the parent and stepparent end up in conflict over alimony, child support, and visitation issues. Finally, the grandparent triangle involves many forms of reactivity to former in-laws and is acted out by rules about grandparenting. In therapy, more realistic expectations for a stepfamily are encouraged and the real hurts and angers are identified and dealt with.

14. *Class discussion.* When addressing the sociocultural explanations of abnormal behavior, point out factors that are associated with high rates of mental illness, such as poverty. Ask students what kinds of clients they would like to serve. Where would they like to practice (a

private practice or an inner-city agency)? Introduce the concept of YAVIS clients (young, attractive, verbal, intelligent, and social)—the kinds of clients most professionals want to see because they (1) are less needy than others, (2) have more resources, (3) are the most like the professionals, and (4) already have many options for getting better. What general societal biases are exhibited by the preference for YAVIS clients?

15. *Lecture addition.* Expand on Rosenhan's study called ***On Being Sane in Insane Places***, which is briefly covered in the text. You can mention that one of the pseudopatients was a professional artist, and the staff interpreted her work in terms of her illness and recovery. At one hospital, games donated by a woman's club were kept locked up so that they would be new-looking if the club ever checked up on their condition. As the pseudopatients took notes about their experience, staff members referred to the note-taking as schizophrenic writing. You can locate more interesting examples in Rosenhan's study.

CHAPTER

3

RESEARCH IN
ABNORMAL PSYCHOLOGY

■

TOPIC OVERVIEW

This chapter explains the role of clinical researchers in efforts to understand topics in abnormal psychology. Students are introduced to the basics of the case study, the correlational method, and the experimental method, and learn more about the advantages and disadvantages of each. The text discusses several quasi-experimental designs.

LECTURE OUTLINE

I. The Task of Clinical Researchers

    A. The use of the scientific method
       1. Researchers systematically acquire and evaluate information through observation.
       2. Researchers seek to gain understanding of the phenomena they study.

    B. The search for general truths
       1. Nomothetic truths are general facts about the nature, causes, and treatment of abnormality.
       2. Idiographic understanding involves assessing, diagnosing, understanding, and treating individuals.

    C. The effort to identify and explain relationships between variables
       1. A variable is any characteristic or event that can vary.
       2. Researchers seek to learn whether variables change together, or if a change in one variable causes a change in another variable.

3. The use of logical thinking to analyze variables can lead to many errors; research methodology is used to minimize the errors.
4. A hypothesis is a tentative explanation about how variables are related.

II. The Case Study

A. The case study: a detailed interpretive description of one person

B. Example: Freud's Little Hans case

C. The value of the case study
   1. The information it provides has implications for the person's treatment.
   2. The case study is a source of ideas about behavior (e.g., Freud's psychoanalytic theory was based on his work with patients).
   3. It can provide tentative support for a theoretical position.
   4. It can also serve as a challenge to a theoretical position.
   5. It can be a source of ideas for new therapeutic techniques (e.g., Anna O. in the development of talk therapy).
   6. It can provide understanding of unusual problems, such as multiple personality.

D. Limitations of the case study
   1. Observations are subjective and unsystematic, and therefore biased.
   2. The case study has low internal validity (e.g., the cause of schizophrenia in the Genain sisters).
   3. It provides little basis for generalization; thus it has low external validity.

III. The Correlation Method

A. Correlational method and experimental method
   1. These methods lack the rich detail of case studies.
   2. They allow researchers to draw broad conclusions and gain nomothetic insights.
   3. They involve observing many individuals with carefully prescribed and uniform procedures and analyzing the results with statistical tests.

B. Basic characteristics of the correlational method
1. The correlational method is used to determine the "co-relationship" of variables.
2. Researchers engage in a process of operationalization, or translating abstract variables into discrete, observable entities or events.
3. Researchers use a representative sample of subjects.

C. The direction of correlation
1. The line of best fit is the one line that best fits all the data points.
2. A correlation can be positive or negative.
3. Unrelated variables have no systematic relationship.

D. The magnitude of correlation
1. The magnitude of a correlation is the strength of the relationship between variables.
2. The greater the magnitude of a correlation, the more accurate the predictions it permits.

E. The correlation coefficient (*r*, or Pearson product moment correlation coefficient)
1. The sign (plus or minus) signifies the direction of the correlation; the number represents its magnitude.
2. +1.00 and –1.00 are perfect correlations.
3. A zero correlation indicates no relationship.
4. The closer *r* is to .00, the weaker the correlation.
5. Example: a correlation of +.53 between recent life stress and depression in a sample of 68 adults.

F. Statistical analysis of correlational data
1. By statistical analysis scientists can determine the real correlation of variables in the general population from a sample of subjects.
2. A correlational study that is statistically significant is one that is probably not due to chance (expressed as $p<.05$).

G. Strengths and limitations of the correlational method
1. A correlational study has more external validity than a case study but shares its lack of internal validity.
2. Researchers can repeat correlational studies on new samples to provide additional support or clarify particular relationships.

3. Correlations enable scientists to describe and predict relationships but not to explain them.
4. Variables may be correlated for any of three reasons: (a) variable A causes variable B; (b) variable B causes variable A; (c) variable C causes both A and B.

H. Special forms of correlational research
   1. Epidemiological studies determine the incidence and prevalence of a disorder in a given population.
   2. Example: An NIMH study to determine the prevalence of mental disorders in this country found that women have higher rates of anxiety disorders and depression, and men have more alcoholism; the elderly have the highest rate of suicide.
   3. Longitudinal studies (also called high-risk or developmental studies) look at the same subjects over a long period of time.
   4. Example: Children of parents with the most severe schizophrenia are most likely to develop a psychological disorder and to commit crimes.

IV. The Experimental Method

A. Basic characteristics
   1. In an experiment a situation is manipulated and the effect is observed.
   2. An experiment tests a hypothesis.
   3. The manipulated variable is the independent variable; the variable observed is the dependent variable.

B. Confounds
   1. Extraneous variables that affect the dependent variable are major obstacles to isolation of the true cause of an observed effect.
   2. Examples: confounds of time and situational variables.

C. The control group
   1. A control group is a group of subjects not exposed to the independent variable (the experimental group is exposed to the independent variable).
   2. The control group reveals the effects of timing and other confounds.
   3. The control group serves as a comparison group for the experimental group(s).

D. Random assignment
   1. Self-selection can result in major differences between control and experimental groups.
   2. Example: Brady's ulcer study of stress and the executive monkey (Box 3-1).
   3. Random assignment greatly reduces the chances of subject bias.

E. Blind design
   1. A blind design can prevent subject bias, as when subjects try to help the experimenter.
   2. Placebos may produce real effects as a result of expectations.
   3. Example: A placebo can release endorphins, which reduce pain (Box 3-2).
   4. Research results can be skewed by experimenter bias, subtle changes in the experimenter's behavior.
   5. This confound is called the Rosenthal effect, after the first psychologist to clarify the effects of experimenter bias.
   6. In double-blind studies, neither subjects nor experimenters know which subjects are the experimental groups and which are the controls.
   7. In triple-blind studies, independent judges assess changes in the subjects without knowing what group they are in.

F. Statistical analysis of experimental data
   1. Statistical analysis enables researchers to determine if differences observed are due to chance.
   2. Findings that are statistically significant increase one's confidence that the differences observed are due to the independent variable.
   3. Statistical significance is influenced by the size of the sample, the extent of the difference observed between the groups, and the central tendency of each group's scores.
   4. The average score of a group is the mean: how widely the scores range within a group is the variability.

G. Variations in experimental design
   1. An experimenter who uses a quasi-experimental design does not randomly assign subjects but uses groups that already exist.
   2. A mixed design involves correlating existing differences with the manipulations of the study.
   3. Example: child-abuse studies.

4. Matched control groups help to eliminate some confounding differences between the experimental and control groups.
5. In natural experiments, nature rather than the experimenter manipulates the independent variable.
6. Natural experiments must be used to study the psychological effects of unusual and unpredictable events, such as floods, earthquakes, and accidents.
7. Example: Survivors of the Buffalo Creek disaster had higher anxiety and depression rates and more sleep disturbances 18 months later than a control group.
8. Natural experiments cannot be repeated at will, and broad generalizations from a single study may be incorrect.
9. In analogue experiments, subjects are induced to behave in ways they believe to be like real-life abnormal behavior.
10. Analogue experiments may use animals (Box 3-3), a practice that poses its own set of ethical issues.
11. Example: Seligman's dog and human studies of learned helplessness.
12. Single-subject experiments use baseline data to compare a single subject's behavior before and after manipulation of the independent variable.
13. The ABAB, or reversal design, looks at a subject's reactions during a baseline period, after introduction of the independent variable, after the removal of the independent variable, and after the independent variable is reintroduced.
14. Example: the effects of reinforcement treatment on a student's loud and disruptive talk during classes.
15. A multiple-baseline design looks at the effect of manipulation of the independent variable on two or more behaviors.
16. Single-subject experiments have greater internal validity than case studies, but have limited external validity.

V. The Limits of Clinical Investigation

A. Clinical subjects have needs and rights that investigators are obliged to respect.

B. The origins of human functioning are very complex.

C. Human beings are changeable.

D. Human self-awareness may influence the results of clinical investigations.

E. Clinical investigators have a special link to their subjects.

LEARNING OBJECTIVES

1. Discuss the problems that can arise in the course of clinical research.
2. Describe the scientific method.
3. Describe the characteristics of the case study method.
4. List the advantages and disadvantages of the case study method.
5. Describe the correlation method and the statistical analysis involved.
6. Know the advantages and disadvantages involved in the correlational method.
7. Describe the experimental method.
8. Know how researchers reduce the effects of confounds by using control groups, random assignment, and blind designs.
9. Describe the variations of experimental designs that are used for ethical and practical reasons.
10. Explain the general limits of clinical investigation.

INSTRUCTION SUGGESTIONS

1. *Class discussion.* The chapter begins by describing clinical psychologists' earlier belief that schizophrenia was caused by cold and domineering mothers who were blind to their children's needs. The introduction of "schizophrenogenic mothers" allows for a class discussion on how psychologists have often blamed mothers (seldom fathers) for causing mental illness. Have students discuss their beliefs and attitudes about the link between mothers and mental illness. Blythe's *Iron John* proposes that because most of a father's time is spent in the workplace, boys win the Oedipal conflict for their mothers' love, with the result that their mothers make them weak and emasculated. The psychoanalyst Melanie Klein proposed that paranoid personality was caused in infancy by a mother with "stony breasts." Ask students to suggest other examples in which moms get the blame. Do they agree?

2. *Lecture additions.* The chapter defines nomothetic and idiographic truths. You may wish to tell a little bit about Gordon Allport's advocacy of the idiographic method as worthy of personality psychologists' attention. You can describe his work with "letters from Jenny," in which he described the personality of one woman by examining her letters.

3. ***Classroom demonstration.*** Hand out to half of the students the
    problem 1 x 2 x 3 x 4 x 5 x 6 x 7 x 8 x 9 and to the other half the
    problem 9 x 8 x 7 x 6 x 5 x 4 x 3 x 2 x 1. Have them guess the solution
    within 5 seconds of receiving the problem (the correct answer is
    362,880). Students who receive the first problem will average lower
    guesses than those who receive the second problem.

    Have half of the students answer the following: Given that there are
    1,000 annual cases of electrocution, how many people do you think die
    from fireworks each year? Give the other half this question to
    answer: Given that there are 50,000 annual deaths from car accidents,
    how many people do you think die from fireworks each year? In one
    study, persons given the first question guessed 77 and those given the
    second question guessed 331. The actual answer is 6.

    Hand out a list of 20 problems to solve. Ask half of the students to
    indicate (before attempting the problems) whether they expect to get
    above or below 18 right and then to estimate the actual number that
    will be correct. Ask the rest to indicate whether they expect to get
    above or below 4 correct and to estimate the actual number. The first
    group will give a higher estimate. Research by Daniel Cervone
    suggests that if you actually allow students to work on the problems,
    the first group will try longer to solve the problems and actually get
    more solved.

    All of these dramatic problems demonstrate the effects of framing, a
    major type of thinking error. Amos Tversky and Daniel Kahneman also
    found that subjects are influenced by the blasting effect of a seemingly
    random number: when subjects spun a wheel of numbers and then
    were asked to estimate the percentage of African countries in the
    United Nations, when the wheel stopped at 10 they estimated an
    average of 25 percent, but when the wheel was on 65 they estimated
    an average of 45 percent.

    In one study, 829,000 high school seniors were asked to rate their
    ability to get along with others. Not one person gave a self-rating of
    below average; 60 percent ranked their ability in the top 10 percent,
    and 25 percent ranked themselves in the top 1 percent. There is a
    strong tendency to rate oneself as better than average. Also, most
    people demonstrate the false consensus effect by overestimating the
    number of people who agree with their views. Another strong bias is
    the self-serving bias, or the tendency to take credit for one's successes
    and to explain one's failures as externally caused. However, not all

people share this bias; depressed persons are likely to blame themselves for their failures and dismiss their successes as matters of luck.

Suggested variation: You can use some of the examples in this selection for student research projects.

4. *Lecture addition.* The chapter introduces the case of Anna O., who initiated "talk therapy." Tell students that the real Anna O. went on to buck the Orthodox Jewish system and establish a high-quality school for girls. When the Nazis overran Europe after Anna's death, Hitler planned to change this school into a whorehouse, with the current students as the prostitutes. All of the students poisoned themselves to escape such a fate.

5. *Class project and discussion.* If possible, have students collect newspaper articles based on correlational studies. Go over the articles with the students and decide if the journalist correctly interpreted the results of the studies or if correlational results were used to indicated causation. If time does not permit the gathering of current articles, discuss the following correlation found by George Snedecor, a statistician at Iowa State University many years ago. Snedecor found a correlation of +.90 between the importation of bananas and the divorce rate. In other words, if the tonnage of bananas delivered to the country rose in a certain year, the number of divorces rose too. Do bananas cause divorces? Or do divorcing people eat more bananas? (Of course, as population increases, more couples divorce and more bananas are consumed.)

6. *Classroom activity.* Bring into the classroom some actual studies involving epidemiological and longitudinal research. Interesting epidemiological research is often reported in the *New England Journal of Medicine* as well as in psychology and sociology journals. You can use either recent studies or classic materials. Have students in small groups find the interesting features in these journal articles. Appropriate material, such as reports on the prevalence of mental disorders and the prevalence of drug use among high school students, can be found also in government publications.

7. *Classroom activity.* Have students read actual (or made-up) titles of research articles and point out which is the independent variable (IV) and which is the dependent variable (DV). Point out that one popular title is "The Effects of (IV) on (DV)." Here are a few actual research titles:

A. "Alteration of type A behavior and reduction in cardiac recurrences in postmyocardial infarction patients."

B. "Alprazolam compared to diazepam and placebo treatment of anxiety."

C. "Relaxation training: Twenty-four-hour blood pressure reduction."

D. "A comparison of cognitive training and response cost procedures in modifying cognitive styles of impulsive children."

E. "The effects of unilateral plethysmographic feedback of temporal artery activity during migraine head pain."

F. "Intensive treatment of psychotic behavior by stimulus satiation and food reinforcement."

G. "The effects of social skills training and peer involvement on the social adjustment of preadolescents."

H. "Depression and the effects of positive and negative feedback on expectations, evaluations, and performance."

I. "The use of meditation relaxation techniques in the management of stress in a working population."

J. "The effect of mianserin on alpha 2 adrenergic receptor functioning depressed patients."

K. "An experimental study of the effect of structured videotape feedback on adolescent group psychotherapy process.

L. "Comparison of effects of marijuana and alcohol on simulated driving experience."

8. *Minilecture: The Rosenthal Effect*

The chapter mentions that experimenter bias is referred to as the Rosenthal effect. You can relate the initial classic work of Rosenthal to illustrate dramatically how experimenters bias studies. At the end of your presentation, you can expand the material into a class discussion of bias effects in the classroom and in the mental health arena.

*Present material about how Rosenthal had graduate students teach rats to run mazes. All rats were run the same length of time daily. Although the rats came from the same litter, students were led to believe that they had either a rat genetically bred to be "maze bright" or genetically bred to be "maze dull." Although genetically similar, those rats whose trainer thought they were "maze bright" did perform better than the supposedly "maze dull" rats. It seems that the students subtly encouraged the rats they expected to do better more than they did the "dull" rats.

*In a related study, the experimenter went into a slow learners' class and gave a pseudotest that was designed to pick out "late bloomers—students who were currently behind their age norms but who had hidden potential. In actuality, "late bloomers" were chosen at random. Near the beginning of the school year, teachers were briefly shown the list of "late bloomers" once. At the end of the year, these "late bloomers" had actually outperformed the rest of the class. Perhaps the moral for teachers is to assume that every student has hidden potential—and perhaps then it will appear.

9. *Class discussion.* Have students discuss other natural experiments, such as research done on the survivors of the Holocaust and on Vietnam vets' PTSD. You might want to include more recent natural disasters, such as the Midwest flood of 1993 and the Los Angeles earthquake of 1994.

10. *Lecture additions.* When lecturing about the use of animals in analogue experiments, you might mention that it was difficult to find laboratory animals that would willingly drink alcohol. Rats and cats learned to prefer their spiked water and spiked milk only under very stressful circumstances, such as receiving repeated electric shocks. At one time the gerbil seemed to be the perfect alcoholic animal—gerbils drank lots of alcohol and got drunk (as one researcher put it, they drank "until they would lie stretched out on their exercise wheel"). However, gerbils did not stay as hung over as humans. It seems that gerbils' livers process alcohol much faster and more efficiently than humans do. Therefore, research with gerbils would not be very relevant to the effects of alcohol on humans. Among other solutions, rats that crave alcohol have been bred.

11. *Minilecture: Early Views on Animal Research*
Your students may be aware that some people are now protesting the use of animals in research (the topic of Box 3-4). You might share some information about the Victorian antivivisectionist movement with your students. These are found in a March 1990 *American Psychologist* article by Dewsbury.

*Around the time that nineteenth-century psychologists were developing an experimental physiology that relied heavily on animal subjects, England and the United States were starting humane and antivivisection movements.

*Henry Bergh founded the American Society for the Prevention of Cruelty to Animals on April 21, 1866.

*William James, the founder of American psychology, sought a balance between the need for animal experimentation and ethical research. James wrote, "Vivisection . . . is a painful duty," and "to taboo vivisection is . . . the same thing as to give up seeking after a knowledge of physiology."

*John Dewey also viewed animal experimentation as a duty. In 1926 he wrote, "Scientific men are under definite obligation to experiment upon animals so far as that is the alternative to random and possible harmful experimentation upon human beings, and so far as such experimentation is a means of saving human life and of increasing human vigor and efficiency."

*The author of the first North American comparative psychology text, John Bascom, favored restricting vivisection so that pain was reduced to the lowest possible amount, doing only important experiments, and limiting repetitive experiments.

*Ivan Pavlov justified his animal research with the statement that "the human mind has no other means of becoming acquainted with the laws of organic world except by experiments and observations on living animals." He added, "When I dissect and destroy a living animal, I hear within myself a bitter reproach that with rough and blundering hand I am crushing an incomparable artistic mechanism. But I endure in the interest of truth, for the benefit of humanity." Yet antivivisectionists accused Pavlov of enjoying the destruction of animals.

*John B. Watson, who did anesthetized surgery on white rats that included removal of eyes, destruction of eardrums, and removal of olfactory bulbs, was called "killer of baby rats" in the media. One reporter wrote, "Now, if the same experiments were tried on the inspired Watson himself, the results would be better, as he could tell us all about it. But he prefers to keep his eyes in his own head. So would the rats."

*An important outcome of this early antivivisection movement was that in 1925 the American Psychological Association appointed a committee to establish research guidelines for animal studies. Today the APA Committee on Animal Research and Ethics (CARE) sets standards for the treatment of animals used in research, ensuring the continuance of humane animal research.

CHAPTER

4

CLINICAL ASSESSMENT, INTERPRETATION, AND DIAGNOSIS

■

TOPIC OVERVIEW

This chapter describes a variety of tools used in clinical assessment, including clinical interviews, clinical tests, projective tests, self-report inventories, psychophysiological tests, neuropsychological tests, intelligence tests, and clinical observations. The chapter covers clinical interpretation, clinical judgment, and diagnosis.

LECTURE OUTLINE

I. Clinical Assessment

    A. Assessment
       1. Clinical assessment is the collection of relevant information on a subject.
       2. It has many uses throughout life.

    B. Clinical assessment techniques
       1. Assessment techniques are used to determine how and why a person is behaving abnormally.
       2. They are also used to assess the effectiveness of treatment.
       3. There are three kinds of assessment techniques: clinical interviews, tests, and observations.

II. Clinical Interviews

    A. Conducting the interview
       1. The interview is often the first contact between the client and the clinician.
       2. Interviewers gather basic data and identify important topics.

    B. Interview formats
       1. Unstructured interviews use open-ended questions.
       2. Structured interviews use a series of prepared questions.
       3. A mental status exam reveals the degree and nature of a client's abnormal functioning.
       4. Psychodynamic and humanistic therapists tend to prefer unstructured interviews; behaviorists tend to prefer structured interviews.

    C. Limitations of clinical interviews
       1. The information supplied is preselected by the client.
       2. It may be self-serving or inaccurate because of distorted perceptions or memories, or unduly pessimistic.
       3. Interviews may use subjective judgments.

III. Clinical Tests

    A. The five kinds of clinical tests are projective tests, self-report inventories, psychophysiological tests, neuropsychological tests, and intelligence tests.

    B. Characteristics of tests
       1. Standardization allows a test score to be compared with others' scores.
       2. Reliability is a measure of consistency of results.
       3. There are four types of reliability: test-retest reliability, alternate-form reliability, split-half reliability, and interrater reliability.
       4. A test's validity is the accuracy of its results.
       5. There are five types of validity: face, predictive, concurrent, content, and construct validity.

    C. Projective tests
       1. A projective test requires the test taker to give interpretive answers to vague stimuli or questions.

    2. The Rorschach Psychodynamic Inkblot Test has at least two phases: a free association or performance phase and an inquiry phase.

    3. The Thematic Apperception Test requires the test taker to tell stories suggested by pictures.

    4. The Sentence-Completion and Draw-a-Person tests are projective tests.

    5. Projective tests, once regarded as primary indicators of personality, are now seen as means to gain supplemental insights.

    6. They do not exhibit great reliability or validity.

D. Self-report inventories

    1. Personality inventories are used to draw broad conclusions about a person's psychological functioning.

    2. The first ones were developed to screen recruits during World War I.

    3. The Minnesota Multiphasic Personality Inventory (MMPI), the most widely used inventory, was constructed using criterion keying and has ten clinical scales.

    4. A person's response set is a tendency to respond in a fixed way.

    5. MMPI-2 updates and broadens the MMPI.

    6. Self-report inventories are designed to collect detailed information about one area of functioning.

E. Narrow self-report inventories

    1. Narrower inventories are designed to collect detailed information about one area of functioning.

    2. Affective inventories measure the severity of one or more emotions.

    3. Social skills inventories ask for responses to a variety of social situations.

    4. Cognitive inventories disclose typical thoughts and assumptions.

    5. Reinforcement inventories look at the nature, intensity, and frequency of various reinforcers in a person's life.

    6. Narrow inventories have the advantages of strong face validity and efficiency, but they are less likely to have been subjected to standardization, reliability, and validity procedures.

F. Psychophysiological tests

    1. Interest grew when physiological changes associated with anxiety were noted.

2. The vaginal plethysmograph and penile plethysmograph (strain gauge) are used to measure sexual arousal.
3. The biofeedback technique gives clients systematic information about key physiological responses.
4. Most psychophysiological tests require expensive equipment that itself may cause anxiety and so may affect results.

G. Neuropsychological tests
   1. Neurophysiological tests include the computerized axial tomograms (CAT scan), electroencephalogram (EEG), positron emission tomogram (PET scan), and magnetic resonance imaging (MRI).
   2. Neuropsychological tests help identify neurological problems by measuring a person's cognitive, perceptual, and motor skills.
   3. The Bender Visual-Motor Gestalt Test consists of nine cards displaying simple designs for subjects to copy and later to draw from memory.
   4. Clinicians often use a battery or comprehensive series of tests.

H. Intelligence tests
   1. In 1905 Alfred Binet and Theodore Simon produced the first modern intelligence test.
   2. The most widely used intelligence tests are the Wechsler Adult Intelligence Scale, the Wechsler Intelligence Scale for Children, and Stanford-Binet Intelligence Scale.

I. Integrating test data
   1. Clinicians usually use a battery of tests to clarify information gathered in the clinical interview.
   2. Information provided by the various tests helps to determine the scope of a client's problems.

IV. Clinical Observations

A. Naturalistic and structured observations
   1. Naturalistic observation involves observing clients in their everyday environments.
   2. Participant observers are key persons in the client's environment who report their observations to the clinician.
   3. When naturalistic observation is not practical, a clinician may observe a client in a structured setting.
   4. Observers may make errors because of overload, observer drift, and observer bias.

     5. A subject's reactivity is the tendency of his or her behavior to be affected by the presence of the observer.

  B. Self-monitoring
     1. To self-monitor is to record the frequency of one's own behavior and the circumstances of its occurrence.
     2. An advantage is that it permits observation of infrequent behavior and may help clients understand the scope of their problems; however, it is subject to reactivity.

V. Clinical Interpretation and Judgment

  A. To interpret assessment data is to transform them into clinical understanding.

  B. Most clinicians use an additive, or linear, model to interpret their data.

VI. Diagnosis

  A. To make a diagnosis is to determine that a person's psychological problems constitute a particular disorder.

  B. The difficulty of diagnosis is shown by the variety of diagnosis offered for Van Gogh's disorder, which ranged from bipolar disorder to schizophrenia.

VII. Classification Systems

  A. A syndrome is a cluster of symptoms.

  B. A classification system consists of a list of mental disorders with descriptions of the symptoms characteristic of each.

  C. The International Classification of Diseases (ICD-10), used by the World Health Organization, covers both medical and psychological disorders.

  D. The Diagnostic and Statistical Manual of Mental Disorders has been revised several times; its current edition is known as DSM-IV.

VIII. DSM-IV

    A. DSM-IV lists more than 200 mental disorders on five axes, or branches of information.

    B. Axis I disorders are clinical syndromes that cause significant impairment.

    C. Axis II disorders are long-standing problems that are frequently overlooked in the presence of the Axis I disorders: the two major categories are mental retardation and personality disorders.

    D. Axis III provides relevant general medical conditions.

    E. Axis IV provides psychosocial or environmental problems.

    F. Axis V is global assessment of functioning (GAF).

IX. Reliability and Validity in Classification

    A. DSM-IV criteria yield more reliable diagnosis than earlier DSM versions.

    B. DSM-IV's predictive and concurrent validities are also improvements.

X. Problems of Clinical Misinterpretation

    A. Clinicians are flawed information processors.

    B. Judgments may be distorted by gender, age, race, and socioeconomic status.

    C. They may make mistakes in their use of assessment information.

    D. They may falsely assume that every client has a disorder.

XI. Dangers of Diagnosing and Labeling

    A. A diagnostic label may be a self-fulfilling prophecy.

    B. The stigma may make it difficult to get a job or enter into social relationships.

C. Professionals, friends, and relatives may continue to apply the label long after the disorder has disappeared.

LEARNING OBJECTIVES

1. Define assessment and discuss the roles of clinical assessment.
2. Discuss clinical interviews and explain how they are conducted.
3. Compare and contrast unstructured interviews and structured interviews.
4. Summarize the limitations of clinical interviews.
5. Describe the five kinds of clinical tests: projective tests, self-report inventories, psychophysiological tests, neuropsychological tests, and intelligence tests.
6. Define the characteristics of useful tests: standardization, reliability, and validity.
7. Explain projective tests and describe the Rorschach Test, the Thematic Apperception Test, the Sentence-Completion Test, and the Draw-a-Person Test.
8. Describe self-report inventories and distinguish between a personality inventory and a narrow self-report inventory.
9. Describe the MMPI.
10. Compare and contrast psychophysiological tests and neuropsychological tests.
11. Describe intelligence tests.
12. Compare and contrast naturalistic observation, structured observation, and self-monitoring.
13. Discuss clinical interpretation and judgment.
14. Describe a diagnosis and classification and judgment.
15. Summarize the history of the DSM and describe the general features of DSM-IV.
16. Explain the dangers of diagnosis and labeling.

INSTRUCTION SUGGESTIONS

1. *Classroom demonstration.* Bring into your class available examples of personality inventories, projective tests, and intelligence tests and share a few aspects of the tests with your students. If possible, include a few of the tests mentioned in this chapter, such as the MMPI, Rorschach Inkblot, TAT, WAIS-R, and Vineland Social Maturity Scale. Have students give their reactions to the contents of the tests.

2. ***Classroom demonstration.*** Bring a copy of DSM-IV to class and point out its features. Read one of the diagnostic criteria sections to the students. Ask them if it is similar to what they thought it would be.

3. ***Class activity.*** Divide students into small groups and tell them to view themselves as counselors. In this role, they are to develop a list of things they would most want to know about a client at the end of the first session together. Then have the groups share their lists and develop one master list. Discuss what their impressions of important information are and why. Two variations are possible: (1) assign different counseling perspectives to the small groups and (2) assign a specific client type (e.g., schizophrenic divorced man, battered woman).

4. ***Class activity.*** Assign students different theoretical orientations and give them a client description. Have some students act out the client role and the other students interview the client from the assigned perspective. Psychoanalytic and behavioral therapists make nice contrasts.

5. ***Class activity.*** For each of the following kinds of validity, have students provide examples that they have experienced in college: face validity, predictive validity, content validity, construct validity. Can students provide examples of situations in which proper validity standards were not met?

6. ***Class project.*** Assign students to find pictures in magazines (***Life, Time, Newsweek***) appropriate for a quick TAT-like test. In pairs, have them take turns telling stories about the pictures and assessing primary themes. Have students express their opinions about the worth of such an approach.

7. ***Class activity.*** Provide colored pencils or crayons and white paper to students and have them try one or more of the following drawing projective tests: (1) draw a mandala; (2) draw a person, a house, and a tree; and (3) draw a picture of their family. Have students write about or talk about one or more of their drawings. You can also provide information about how therapists use such pictures.

8. *Classroom demonstration.* Locate and bring to class some older inventories and describe changes over the years. (In older journals you may find questionnaires that measure neuroticism, for example; or you might look at Sheldon's inventories measuring ectomorphs, endomorphs, and mesomorphs.)

9. *Classroom demonstration.* Collect (or have students assemble) some questionnaires from popular magazines or self-help books. Compare these items with the more standardized, classical personality inventories, such as the MMPI.

10. *Class discussion.* One response set recognized by the MMPI is social desirability. Bring in the items from the social desirability scale and read them to the class. Have them discuss why this response set occurs frequently.

11. *Class project.* Have students develop and try out a Q-sort technique. One possible way is to list items that can be assessed as "True of the real me" and "True of my ideal me." Have students try their new test and evaluate what they learned about test construction and about themselves from the activity.

12. *Classroom demonstration.* Bring in and demonstrate biofeedback equipment (some inexpensive ones, including programs for computers, might be purchased by your psychology department). You can also use stress dot cards, which indicate level of stress by the color of the dot after it has been held for ten seconds.

13. *Classroom demonstration.* A growing area of assessment is neuropsychological testing. Demonstrate the Bender Visual-Motor Gestalt Test or the Halstead Reitan Neuropsychology Battery. Other simple tests can be found and adapted to the classroom.

14. *Classroom demonstration.* Have a neurologist or a psychologist who does neuropsychological assessment come and speak to your class.

15. *Class discussion.* Self-monitoring helps to reduce a bad habit as an effect of subject reactivity. The person who writes a checkmark each time she lights a cigarette, for example, is likely to smoke fewer cigarettes. An expensive pocket computer can also be used to monitor (and later adjust) one's smoking habits. Do students think that the computer will produce better results than mere markings on paper? Why, or why not? You can also discuss how to take other simple counseling ideas and use technology to develop a marketable product.

16. *Lecture addition.* When you discuss self-monitoring, you might want to address the differences between automatic and controlled processing. Habits are automatic, and therefore inflexible and hard to modify. Therapeutic intervention to change a habit makes use of controlled processing, which is changeable and flexible. One of the difficulties of effecting a long-term change of habit is that automatic processing can easily intervene. Controlled processing takes continual effort. So one person diets successfully for two weeks, keeping vigilant watch over fat content, number of calories, and so forth. Then one slip-up, and automatic processing wipes out much of the constructive results.

17. *Classroom demonstration and discussion.* Bring in DSM-I, DSM-II, DSM-III, and DSM-III-R along with DSM-IV. The impact of seeing how much longer the successive versions have become since that slim DSM-I is quite dramatic. Have students discuss why each edition is longer than the one before.

5

TREATMENTS FOR ABNORMAL PSYCHOLOGICAL FUNCTIONING

■

TOPIC OVERVIEW

This chapter focuses on the client-therapist relationship and then discusses the major systems of therapy: psychodynamic, humanistic, existential, behavioral, cognitive, and biological. Next, the different formats of therapy are covered: individual, group, family, and couple. Finally, the chapter discusses the effectiveness of therapy.

LECTURE OUTLINE

I. Clients and Therapists

    A. Characteristics shared by all therapies
        1. A sufferer seeks relief from a healer.
        2. The healer is trained and socially sanctioned.
        3. Their contacts are structured.

    B. One-fifth of adults suffering from psychological problems are in counseling.

    C. A greater variety of problems are now being treated by counselors.

    D. The most prevalent counseling problems are anxiety and depression, but 10 percent of clients have schizophrenia and 5 percent have substance abuse disorders.

E. Clients are no longer just the privileged; they now cover a wide socioeconomic range.

F. The typical client waits more than two years before seeking counseling.

G. The length of counseling varies; more than half of all clients see counselors fewer than fifteen times.

II. Global Therapy

A. Psychodynamic therapies
1. Today's disorders result from earlier emotional traumas.
2. Insight therapy seeks to uncover old traumas.
3. Its main technique is free association.
4. The therapist interprets clues provided by the patient, especially of resistance, transference, and dreams.
5. Catharsis, or emotional insight, is important.
6. Shorter versions of psychodynamic therapies have been developed.
7. The strongest support for psychodynamic therapies is provided by case studies rather than by systematic research.

B. Humanistic and existential therapies
1. Client-centered therapy emphasizes the counselor's unconditional positive regard, accurate empathy, and genuineness.
2. Gestalt therapy involves skillful frustration, role-play, and exercises and games.
3. Existential therapists encourage clients to take responsibility for their lives, make choices freely, and live authentic lives.

III. Problem-Based Therapies

A. Behavioral therapies
1. Classical conditioning techniques include systematic desensitization and aversion therapy. Operant conditioning techniques are designed to modify behavior through rewards and punishments, and include token economies.
2. Modeling therapy is another type of behavioral therapy.
3. Behavioral therapies have been shown to be effective for specific problems, such as reducing specific fears and social deficits.

B. Cognitive therapies
1. Rational-emotive therapy uncovers irrational assumptions and challenges and modifies them.
2. Cognitive therapy is most frequently used to treat depression.
3. Cognitive-behavioral therapists view cognitions as responses that can be altered by systematic regard or punishment.
4. These strategies appeal to therapists of many persuasions and perform well in research studies.

C. Biological therapies
1. Effective psychotropic drugs have been available since the 1950s.
2. Drug categories include antianxiety drugs (or minor tranquilizers), antidepressant drugs, antibipolar drugs (primarily lithium), and antipsychotic (or neuroleptic) drugs.
3. Electroconvulsive therapy (ECT), developed in the 1930s, is still widely used to treat depression; the current form of bilateral ECT has fewer serious adverse effects.
4. Few lobotomies have been performed since the 1950s; today's psychosurgery is much more precise.

IV. Formats of Therapy

A. Individual therapy
1. Individual therapy was the first form of modern therapy.
2. The number and length of sessions vary, as do techniques.

B. Group therapy
1. Group therapy grew in popularity after World War II because it is efficient, time-saving, and relatively inexpensive.
2. Many therapy groups are often composed of a particular client population.
3. Group therapy's curative features include guidance, identification, group cohesiveness, universality, altruism, catharsis, and skill building.
4. Psychodrama involves role-playing techniques such as mirroring, role reversal, and magic shop.
5. Self-help groups are made up of people with similar problems who come together to help and support each other without direct leadership by a professional.

C. Family therapy
1. Family systems theory states that each family has its own implicit rules, relationship structure, and communication patterns.
2. Structural family therapy focuses on family power structures.

D. Couple therapy
1. Couple therapy can incorporate any major therapy system.
2. Behavioral marital therapy helps spouses identify and change problem behaviors.
3. Intimacy can be reestablished by use of core symbols.

V. Is Treatment Effective?

A. General effectiveness
1. Research has supported the effectiveness of behavioral, cognitive, and biological therapies.
2. Psychodynamic and client-centered therapies have received some research support.
3. Any type of therapy seems to be more effective than being in a control group.

B. Particular therapies for particular disorders
1. Behavioral therapies are most effective for phobic disorders.
2. Drug therapy is most effective for schizophrenia.
3. Cognitive-behavioral therapies are very effective for sexual dysfunctions.
4. Cognitive therapy and drug therapy are often successful for depression.
5. Combined therapy approaches are often superior to any single approach.

LEARNING OBJECTIVES

1. Know what all forms of therapy have in common.
2. Compare and contrast the features and goals of global therapies and specific therapies.
3. Describe the procedures and techniques of psychodynamic therapies.
4. Know the primary characteristics of humanistic-existential therapies.
5. Compare and contrast client-centered therapy, gestalt therapy, and existential therapy.
6. Know the behavioral technique categories of classical conditioning, operant conditioning, and modeling.

7. Understand the premises of cognitive therapies and how cognitive therapies are conducted.
8. Know the three main kinds of biological therapy: drug therapy, electroconvulsive therapy, and psychosurgery.
9. Compare individual therapy and group therapy.
10. Describe family systems theory, family therapy, and marital therapy.
11. Evaluate the effectiveness of therapy.

INSTRUCTION SUGGESTIONS

1. *Class activity.* Find recent surveys on people's attitudes toward therapy. You can locate such material in recent journal articles or the *APA Monitor.* You can also contact your local chapter of the National Association for the Mentally Ill (NAMI) for information on changing attitudes. Its 1991 newsletter featured information concerning the significantly more positive attitudes of the American population toward counseling for other people and for oneself. Have students formulate a simple opinion survey on attitudes toward therapy (incorporate some of the questions from surveys you discuss in class). Ask students to answer the poll anonymously and compare the results from year to year.

2. *Minilecture: Brief Therapies*
   Growing in popularity is the brief therapy format, which developed from professionals' belief that significant progress can be made on a specific problem and in response to insurance policies that will pay for only a limited number of sessions. Brief therapies tend to be problem-focused and action-oriented, and deal with a limited number of problems. Many brief therapists rely most heavily on behavioral and cognitive techniques.

   For example, the brief therapist may ask the client to deal with the most important concern in the client's life and to divulge only information that affects this concern. The therapist will ask about the client's past and current strategies for dealing with the problem and how these approaches have worked. Then the therapist and client work together to produce a new behavioral approach and evaluate the results.

   The brief therapist asks the client to address these questions: (1) What is the significant problem with which you are dealing? (2) What have you tried that has not worked? (3) Are there times when these failed strategies have had positive results? If so, is there anything you can remember that was different during those times? (4) What can be tried at a different level or with some modification? (5) What could be tried that has not yet been tried? (6) How can you think differently about this situation? Behave differently? Feel differently?

Brief therapy can be highly effective in working out specific life problems. Research has also shown, however, that long-term counseling continues to bring increasing benefits to the client.

3. *Class activity.* Gather books that deal with dream symbolism and use these pictures and words to discuss dream analysis with your class. You could also ask students (ahead of time) to write down anonymously a couple of dreams they have had and have students attempt to interpret them. Point out the different ways in which Sigmund Freud, Carl Jung, and Fritz Perls approached the analysis of dreams. Some classes can get into a lively discussion of the value of dream interpretation.

4. *Class discussion.* Have the class discuss their beliefs about whether or not symptom substitution occurs. Be ready to provide some examples if students just dismiss the possibility. For example, is oral substitution at work when a person who has quit smoking starts to eat more? What other explanations are there?

5. *Class activity.* You may use student volunteers to demonstrate the various gestalt techniques. Give them a specific situation to role-play (e.g., anger at a father who abandoned the family, depression after the death of a sibling, coming to terms with poor grades at college) so that no student is made to reveal sensitive information. Demonstrate the exaggeration game, the hot seat, and the empty chair.

6. *Class demonstration.* Here or in conjunction with Chapter 7, consider demonstrating systematic desensitization. You can perhaps have your students develop a hierarchy for a college issue (anxiety about speaking in class or about midterm examinations) and take them through progressive relaxation training (stop short of the process of pairing the hierarchy and the relaxation; instead describe what the future steps would be).

7. *Class discussion.* Put this quotation on the board: "Anything worth doing is worth doing badly.—Oscar Wilde." Ask for students' reactions to this quote. Most students will dislike it and criticize it. Then suggest that there are many things that they would like to try but they tell themselves, "I don't have time to be good at it" or "It's too late to learn that well" or "I should have taken lessons as a kid." As adults we may tell ourselves, "It's too late to go to college" or "Even though I would love to take an art class I'd probably only get a C." Each of us limits our pleasure because we can't do that pleasurable activity well. If you're 50, take piano lessons if you always wanted to learn, even though it's not going to get you to Carnegie Hall. If you're really interested in chemistry, take that class, even though your ability may lead to a C and a small dent in your grade point average. Go ahead and sing that hymn during the church service, even though your voice is not angelic. Wilde's real message is that it's OK to try something at which you may fail. It's OK to work on something even if the very best you can ever be at it is mediocre.

8. *Class demonstration.* Bring in a copy of the Physician's Desk Reference (PDR) and share the effects of a few psychoactive drugs with the class. You might want to choose a few selections ahead of time (e.g., meprobamate, or Miltown; diazepam, or Valium; fluoxetine hydrochloride, or Prozac; chlorpromazine, or Thorazine; haloperidol, or Haldol).

9. *Class demonstration.* Begin a collection of literature and information about self-help groups, especially those that meet locally. You may wish to share a list of local groups with class members. If school counselors run groups or have information about groups in the community, let students know that this information is available.

10. *Class activity.* On the blackboard write "Professional counseling" and "self-help groups." Have students generate lists of advantages and disadvantages of each of these formats. You may need to help these lists grow by asking such questions as "Which of these formats ensures confidentiality?"

6

ANXIETY DISORDERS

■

TOPIC OVERVIEW

This chapter covers the topics of stress, coping, and anxiety response, and then discusses phobic disorders, generalized anxiety disorders, panic disorders, and obsessive compulsive disorders. Finally, the chapter covers acute stress disorders and posttraumatic stress disorders.

LECTURE OUTLINE

I. General Introduction

   A. Fear and anxiety
       1. Fear is a state of tension or alarm in response to a serious threat.
       2. Anxiety is a response to an unspecified threat.
       3. Fear and anxiety have the same clinical features—accelerated breathing, muscular tension, perspiration.
       4. Both fear and anxiety prepare one for "flight or fight."

   B. Anxiety disorders
       1. Anxiety becomes a disorder when it is continuous and disabling and is too severe, too frequent, too long-lasting, and too readily triggered.
       2. Anxiety disorders are the most common mental disorders in the United States.
       3. In a year's time, about 15 percent of the U.S. population suffer one of the DSM-IV's six anxiety disorders.

4. Anxiety disorders account for about one-third of all mental health costs: $46.6 billion.

C. Historical information
1. Anxiety disorders used to be called neuroses.
2. Freud believed a neurosis to be caused by the inability of ego defense mechanisms to prevent or reduce anxiety aroused by unconscious conflicts.
3. Anxiety was apparent in phobic, anxiety, and obsessive compulsive disorders.
4. Anxiety was hidden in hysterical, neurasthenic, depersonalization, depressive, and hypochondriacal neuroses.
5. Now DSM-IV defines disorders by symptoms rather than by possible causes.
6. Anxiety is now recognized as the central symptom of anxiety disorders; other symptoms lead to a diagnosis of mood disorders, somatoform disorders, or dissociative disorders.

II. Stress, Coping, and the Anxiety Response

A. Stress
1. We experience stress when we are confronted by demands, constraints, or opportunities that require us to change.
2. Stressors are events that create such demands.
3. Stress response is one's idiosyncratic reaction to stressors.
4. Hassles are common, everyday life stressors.
5. Stressors can be major life events or transitions.

B. Appraisal of stressors
1. In the primary appraisal stages one interprets a situation as threatening or harmless.
2. In the secondary appraisal stage one assesses the needed response and one's ability to cope.

C. The autonomic nervous system (ANS)
1. The ANS generates the fear in the fear and anxiety response.
2. It regulates the involuntary activities of one's organs.
3. The sympathetic nervous system is the "fight or flight" system that prepares a response to danger.
4. The parasympathetic nervous system restores the body to normal when perceived danger passes.
5. The sympathetic and parasympathetic nervous systems are complementary.

D. Trait and state anxiety
   1. Trait anxiety is one's general level of anxiety.
   2. Some psychologists believe that trait anxiety is learned in early childhood; others view it as biologically determined.
   3. Situation or state anxiety consists of variations on trait anxiety produced by specific situations.

III. Phobic Disorders and Generalized Anxiety Disorders

A. Phobic disorders
   1. A phobia is a persistent, unreasonable fear of a specific object, activity, or situation.
   2. Example: fear of the dentist.
   3. A typical coping strategy is to avoid the feared object or situation and not to think about it.
   4. Phobias tend to vary by age; fear of crowds, or injury, and of separation is more prevalent among the elderly, whereas fear of snakes, heights, and storms is more common among young adults.
   5. Phobic disorders are more disruptive, intense, and persistent than phobias; they interfere with personal, social, or occupational functioning.
   6. DSM-IV distinguishes three categories: agoraphobia, social phobias, and specific phobias.
   7. Agoraphobia is fear of public places and situations from which escape seems difficult should a physical symptom, such as dizziness or diarrhea, develop.
   8. Agoraphobia affects 4 percent of the adult population, and twice as many women as men.
   9. People with agoraphobia avoid crowded streets and stores, tunnels and bridges, public transportation, and elevators; some become prisoners in their own homes.
   10. Some agoraphobic patterns are combined with panic disorder.
   11. Social phobias, which involve incapacitating anxiety under exposure to scrutiny, may be specific (e.g., fear of public speaking or eating in public) or general.
   12. About 8 percent of the population—slightly more women than men—have social phobias.
   13. The majority of phobias are specific phobias, such as fear of thunderstorms, insects, and heights.
   14. Eleven percent of the population have a specific phobia at some time, with an annual incidence of 9 percent; these disorders are twice as common among women as among men.

15. The impact of a specific phobia depends on how easy it is to avoid the object one fears.
16. Animal phobias are more common among children.
17. Many childhood phobias gradually disappear, but those that begin or persist in adulthood usually yield only to treatment.

B. Generalized anxiety disorders
1. These disorders are characterized by free-floating anxiety, or excessive worry about a wide range of things.
2. Nearly 4 percent of the general population—twice as many women as men—have the symptoms in any given year.
3. Generalized anxiety disorders most commonly appear in childhood and adolescence.
4. These disorders are characterized by muscular tension, sleep disturbances, difficulty in concentrating, restlessness, and fatigue over a period of at least six months.
5. The majority of people with these disorders develop other disorders, such as a phobia or depression.
6. Pervasive anxiety is frustrating for the family and friends as well as for the sufferer.

C. Explanations of phobic and generalized anxiety disorders
1. Sociocultural explanations focus on the role of dangerous situations and societal pressures.
2. People in highly threatening environments are more likely to develop feelings of tension, anxiety, and fatigue, exaggerated startle reactions, sleep disturbances, specific fears, and avoidance behaviors.
3. Example: The Three Mile Island nuclear power plant accident resulted in long-term elevated anxiety and depression levels in those living nearby.
4. Societal changes increase anxiety symptoms, and the prevalence of phobic and generalized anxiety has increased from 1.4 and 2.5 percent, respectively, to 11.0 and 3.8 percent since 1975.
5. Cross-cultural studies indicate that anxiety symptoms increase with a variety of societal changes, including war, political oppression, and modernization.
6. One growing problem is "technophobia," a fear of interacting with modern technological products.
7. Poor people have higher rates of phobic and generalized anxiety disorders.

8. Generalized anxiety disorders and phobic disorders are more common among African Americans than among white Americans.

9. Freud's initial psychodynamic explanation distinguished three kinds of anxiety: realistic, neurotic, and moral.

10. Freud thought people attempt to control unacceptable impulses by using ego defense mechanisms.

11. Psychodynamic theory explains phobic disorders as resulting from overreliance on defense mechanisms, whereas it attributes generalized anxiety disorder to a breakdown of defense mechanisms.

12. Most phobias involve the defense mechanisms of repression and displacement (e.g., Little Han's fear of horses is seen as displaced castration anxiety).

13. Object relations theorists link generalized anxiety disorders to overstrict or overprotective parents.

14. Self theorists believe that children develop disintegration anxiety when their parents fail to treat them in a confident, supportive manner, and the defensive structures they develop break down under the stresses of adult life; in the resultant state of self-fragmentation they are prey to constant anxiety.

15. Researchers have found that people employ repression and related defense mechanisms in the face of fear and anxiety, and anxious patients often forget or change the topic when asked to discuss anxiety-arousing experiences.

16. Cross-cultural research suggests a correlation between restrictive child-rearing practices and anxiety in adulthood.

17. Psychodynamic research findings could be explained in other ways, and not all such findings support the theory.

18. The humanist Carl Rogers believed that anxiety disorders are caused by harsh self-standards, or conditions of worth, developed in people who as children did not receive unconditional positive regard.

19. Existential anxiety is the fear of limits and of the responsibilities of existence.

20. Behaviorists believe that anxiety disorders may be learned through conditioning; fears can be classically conditioned or modeled, and avoidance behaviors develop through vicarious conditioning.

21. Fears undergo extinction after repeated exposure to the feared object brings no harm, but people with phobias develop avoidance behaviors through operant conditioning.

22. Through stimulus generalization, specific learned fears can become a generalized anxiety disorder.
23. Analogue experiments with animals and humans have supported behavioral explanations of anxiety disorders.
24. The frequency of some common phobias suggests the possibility of genetic or cultural preparedness for some phobias.
25. Cognitive explanations focus on maladaptive assumptions and faulty thinking processes, such as automatic thoughts.
26. Unpredictability increases fear and generalized anxiety.
27. The biological explanation was first supported by the effectiveness of benzodiazepines in the treatment of anxiety.
28. Generalized anxiety disorder is associated with the anxiety feedback system involving GABA and GABA receptors.
29. There may be inborn differences in arousal styles.
30. Generalized anxiety disorder runs in families, and biological or environmental explanations can be offered.

IV. Panic Disorders

   A. Panic attacks
     1. Panic attacks are periodic, discrete bouts of panic that occur abruptly and reach a peak within ten minutes.
     2. Common symptoms: palpitations, tingling in hands or feet, shortness of breath, sweating, hot and cold flashes, trembling, chest pains, choking sensations, faintness, dizziness, and feelings of unreality.
     3. Anyone can panic in an emergency, but people with a panic disorder do so frequently, unpredictably, and without apparent cause.
     4. Panic disorder requires a certain level of physical or cognitive maturity.

   B. Diagnosis of panic disorder
     1. According to DSM-IV, after at least one unexpected panic attack a person spends at least a month worrying persistently about having another attack or about its consequences, or changes behavior markedly.
     2. Some medical conditions, such as mitral valve prolapse, a cardiac condition marked by periodic heart palpitations, and thyroid disease may be misdiagnosed as panic disorder.
     3. Panic disorder is more common in young adulthood, and is diagnosed twice as often among women as among men.

4. When panic disorder occurs with agoraphobia, the agoraphobic pattern usually emerges from the panic attacks.
5. Some clinicians believe that most cases of panic disorder are accompanied by agoraphobia, but DSM-IV recognizes a category of panic disorder without agoraphobia.

C. Biological explanations
1. In the 1960s an antidepressant drug that affected norepinephrine activity was shown to alleviate panic symptoms.
2. Norepinephrine activity, especially in the locus coeruleus, is irregular in people with panic attacks.
3. Yohimbine, which alters norepinephrine functioning, especially in the locus coeruleus, can trigger panic symptoms even in people with no history of panic attacks.
4. The blood pressure medicine clonidine affects norepinephrine activity and reduces panic symptoms.

D. Cognitive-biological explanations
1. Panic-prone people are highly sensitive to physical sensations and overinterpret them as signaling disaster.
2. People with a high degree of anxiety sensitivity are preoccupied by their bodily symptoms, worry about losing control, expect the worst, and lose perspective.
3. Panic-prone people tend to hyperventilate in stressful situations.
4. Some people with medical problems are incorrectly diagnosed as having a panic disorder.

V. Obsessive Compulsive Disorders

A. General information
1. Obsessions are invasive repetitive thoughts, ideas, impulses, or mental images.
2. Compulsions are repetitive and rigid behaviors that a person feels compelled to perform.
3. Minor obsessions and compulsions may be adaptive.
4. Obsessive compulsive disorders are classified as anxiety disorders because obsessions cause intense anxiety and compulsions prevent or reduce it.
5. Example: Georgia's cleanliness pattern.
6. Up to 2 percent of Americans have these disorders.
7. They are equally common in males and females.

      8. They usually begin in childhood, adolescence, or the early 20s.

      9. They may also involve depression or an eating disorder.

B. Obsessions
  1. Obsessions are thoughts that feel both involuntary (ego dystonic) and foreign (ego alien).
  2. Attempts to ignore or dismiss such thoughts arouse more anxiety.
  3. People with obsessions are aware that their cognitions are excessive and inappropriate.
  4. Kinds of obsessions: obsessive thoughts and wishes, obsessive impulses or urges, obsessive images, obsessive ideas, obsessive doubts.
  5. The most common theme is dirt or contamination (59 percent).
  6. Other common themes: violence and aggression (25 percent), orderliness (23 percent), religion (10 percent), and sexuality (5 percent).
  7. Contamination is the most common theme in Western populations, and aggression, orderliness, and sexual obsessions are quite common as well.

C. Compulsions
  1. People with compulsions feel compelled to perform certain behaviors to prevent something terrible from happening, though they know the behavior is excessive and unreasonable.
  2. Compulsive rituals are detailed, elaborate performances of the compulsion.
  3. Common forms of compulsion: cleaning; checking; symmetry, order, or balance; touching; verbal rituals; counting.

D. Relationship between obsessions and compulsions
  1. Most people who have obsessions also have compulsions, although either disorder can occur alone.
  2. In 61 percent of cases, compulsions represent a yielding to obsessive doubts, ideas, or urges.
  3. In 6 percent of cases, compulsions serve to control obsessions.
  4. Many people with obsessive compulsive disorders worry that they will act out their obsessions.
  5. Obsessions do not usually lead to acts of violence or immorality, but often lead to compulsive acts.
  6. Examples: Samuel Johnson and Howard Hughes (Box 6-4).

E. Explanations of obsessive compulsive disorders
   1. Until recently, these were among the least understood of the mental disorders.
   2. The psychodynamic view is that these disorders represent a battle at the unconscious level between anxiety-provoking id impulses and anxiety-reducing defense mechanisms.
   3. Three commonly used defense mechanisms: isolation, undoing, reaction formation.
   4. Freud believed that children's rage at premature or harsh toilet training can lead to aggressive id impulses, which punishment then teaches them to seek to control, thus establishing a conflict between id and ego that may develop into an obsessive compulsive disorder.
   5. Many people with obsessive compulsive disorders do seem to have rigid and demanding parents.
   6. Object relations theorists propose that disturbed relationships lead some children to believe that everything is either all good or all bad, and they develop obsessions as a way of dealing with negative feelings.
   7. Ego psychologists believe that obsessive people's aggressive impulses represent efforts to fulfill a need for self-expression or to overcome feelings of insecurity.
   8. Cognitive-behavioral theorists propose that some persons are so distressed by perfectly normal unpleasant and intrusive thoughts that they engage in neutralizing thoughts or behaviors to "put matters right" internally.
   9. Factors associated with this pattern: depressed mood, strict code of acceptability, dysfunctional beliefs about responsibility and harm, dysfunctional beliefs about the control of thoughts.
  10. Researchers have found that frequent intrusive thoughts are indeed normal, and that people who develop obsessive compulsive disorders do develop elaborate neutralizing strategies.
  11. Recent research suggests that biological factors are involved in the onset and maintenance of these disorders.
  12. Serotonin seems to be involved because clomipramine, which increases serotonin activity, reduces obsessive and compulsive symptoms.
  13. Abnormal functioning in the orbital region of the frontal cortex and the caudate nuclei (parts of the basal ganglia) seem to be involved; these parts control the conversion of sensory input into cognitions and actions.

14. Symptoms may arise or subside after damage to the orbital region or the caudate nuclei (example: an obsessive compulsive patient who shot himself in the head experienced a dramatic decrease in symptoms).
15. PET scans reveal rapid glucose metabolism in these areas among obsessive compulsive patients.
16. Serotonin plays a very active role in these areas of the brain.

VI. Acute Stress Disorder and Posttraumatic Stress Disorder

   A. Distinguishing the two disorders
     1. Both are reactions to a traumatic event (e.g., combat, earthquake, airplane crash).
     2. Acute stress disorder is diagnosed if symptoms begin within four weeks of the traumatic event and last 2 to 28 days.
     3. Posttraumatic stress disorder can begin shortly after a traumatic event or be delayed, and continue longer than 28 days.

   B. Common symptoms
     1. Reexperiencing the traumatic event, as in recurring recollections, dreams, or nightmares.
     2. Avoidance of activities or situations that are reminiscent of the traumatic event.
     3. Reduced responsiveness, often called "psychic numbing" or "emotional anesthesia"; may involve dissociation, loss of memory, derealization, or depersonalization.
     4. Increased arousal, anxiety, and guilt, possibly with hyperalertness, an exaggerated startle response, and sleep disturbances.

   C. Acute and posttraumatic stress disorders caused by combat
     1. In the past, symptoms of anxiety during combat were called nostalgia, shell shock, and combat fatigue.
     2. Up to 31 percent of men and 26 percent of women who served in Vietnam experienced serious symptoms after combat—80 percent of soldiers who were prisoners of war.
     3. One-quarter of 1.5 million Vietnam combat vets were arrested within two years of their return, and 200,000 were dependent on drugs.
     4. Vietnam veterans had elevated rates of divorce and suicide.

5. Veterans with PTSD had intrusive and repeated recollections of war experiences in the form of flashbacks, night terrors, nightmares, and persistent images and thoughts.
6. These recollections were triggered by similar stimuli, combat scenes, and war news.
7. Six months after the Persian Gulf War, over a third of combat veterans were having nightmares and drinking more than before.

D. Acute and posttraumatic stress disorders caused by other traumas
   1. Symptoms of PTSD are common after natural and accidental disasters; 10 percent of victims of serious traffic accidents experience them.
   2. Symptoms are especially common among people who have come close to dying or who have lost family members.
   3. Examples: Buffalo Creek flood (1972); Hurricane Andrew (1992).
   4. By the 1990s, 46 percent of survivors of Nazi concentration camps fit the diagnostic criteria for PTSD.
   5. About 683,000 adult women are raped each year, and 31 percent have symptoms of PTSD even years afterward.

E. Explanations of posttraumatic stress disorders
   1. Susceptibility is increased by a childhood characterized by poverty, the separation or divorce of parents, or assault, abuse, or catastrophe, or by a history of mental disorders among family members.
   2. Abused children may learn to dissociate as a habitual way of dealing with traumatic events.
   3. Those with poor relationships, or who view aversive events as beyond their control, develop more severe symptoms.
   4. Hardiness—a set of positive attitudes—helps some people respond to stress with a sense of fortitude, control, and commitment.
   5. Symptoms are less severe if the person has a strong support system.
   6. A severely stressful situation will override a positive personal and social context.

VII. The State of the Field: Anxiety disorders

   A. Anxiety disorders are the most common mental disorders in the United States, and are more common among women than among men.

   B. Clinicians have improved their ability to identify significant differences among the various anxiety disorders.

   C. Phobic disorders are the best understood of the anxiety disorders.

   D. Great strides have been made in understanding panic disorders and obsessive compulsive disorders.

   E. Less is known about generalized anxiety disorders; only their biological correlates are coming to be clearly understood.

   F. All of the models of psychopathology have contributed to our understanding of these disorders, but all have limitations.

   G. The current trend is to combine theoretical views in efforts to understand anxiety disorders.

LEARNING OBJECTIVES

1. Distinguish between fear and anxiety.
2. Describe the anxiety disorders and how common these disorders are.
3. Define stress and compare primary appraisal and secondary appraisal of stressors.
4. Explain the role of the sympathetic and parasympathetic nervous system in the anxiety response.
5. Distinguish between trait anxiety and state anxiety.
6. Define "phobia" and describe agoraphobia, social phobia, and specific phobia.
7. Describe the major features of generalized anxiety disorders.
8. Compare and contrast the various perspectives' explanations of phobic disorders and generalized anxiety disorders.
9. Describe the features of panic disorder and discuss the biological and cognitive-biological explanations of this disorder.
10. Distinguish between obsessions and compulsions.
11. Compare and contrast the psychodynamic, cognitive-behavioral, and biological explanations of obsessive compulsive disorder.

12. Define acute stress disorder and posttraumatic stress disorder, list typical symptoms, and provide psychological explanations for them.
13. Summarize the current state of the field of anxiety disorders.

INSTRUCTION SUGGESTIONS

1. *Class demonstration.* Bring in DSM-IV and read one or more descriptions of various anxiety disorders. If you have access to the DSM-II version, bring it into class and compare the current description of generalized anxiety disorder and the older description of anxiety neurosis. Elicit or point out the differences between the two. One significant difference to discuss is that the current manual is the first to suggest how long and how often symptoms should be present before a specific diagnosis is made.

2. *Class demonstration.* Get a copy of Charles Spielberger's State-Trait Anxiety Inventory (STAI) and use it to help you discuss the difference between trait anxiety and state anxiety. You might use college student examples to illustrate these differences. For example, students can identify basic differences among college friends in their typical anxiety level; these differences represent trait anxiety. You can illustrate state anxiety by having students draw a graph of the anxiety levels they experienced in the course of the semester. They will probably have a couple of "peak weeks," especially at midterms and finals. These differences illustrate the effects of state anxiety.

3. *Lecture additions.* The text points out that "phobia" comes from the Greek word for fear. You can add that Phobos was the Greek god of fear. In fact, the scary face of Phobos was painted on the shields of Greek warriors to strike fear into the hearts of their opponents.

4. *Lecture additions.* The text mentions that many people with agoraphobia (and some with other phobias) avoid driving through a tunnel or across a bridge. Those who must do so usually experience a buildup of anxiety, which generally disappears once the "danger" is past. The question then becomes: What do such people experience if they must travel across a very long bridge?

One such bridge crosses Chesapeake Bay. This bridge is long enough to include a stopping area for a scenic view and roadside restrooms, and even people who never panicked on a bridge before have found themselves white-knuckled and paralyzed by fear along the side of the road. Authorities eventually solved some difficult problems by hiring experienced drivers to travel in vans until they notice an incapacitated driver. They then move the scared driver to a passenger seat and drive the car the rest of the way across the bridge.

5. *Class activity.* Refer students to Box 6-1 and ask them to peruse the list of phobia names. Have students speculate on why phobias were given such fancy names. Our favorite explanation is that when professionals can't treat and understand something, we give it a name hard to pronounce so that the patient feels that progress is being made; and until behavioral therapy techniques proved very successful, phobias were quite resistant to change. An interesting classroom alternative or addition is to select a few of these phobia names and write each on a separate card. Choose words that some students will be able to figure out because the word's root is familiar or because some common word looks similar and means about the same. Have students figure out what these phobias represent. For example, you could choose the following phobias for this exercise:

AEROPHOBIA (air) - aerogram, aeroplane
APIPHOBIA (bees) - apiary
PHOBOPHOBIA (fear) - phobia
MONOPHOBIA (being alone) - monotone, monopoly, monogram
ORNITHOPHOBIA (birds) - ornithology
HEMATOPHOBIA (blood) - hematology, hemophilia
BIBLIOPHOBIA (books) - bibliography, bibliophile
CANCEROPHOBIA (cancer) - cancer, cancerous
ECCLESIAPHOBIA (churches) - ecclesiastic
FRIGOPHOBIA (cold) - frigid, Frigidaire
CHROMATOPHOBIA (color) - trichromatic theory, Kodachrome, chromatic
CRYSTALLOPHOBIA (crystals) - crystals
DEMONOPHOBIA (devils) - demon, demonic
PHARMOCOPHOBIA (drugs) - pharmacy, pharmaceutical
CHRONOPHOBIA (duration) - chronicity, chronological, chronicle, chronic
ACROPHOBIA (heights) - acrobat, acropolis
CLAUSTROPHOBIA (enclosed space) - closet
ANGLOPHOBIA (England/English) - Anglo-Saxon, Anglo-American
ELECTROPHOBIA (electricity) - electric, electrify

6. ***Class activity.*** Take a tally of phobias of class members (you can have them write them down to preserve anonymity) and discuss the most common irrational fears. If the class is typical of the American population, public speaking will rank first (or may be expressed as "speech class" among college students). It is also good to have class members determine which of the fears are specific phobias and which are social phobias. Sometimes this is easy (e.g., fear of storms, fear of spiders, and fear of bats are specific phobias), but social phobias may be mislabeled as specific phobias (e.g., fear of eating in restaurants and fear of blushing).

7. ***Class demonstration.*** Ask a Vietnam vet, a worker at a vets' center, a Red Cross volunteer, or a survivor of a natural catastrophe to speak to your class and discuss the experience and what helped him or her to cope.

8. ***Class discussion.*** Propose some legal situations in which a victim of PTSD is involved and have the class discuss how PTSD affects the way they would resolve the legal problems. Give a variety of situations and initial traumas—some that occurred over time and some that were an overwhelmingly intense single event. For example, would a wife who has been physically and emotionally battered for seven years be considered a victim of PTSD? Why, or why not? As jury members, would they consider this experience when they assessed the guilt of a woman who had shot and killed her husband during or after a battering?

    Propose a situation in which a combat veteran has a flashback to a battle situation and assaults an ordinary citizen. Would your students put the veteran on trial? If they were on the jury, would his experience affect their decision? If he were convicted, what sentence would they recommend?

    You can use examples from actual recent cases, such as the teenage sons who killed their parents after repeated abuse or the battered and raped wife who severed her husband's penis. You can bring in news articles about the legal cases.

    You could also have small groups come up with a variety of legal situations and then discuss these class-generated situations as a whole.

9. *Lecture additions.* Box 6-4 provides an interesting look at Howard Hughes's obsessive compulsive behavior. You can add this information about his odd behavior:

 *Hughes would not touch any object unless he first picked up a tissue (which he called insulation) so that he would never directly touch an object that might expose him to germs.

 *Hughes saved his own urine in mason jars; hundreds of them were stored in his apartment. From time to time a staff member would covertly empty some of the filled jars.

 *Hughes saves his newspapers in high stacks, so many of them that visitors sometimes had to weave carefully through a room to avoid toppling them.

 *Hughes sometimes watched one film (his favorite was Ice Station Zero) more than a hundred times in a row before switching to another film. Likewise, he might have gone for days eating the same couple of foods (e.g., chicken noodle soup and one flavor of Baskin-Robbins ice cream) and no others.

 *Hughes used heroin and other drugs.

10. *Class discussion.* Talk about dual diagnosis and multiple diagnosis. No individual is necessarily limited to just one diagnosis. After presenting the additional information about Howard Hughes, you can have the class discuss what diagnoses Hughes might have qualified for. Have students consider obsessive compulsive disorder, agoraphobia, a specific phobia, a social phobia, substance abuse, schizophrenia, paranoia, and a personality disorder.

11. *Class activity.* Have students generate a list of college situations that encourage anxiety symptoms and mini-solutions that mimic phobias, obsessions, compulsions, free-floating anxiety, and so on. For example, does one write a better term paper if one hits upon a "healthy adaptation" of some obsessive compulsive strategy?

12. *Class discussion.* When you discuss habits vs. compulsions, you might consider when cleaning becomes compulsive behavior. For example, find out how many students make their beds each day. Is this just a habit, or is it a compulsion? For fun, have them guess what percentage of Americans make their beds every day. According to a 1994 Roper poll published in the April 1994 issue of *Good Housekeeping*, making one's bed is becoming less of a national

pastime. Only 45 percent of women under the age of 45 say they make their beds every day; among women over 45, however, 71 percent make their beds every day. Surprisingly, not making the bed is not a major source of guilt. Only 15 percent of the women polled admitted to much guilt over an unmade bed. Only about 10 percent of men make their beds every day. In fact, 60 percent of husbands never make a bed. Children do slightly better: 19 percent of those from 10 to 17 years old make their beds daily.

13. *Minilecture: Choking Under Pressure*
    The material for this minilecture is from Chapter 3 of *Your Own Worst Enemy* by Steven Berglas and Roy F. Baumeister (Basic Books). Other chapters provide more examples for lecture material.

    Choking, or the paradoxical incentive effect, involves performing badly when rewards are linked to superior performance. When people choke, they do the opposite of what is in their best interests.

    In an experiment Baumeister gave subjects time to learn a simple skill task and then to perform it as well as they could. Subjects in the experimental condition would receive a cash reward if they matched their best previous performance; the control group, of course, had no incentive. The control group ended up performing better than the experimental group. In other words, randomly chosen persons choked under the pressure of a cash reward.

    As individuals learn skills, they move from consciously attending to each step and slow, measured efforts to being able to perform without thinking about the performance. A well-learned task is done without conscious thinking. Choking can occur when well-learned, automatic processes are interfered with by the conscious mind. In other words, there is an unfortunate shift in attention when it is important to do well at something. Choking under pressure is not a reduction in effort but a failure of skill.

    Several things can capture one's attention and produce choking. We have seen that a monetary incentive can produce choking. So can a grade incentive or an award incentive. A crowd may pay a role in choking. Compliments can also increase self-consciousness and lower performance. This is particularly the case when a compliment raises self-consciousness without boosting one's confidence (as when someone compliments your appearance rather than your speaking skill at a debating contest).

Not all tasks are equally likely to be interfered with by choking. Skill tasks are more affected than effort tasks. When pressure is high, self-awareness often helps people do better on tasks that depend mainly on effort. Incentives, awards, and the presence of other people can increase persistence, muscular exertion, and determined concentration.

People who are low in self-consciousness are most likely to choke because when pressure makes them self-conscious they do not know how to handle it well. On the other hand, individuals who are typically self-conscious learn to cope with it and are therefore less likely to choke than those low in self-consciousness.

TREATMENTS FOR ANXIETY DISORDERS

■

TOPIC OVERVIEW

This chapter explores a wide range of therapies that are typically used in treating anxiety disorders. It opens with the global therapies: psychodynamic therapies and humanistic and existential therapies. Then the chapter covers the specific therapies used in the behavioral, cognitive, and biological approaches. Systematic desensitization, flooding and implosive therapy, modeling, social skills training, cognitive therapies, stress management training, exposure and response prevention, and drug therapies are discussed.

LECTURE OUTLINE

I.   Global Therapies

   A. A global therapy is a general procedure that the therapist follows regardless of the client's particular disorder.

   B. Psychodynamic therapies explore the impact of past events and search for deep-seated conflicts in the expectation that insight fosters recovery.

   C. Humanistic and existential therapies help clients become more aware and accepting of their true thoughts and feelings.

   D. Global therapies emphasize the role of insight.

II. Psychodynamic Therapies

    A. Psychodynamic therapists attribute anxiety disorders to fear of id impulses and lack of success in controlling them.

    B. The therapist's aim is to have clients uncover and understand unconscious issues.

    C. Controlled research has not consistently supported this approach as effective with anxiety disorders.

    D. This approach is modestly helpful for generalized anxiety disorder but not for other anxiety disorders.

    E. Freud thought it important to face one's phobia in addition to undergoing psychoanalysis.

    F. Free association and interpretation techniques may increase an obsessive compulsive pattern.

    G. Short-term psychodynamic therapies, which are more direct and action-based, may work with obsessive compulsive disorders.

III. Humanistic and Existential Therapies

    A. Client-centered therapists show unconditional positive regard, empathy, and genuine acceptance and concern.

    B. Their goal is to help clients experience themselves, to trust themselves completely and to be more open and honest.

    C. They view therapy as a safe relationship.

    D. Research does not support the effect of these therapies with anxiety disorders.

IV. Problem-Based Therapies: Behavioral, Cognitive, and Biological Approaches

    A. General information
        1. Specific therapies are tailored to the idiosyncratic features of each disorder.

2. Behavioral approaches are most successful with phobic disorders.
3. Behavioral, cognitive, and biological approaches have made substantial contributions to the treatment of the other anxiety disorders.

B. Specific phobias
   1. The major behavioral approaches, called exposure treatments, are desensitization, flooding, and modeling.
   2. Wolpe's systematic desensitization involves learning to relax while one is confronted with feared objects or situations.
   3. Systematic desensitization has three phases: relaxation training, construction of a fear hierarchy, and graded pairing of feared objects and relaxation responses, which results in reciprocal inhibition.
   4. An actual physical confrontation with feared events is in vivo desensitization: the use of mental images is called covert desensitization.
   5. In flooding and implosive therapy, clients stop fearing things because repeated, intensive exposure to those feared objects teaches them that they are actually harmless.
   6. Flooding procedures can be in vivo (flooding) or imaginal (implosive therapy).
   7. Flooding is an intense therapy, and it should be conducted by a properly trained therapist so that harm is avoided and clients are actually helped to overcome their phobias.
   8. Modeling can involve vicarious conditioning, in which the therapist confronts the feared object or situation while the client observes.
   9. The most effective modeling technique is participant modeling, or guided participation.
   10. Research supports behavioral approaches for specific phobias.
   11. The first controlled experiments on desensitization were snake phobias studies, in which about 75 percent of subjects improved; 92 percent improved with live modeling and guided participation.
   12. Prolonged exposure combines the gradualism of desensitization, the nonrelaxation of flooding, and the supportive modeling of guided participation.

C. Agoraphobia
   1. A variety of in vivo exposure approaches offer some relief to many people.

2. Agoraphobic people who join a support group go together into exposure situations for several hours.
3. Another approach consists of home-based self-help programs.
4. Between 60 and 80 percent of clients are significantly helped by exposure-based treatment.
5. Relapses occur in as many as 50 percent of successfully treated clients.
6. Exposure-based treatment is less helpful to clients whose agoraphobia is combined with panic disorder.

D. Social phobias
   1. Therapists either try to reduce social fears, provide social skills training, or both.
   2. Stage fright (Box 7-1) is lessened when one decides on specific objectives, puts oneself in the audience's place, uses only brief notes, speaks to one person at a time, avoids thinking about one's hands or expression, talks slowly, speaks the way one normally talks, and asks for advice and criticism.
   3. Exposure therapies are used to reduce social fears, sometimes in a group therapy setting.
   4. Ellis's rational-emotive therapy involves finding and altering irrational assumptions and doing homework assignments.
   5. Cognitive approaches have been shown to reduce social fears even five years later.
   6. Social skills training combines role playing, assertiveness training, and learning of social interaction skills.

E. Generalized anxiety disorders
   1. About 27 percent of people with generalized anxiety disorders seek treatment each year.
   2. Global therapies are modestly helpful with this disorder.
   3. Cognitive therapies, management training, and antianxiety drugs are somewhat more helpful.
   4. Beck suggests that these people's assumptions are dominated by themes of imminent danger.
   5. They need to alter such automatic thoughts as "What if I fail?" and "I'm falling behind."
   6. Some therapists teach stress management skills that the client can apply during stressful times.
   7. Self-instruction training, or stress inoculation training, is intended to replace negative self-statements with coping self-statements; it is of modest helpfulness.
   8. Relaxation training and biofeedback are of modest help.

9. The electromyograph (EMG) provides feedback about the level of muscular tension, which produces a modest reduction of anxiety for normal and anxious subjects.
10. Production of increased alpha brain waves by use of an electroencephalograph (EEG) is not successful.
11. The first antianxiety medications were sedative-hypnotic drugs (e.g., barbiturates), which led to physical dependence, drowsiness, and risk of overdose.
12. Meprobamates (e.g., Miltown) were less dangerous but still caused drowsiness.
13. The family of drugs called the benzodiazepines (e.g., chlordiazepoxide and diazepam, or Valium) reduced anxiety and were relatively nontoxic except in combination with other drugs.
14. GABA receptors (especially GABA-A) receive benzodiazepine drugs, which inhibit neuron firing, thus slowing physical arousal throughout the body.
15. Benzodiazepines reduce the symptoms of generalized anxiety disorder but are not helpful with specific phobias or obsessive compulsive disorders.
16. When benzodiazepines are stopped, the anxieties return; and when these drugs are taken in large doses for an extended time, patients become physically dependent on them.
17. Benzodiazepines produce the adverse effects of drowsiness, lack of coordination, impaired memory, depression, and aggressive behavior.
18. Benzodiazepines potentiate (increase the effects of) other toxic drugs, including alcohol.
19. Family physicians prescribe more benzodiazepines than psychiatrists do.
20. Beta blockers bind to receptors called B-adrenergic receptors and block the reception of norepinephrine, reducing palpitations and tremors.
21. Buspirone, which is an azaspirone, is better than beta blockers at reducing anxiety and is less addictive.

F. Panic disorders
   1. About 54 percent of all Americans with panic disorder receive treatment for it each year.
   2. Success in treatment is a recent phenomenon.
   3. Global therapies and stress management techniques are not helpful.

4. Antianxiety drugs do not reduce the frequency or intensity of panic attacks.
5. In 1962, Klein and Fink found that antidepressant drugs prevented or lessened panic attacks.
6. Alpraxolam (Xanax), although a benzodiazepine drug, is effective in treating panic disorders.
7. It seems that antidepressant drugs restore norepinephrine activity in the locus coeruleus.
8. Antidepressant drugs and alpraxolam help with panic disorder that occurs in conjunction with agoraphobia.
9. A problem is the client's anticipatory anxiety, which can be helped with behavioral exposure treatments.
10. Drugs, or drugs combined with exposure therapy, bring improvement to 80 percent of clients, and 40 percent reach full recovery.
11. Misinterpretation of physical symptoms as a panic attack can become a self-fulfilling prophecy.
12. Cognitive therapists provide accurate information about symptoms (e.g., sudden faintness is a faulty adjustment of the blood pressure mechanism to changes in posture).
13. Biological challenge procedures induce panic symptoms and clients practice interpreting them appropriately; research has shown these procedures to be at least as useful as drug therapy.

G. Obsessive compulsive disorders
   1. About 41 percent of Americans with an obsessive compulsive disorder receive treatment for it each year.
   2. Fewer than 60 percent improve with treatment.
   3. Prevention of compulsive acts can lead to a reduction in their occurrence.
   4. Therapists who use an exposure and response-prevention procedure repeatedly expose clients to objects or situations that elicit fears but instruct them to refrain from their compulsive acts; 60 to 90 percent show improvement.
   5. Thought stopping, or saying "stop" to interrupt obsessive thoughts, may lead to an intensification of obsessive thoughts.
   6. Therapists who engage in habituation training evoke a client's obsessive thoughts again and again.
   7. Covert-response prevention teaches clients to identify, prevent, or distract themselves from carrying out any neutralizing thoughts or actions that emerge during habituation training.

8. Some clinicians believe clients must challenge and change their underlying dysfunctional beliefs about unwanted negative thoughts.

9. Antianxiety drugs are not useful for clients with these disorders.

10. Certain antidepressants, especially clomipramine, are helpful to 50 to 80 percent of patients.

11. Trichotillomania, or pulling and yanking of the hair, and onychophagia, or nailbiting, are helped by clomipramine (but not by despiramine, which does not effect serotonin).

12. Antidepressants help by increasing serotonin activity.

13. Lower, more normal levels of metabolic activity in the right caudate nucleus are produced by antidepressants that affect serotonin and by exposure and response-prevention treatment.

H. Acute stress disorders and posttraumatic stress disorders

1. The treatment goals are to reduce or overcome lingering symptoms, to gain perspective on the trauma, and to return to constructive living.

2. Antianxiety drugs and antidepressant drugs are used to reduce tension, lessen nightmares, and reduce depression.

3. Exposure techniques are applied to reduce symptoms.

4. Talking and writing about suppressed traumatic experiences can reduce symptoms.

5. Many PTSD sufferers deal with guilt, rage, and overresponsibility in group therapy.

6. 150 small counseling centers and treatment programs in Veterans Administration hospitals specialize in helping veterans heal their psychological wounds through group and individual therapy.

V. The State of the Field: Treatments for Anxiety Disorders

A. Treatment for anxiety disorders has changed in many ways in the past fifteen years.

B. Behavioral, cognitive, and drug therapies dominate the treatment picture.

C. Behavioral therapy is effective with specific phobias, agoraphobia, and obsessive compulsive disorders.

D. Cognitive approaches are helpful with panic and obsessive compulsive disorders, and somewhat helpful with generalized anxiety disorder and social phobias.

E. Antianxiety drugs are an important adjunct in the treatment of generalized anxiety disorder.

F. Antidepressant drugs have a major impact on panic disorders and obsessive compulsive disorders.

G. Global therapies are sometimes helpful with generalized anxiety disorder and acute and posttraumatic stress disorders.

H. Clinicians now make greater efforts to match anxious clients to particular forms of treatment.

I. Research helps clarify and alter treatment.

LEARNING OBJECTIVES

1. Explain the characteristics of global therapies and compare psychodynamic therapies with humanistic and existential therapies.
2. Know how psychodynamic therapists explain anxiety disorders and what procedures they use.
3. Describe the three exposure-based behavioral therapies used in treating phobias: desensitization, flooding, and modeling.
4. Describe the treatment for agoraphobia.
5. Describe the exposure techniques, cognitive therapy, and social skills training used in treating social phobias.
6. Explain why generalized anxiety disorders are least responsive to treatment.
7. List and describe the cognitive approaches, stress management training techniques, and the actions of benzodiazepine drugs in the treatment of generalized anxiety disorders.
8. Know how biological and cognitive interventions alleviate panic disorders.
9. Describe exposure with response prevention, thought stopping, habituation training, and covert response prevention, and tell how they are used to help individuals with obsessive compulsive disorders.
10. Know what drugs are helpful for obsessive compulsive disorders.
11. Describe treatment programs for acute and posttraumatic stress disorders.
12. Summarize the current state of treatments for anxiety disorders.

INSTRUCTION SUGGESTIONS

1. *Class project.* Assign students to engage in (and record) a ten-minute attempt at free association. Have them begin with the thought "One of the things I remember about the experience of anxiety is that . . ." Tell them to write about the experience of free association and to estimate their success at talking without censorship. At this point they should listen to their ten-minute session to refresh their memory of what they did think about. Then they should write about the cognitive flow during the free association. Did they change topics? Did some surprising topics come up? What are their reactions to their chain of associations? Finally, they should state their opinions about the usefulness of free association in therapy. Would they like to enter therapy in which they were requested to engage in free association?

2. *Class activity.* As a class or in small groups, have students construct a hierarchy of fears for a situation other than one described in the chapter; for example, (1) a job interview, (2) a midterm exam, (3) giving a speech in class. You may wish to instruct students about a muscle tension-relaxation exercise. Finally, describe the pairing of tension and relaxation but do not carry out this step during class.

3. *Class activity.* After emphasizing how vivid and detailed a therapist's description of a feared object must be to help someone with a germ phobia and obsession, assign each small group the task of writing a graphic passage for one of the following examples. Check on their progress and suggest that they add more vivid and disgusting detail (e.g., "Don't forget to describe the green mold that's growing on the slimy tomato left on that dirty dish in that filthy dishwater"; "Don't forget to describe those huge, mangy, flea-bitten, dirt-caked rats that run in and out of all that disgusting, smelling, leaking garbage at the dump"). At the end, dramatically read the passages they have produced, commenting that in actual flooding and implosive therapy the descriptions would be much longer. Ask students how these passages made them feel and what hearing a couple of hours of such descriptions would do.
   A. A sinkful of dirty dishes that have gathered over a two-week period.
   B. A look into one of the most disgusting full garbage cans imaginable.
   C. A kitchen floor that has been unscrubbed and unswept for at least three months.

    D. Walking around a community junkyard.

    E. Taking a tour of a garbage dump.

    F. Viewing an underground sewer system.

    G. Looking into the refrigerator vegetable crisper after returning from a three-week vacation.

4. *Lecture additions.* Here is a brief additional case of agoraphobia. Polly, a homemaker with two small children, developed agoraphobia around the age of 20. Eventually she could not enter the back of a grocery store for fear that she would faint. She would not allow non-family members in her car because of her belief that their presence would trigger a panic attack. She did not go to concert halls, restaurants, or other public places because she believed physical symptoms would develop that would result in a loss of control. Malls especially were intolerable to her, and she gave up the shopping sprees she had enjoyed as a teenager. In reality, Polly had fainted only twice.

Polly developed ingenious ways to cope with her agoraphobia. She had her best friend choose groceries located in the back of the store. Rather than visit her friends, she had them come to her home, and she became quite a skilled hostess, cook, and entertainer. Friends were important to her and she honed her skills as a storyteller so that her agoraphobia did not leave her lonely. She did most of her shopping through catalogs.

Yet Polly realized that she needed help when her 7-year-old daughter, Molly, needed new gym shoes. She sent Molly into the mall alone with a credit card to buy the shoes. Molly succeeded, and Polly thought that she needed to learn to be as courageous as young Molly.

By means of a variety of therapy techniques that gradually expanded her world, the therapist helped Polly build her self-esteem until she was ready to try to attend college. However, she enrolled in a chemistry course because "I'd show my therapist that I wasn't smart enough for college and be done with this hard work of getting better," and she enrolled in a night class "so if I fainted not as many people would see me embarrass myself." Polly never did faint, and she managed a B in that first chemistry class. A year and a half later Polly had her A.A. degree; just over a year later she had a B.A. in psychology, and within two more years an M.A. in counseling.

5. *Class activity.* Get students to design a combined cognitive therapy and social skills training program for a client with a fear of blushing.

6. *Class demonstration.* Bring in a copy of the Physician's Desk Reference (PDR), look up information on some of the medications mentioned in this chapter, and discuss the material in class.

7. *Class activity.* Have the class generate automatic thoughts that students typically engage in during a test, such as "You'll never finish," "Stupid jerk," "Everybody else can do this." Discuss the origin of the unhelpful automatic thoughts and how to reduce their power over us.

8. *Class activity.* Discuss the material on stress inoculation and have students adapt this training for learning to cope better with midterm exams (or some other threatening aspect of the semester). The four steps are (1) preparing for a stressor (e.g., How many tests do I have? Which of them are comprehensive? What kinds of questions will be asked? How are the various tests scheduled? What's my realistic plan of attack? Remember that I need to focus on what I can do to prepare for them); (2) confronting and handling a stressor (e.g., I need to turn this stress into studying energy. Relax and be in control—remember to take deep breaths while studying and during the test); (3) coping with the feeling of being overwhelmed (e.g., It's normal to feel scared while the tests are being passed out—just let the feeling subside; I don't have to eliminate all my test anxiety—just keep it manageable); (4) reinforcing self-statements (Way to go, you aren't dying! Hey, I recognize this one—seems I have learned a lot!)

9. *Class demonstration.* Demonstrate biofeedback or stress cards in class. If you have stress dots, get students to wear them for one day and note what situations appear to be the most stressful and the most relaxing.

10. *Class demonstration.* Ask a pharmacist, chemical dependency counselor, or physician to speak to your class about prescription drug addictions and the dangers of overdosing on prescribed drugs and over-the-counter medications.

11. *Class discussion.* Have the class discuss how paradoxical intention might be applied to learning to cope better with one aspect of being a student.

12. *Class demonstration.* Have a speaker from a veterans' center or some other crisis center address the role of group therapy in the treatment of PTSD.

13. *Class project.* Have students keep a worry journal for two weeks. At the end of that time either discuss the exercise in class or have them write a two- or three-page reaction to the experience of writing about their daily fears and anxieties.

MOOD DISORDERS

■

TOPIC OVERVIEW

This chapter explores both unipolar patterns of depression and bipolar disorders. Beginning with the clinical picture of depression, the chapter discusses diagnosing unipolar patterns of depression and explanations that have been proposed for them. The chapter also looks at the clinical picture of mania, the diagnosis of bipolar disorders, and explanations of bipolar disorders.

LECTURE OUTLINE

I. General Information

    A. Most people have transient moods, but people with mood disorders have moods that last a long time, that greatly affect their interactions with the world, and that disrupt normal functioning.

    B. Depression is a low, sad state in which life seems bleak and challenges seem overwhelming.

    C. Mania, the extreme opposite of depression, is a state of euphoria and frenzied energy.

    D. Unipolar depression, which is not accompanied by a manic state, is more common than bipolar or manic-depressive disorder.

    E. Mania without depression is rare except when it is caused by a medical condition.

II. Unipolar Patterns of Depression

A. Normal dejection
   1. All people experience dejection at times.
   2. It is seldom so severe that it significantly alters daily functioning.
   3. It is beneficial if it encourages healthy self-exploration.

B. The prevalence of unipolar depression
   1. About 5 to 10 percent of adults in the United States suffer unipolar depression and another 3 to 5 percent suffer mild forms of it.
   2. Worldwide, between 6 and 16 percent of adults experience a severe episode of unipolar depression at some time.
   3. The prevalence of unipolar depression is increasing, and the age of onset is becoming younger.
   4. Twice as many women as men have severe unipolar depression, and women also have more mild episodes (Box 8-1).
   5. There is no difference between girls and boys in the incidence of unipolar depression.
   6. The incident rate is fairly steady across all socioeconomic classes.
   7. Between the ages of 30 and 64, white Americans have higher rates than African Americans.
   8. Approximately two-thirds recover within 6 months and at least 80 percent within 5 years; but they are at an increased risk of becoming depressed again.

C. The clinical picture of depression
   1. The emotional symptoms include intense sadness, dejection, feelings of emptiness, loss of pleasure, loss of humor, crying spells, and sometimes anxiety and anger.
   2. Patients experience a loss of motivation to participate in their usual activities, a loss of drive and initiative, a paralysis of will.
   3. Between 7 and 15 percent of depressed persons commit suicide (compared to 1 percent of nondepressed people); they account for half of all suicides.
   4. Behavioral symptoms include a dramatic decrease in activity level, doing less and getting less done, slow movement, lack of energy.
   5. Cognitive symptoms involve a view of oneself as inadequate, undesirable, inferior, unattractive, and perhaps evil.

6. Depressed persons blame themselves for nearly every negative event and rarely credit themselves for positive achievements.
7. They take a negative view of the future, do not expect things to improve, and feel hopeless.
8. They often complain that their intellectual ability, memory, and problem-solving abilities are deteriorating.
9. Depressed persons do as well as nondepressed persons in solving problems but predict poorer performances and evaluate themselves less favorably.
10. Research has found that depressed persons are less able to remember events of the distant past.
11. Depression may be accompanied by such physical complaints as headaches, indigestion, constipation, dizziness, and pain.
12. Disturbances in appetite and sleep are common, as is fatigue.
13. About 9 percent of depressed people sleep excessively; the majority get less sleep than normal and awaken frequently during the night.

D. Diagnosing unipolar patterns of depression
1. According to DSM-IV, a major depressive episode is severely disabling, lasts at least two weeks, and has at least five of the symptoms of depression.
2. One must be able to rule out drugs, medical conditions, and recent loss of a loved one as a cause.
3. A small percentage of depressed persons have psychotic symptoms; that is, they lose contact with reality and experience delusions or hallucinations.
4. A diagnosis of major depressive disorder, single episode indicates the patient's first depressive episode and no manic episode.
5. If the episode is not the first, the diagnosis is major depressive disorder, recurrent.
6. A diagnosis of seasonal depressive disorder indicates that the patient's mood fluctuates with seasonal changes.
7. A depressive disorder is labeled catatonic if it is accompanied by either motor immobility or excessive motor activity.
8. It is labeled postpartum if it occurs within 4 weeks of giving birth.
9. It is diagnosed as melancholic if the person is almost totally unaffected by pleasurable events, suffers significant motor disturbances, experiences loss of sleep and appetite, and feels excessive guilt.

10. A less disabling depression characterized by fewer than five symptoms for at least two years is called dysthymia; it has a recovery rate of only 40 percent.

11. Dysthymia leading to a major depression is called double depression.

12. A depressive pattern that causes significant impairment but does not fully meet the criteria of major depressive disorder or dysthymic disorder is called depressive disorder not otherwise specified.

E. Recent life events and unipolar depression

1. Depressed persons tend to have experienced a large number of stressful life events just before the episode.

2. People whose lives are generally stressful and isolated seem more likely than others to become depressed when stresses multiply.

3. Depressed people who lack support tend to remain depressed longer than those who live in a supportive environment.

4. At least 30 percent of depressed persons did not report undesirable events before the onset of their depression.

5. A reactive depression follows precipitating events; an endogenous depression is assumed to have an internal cause.

6. DSM-IV does not require diagnosticians to determine whether an individual's depression is externally or internally caused.

7. Most unipolar depressions are assumed to have both internal and situational components, while melancholic depressive episodes represent an endogenous form.

F. Explanations of unipolar patterns of depression

1. Freud and Abraham compared depression with grief at the loss of a loved one (Box 8-3), in the first stage of which the mourner refuses to accept the loss and regresses to the oral stage of development.

2. Introjection of the loved one leads the mourner to experience all feelings toward the loved one as feelings about self.

3. As the grief reaction worsens, the person feels empty, avoids relationships, becomes preoccupied with the sense of loss, and experiences self-hatred as a result of anger at the loved one for departing.

4. Freud believed that people whose parents failed to meet their needs at the oral stage or overgratified them are particularly prone to depression.

5. Freud thought that depression without the actual loss of a loved one was due to an imagined or symbolic loss.

6. Psychodynamic theorists vary in their emphasis on hostility turned inward, oral fixation, anal and phallic problems, and loss of self-esteem.

7. Object relations theorists link depression to people's inner representations of relationships that leave them feeling unsafe and insecure, especially if their parents pushed them toward either excessive dependence or excessive self-reliance.

8. Studies confirm that separation from the mother before the age of 6 is often accompanied by depression, a pattern called anaclitic depression.

9. Harry Harlow's studies of separation and isolation in young monkeys showed a protest-despair reaction.

10. The dreams of depressed persons reveal higher levels of hostility and masochism.

11. Many depressed persons were raised by parents who treated them with low care and high protection, or "affectionless control."

12. Behaviorist Peter Lewinsohn proposed that depression is related to people's tendency to engage in progressively fewer positive behaviors when the expected rewards dwindle.

13. When the rate of reinforcement rises, particularly social reinforcements, depressed persons improve.

14. This system also works in reverse: a depressed mood changes one's behaviors, and then the reinforcement rate drops.

15. Beck's cognitive view suggests that negative thinking (maladaptive attitudes, the cognitive triad, errors in thinking, automatic thoughts) lies at the heart of unipolar depression.

16. The cognitive triad consists of negative interpretation of one's experiences, oneself, and one's future.

17. Typical errors in thinking include arbitrary inference, selective abstraction, overgeneralization, magnification and minimization, and personalization.

18. Beck believes that the emotional, motivational, behavioral, and somatic aspects of depression all follow from cognitive processes.

19. Ruminative responses during a depressed mood are associated with longer periods of depressed mood.

20. Beck's cognitive theory has received good support from research.

21. Martin Seligman suggests that helplessness is at the center of depression: people perceive a loss of control over reinforcements and hold themselves responsible for their helplessness.
22. One can reverse helplessness by attributing loss of control to an external cause or to an internal cause that is specific or unstable.
23. Compelling evidence has been found that biological abnormalities contribute to the development of unipolar depression.
24. Support for the genetic view comes primarily from family pedigree studies, twin studies, and adoption studies.
25. As many as 20 percent of close relatives of a depressed person (a proband) are depressed, compared to 5 percent of the general population.
26. Among monozygotic twins, when one twin is depressed, 43 percent of the other twins are depressed; for dizygotic twins the figure is 20 percent.
27. A Danish study found a higher incidence of severe depression among the biological parents of depressed adoptees than among the biological parents of nondepressed adoptees.
28. The catecholamine theory attributes depression to a low level of norepinephrine.
29. The idoleamine theory attributes depression to a deficiency in serotonin.
30. Current theories propose that a deficiency of either norepinephrine or serotonin (or of both) produce depression.
31. Acetylcholine may be another neurotransmitter involved in depression.

III. Bipolar disorders

A. The clinical picture of mania
   1. Manic episodes are characterized by exaggerated feelings of joy and well-being, immoderate activity, and expansive emotions but also irritability, anger, and annoyance.
   2. Manic people seek constant excitement, involvement, and companionship.
   3. Their behavior is described as hyperactive, loud, fast, and flamboyant.
   4. Manic persons display poor judgment and planning and may have grandiose self-esteem; they may have so much trouble keeping their thoughts on track that they become incoherent.

    5. Manic people are easily distracted by random stimuli from the environment.

    6. Manic persons get very little sleep, yet are wide awake and energetic.

B. Diagnosing bipolar disorders

    1. According to DSM-IV, a manic episode is an abnormally elevated, expansive, or irritable mood accompanied by at least three other symptoms for at least one week.

    2. Manic episodes vary from moderate to extreme in severity and may include a hypomanic episode.

    3. An episode that is less severe, is of shorter duration, and displays fewer symptoms is called a hypomanic episode.

    4. DSM-IV distinguishes two general kinds of bipolar disorders: bipolar I and bipolar II disorders.

    5. In bipolar I disorders, manic episodes alternate with major depressive episodes.

    6. Depressive and manic episodes usually alternate, but some people experience mixed episodes of both manic and depressive symptoms in the same day.

    7. In bipolar II disorders, hypomanic episodes alternate with major depressive episodes.

    8. If a patient experiences the four or more episodes of mood disturbance within a year, the disorder is further classified as rapid cycling.

    9. If a patient's mood episodes vary with the seasons, the disorder is further classified as seasonal.

C. The incidence of bipolar disorders

    1. Between 0.4 and 1.3 percent of all adults worldwide suffer from a bipolar disorder in any given year; bipolar I disorders are more common.

    2. These disorders are equally common in women and men.

    3. They usually begin between the ages of 15 and 44 years.

    4. They are equally common in all socioeconomic classes and ethnic groups.

    5. Up to 60 percent of these disorders begin with a manic or hypomanic episode.

    6. In the typical untreated case, manic and depressive episodes last for several months, with intervening periods of normal mood lasting two or more years.

7.   Cyclothymic disorder, marked by numerous periods of hypomanic and wild depressive symptoms, affects 0.4 percent of the population.

D. Explanations of bipolar disorders
1.   Through the first half of this century, the study of bipolar disorders made little progress.
2.   The psychodynamic view is that depressed reactions are introjection of a loss object and manic reactions flow from the denial of the loss of a loved one; this view is not supported by research.
3.   The theory that mania is related to an oversupply of norepinephrine is supported by research with reserpine and by the effectiveness of lithium, which reduces norepinephrine activity.
4.   Mania, like depression, is associated with a low level of serotonin, which is shown by spinal fluid levels of 5-HIAA (the serotonin metabolite) and by the fact that lithium increases brain serotonin activity.
5.   A "permissive theory" suggests that low serotonin activity sets the stage for a mood disorder and norepinephrine activity defines the particular form it takes.
6.   Another possibility is defective transportation of sodium ions at certain neuron membranes; this hypothesis is derived from the effectiveness of lithium.
7.   Pedigree studies find that close relatives of a person with a bipolar disorder have as much as a 25 percent likelihood of developing the same or a related mood disorder, compared to the 1 percent prevalence rate in the general population.
8.   The likelihood is as high as 70 percent for an identical twin (less than 20 percent for a fraternal twin).
9.   Genetic linkage studies, such as those done with Israeli, Belgian, and Italian families, have found bipolar disorders linked to red-green color blindness and to a medical abnormality called G6PD deficiency (both transmitted by genes on the X chromosome).
10. A genetic linkage study with Amish families found a different chromosomal area, a region on chromosome 11 near the insulin gene and the Ha-ras-1 gene.
11. Attempts to replicate the genetic linkage studies have failed.

IV. The State of the Field: Mood Disorders

    A. Clinicians have a lot of information about mood disorders, yet much is not yet understood.

    B. Patterns of unipolar depression are quite prevalent and subside eventually even without treatment.

    C. Bipolar disorders are less common but are unlikely to subside fully without treatment and are more likely to recur without treatment.

    D. Many important factors in unipolar disorders have been identified but only biological factors are consistently found in association with bipolar disorders.

    E. If one factor is the key cause of unipolar depression, cognitive and biological factors are the leading candidates.

    F. Alternatively, any of the leading factors may be capable of initiating a unipolar pattern of depression, and any initial cause may move toward a "final common pathway" of unipolar depression.

    G. Or an interaction between two or more factors may be necessary to create an episode of unipolar depression.

    H. Or various factors may play different roles in unipolar depression.

LEARNING OBJECTIVES

1. Be able to differentiate between moods and mood disorders.
2. Contrast depression and mania, and contrast unipolar depression and bipolar disorders.
3. Know the primary symptoms of depression and the relationship between depression and suicide.
4. Discuss the incidence of depression, and explain why more women than men experience depression.
5. Compare and contrast reactive depression and endogenous depression.
6. Discuss the role of recent life events in unipolar depression.
7. Describe the psychodynamic view of depression.
8. Describe the behavioral view of depression.

9. Define the four cognitive processes that generate depressive symptoms: maladaptive attitudes, the cognitive triad, errors in thinking, and automatic thoughts.
10. Explain the learned helplessness theory of unipolar depression.
11. Summarize biological evidence from family pedigree studies, twin studies, and adoption studies.
12. Describe the possible roles of the neurotransmitters norepinephrine, serotonin, and acetylcholine in unipolar depression.
13. Define mania and describe its typical symptoms.
14. Describe bipolar disorders and know who is typically affected by them.
15. Distinguish between bipolar disorder and cyclothymic disorder.
16. Know how biological research helps explain bipolar disorders.

INSTRUCTION SUGGESTIONS

1. *Class activity.* Discuss with your class why depression is so common. List reasons on the blackboard. Then have students choose which of the factors are most common in the lives of college students. Can they identify additional factors that pertain principally to college students?

2. *Small-group discussion.* Have students in groups of 3 to 6 share some of their own personal experiences with the emotional, motivational, behavioral, cognitive, and somatic symptoms of depression.

3. *Class activity.* Have the class help you develop a study aid that will help distinguish various types of major depression and dysthymia (visual imagery is one possible tool).

4. *Lecture additions.* Talk about the effects of anniversaries on depression. Explain how people may remourn a significant loss around the same time each year. If we lose a loved one around Christmas, every Christmas is then touched with sadness. Similar weather may also retrigger the emotion. It seems that the body may mourn even if cognitively one does not at first recognize the original loss. If one is depressed "just out of the blue," it might be a good idea to think about what loss occurred at this time of year. Reacknowledging the loss and conducting a grieving ritual will help to reduce the length and intensity of the sadness. The loss is most often a person but it can be a career change, a significant property loss, or a major disappointment.

Anniversary reactions are also associated with the commencement of schizophrenic episodes.

5. ***Lecture additions.*** When you discuss the psychodynamic view that depression involves hostility turned against oneself, you might want to mention Karl Menninger's book ***Man Against Himself***, which views all risk-taking behaviors as a "touch of suicide." Moreover, you might want to describe the Menninger Foundation and the Menninger Clinic in Topeka, Kansas, an institution that is the psychiatric version of the Mayo Clinic. Incidentally, if your college is within a few hours' drive of Menninger, consider making arrangements to take psychology majors (or Psi Beta or Psi Chi members) on an arranged visit there. Students will learn much from the tour.

6. ***Minilecture: The Monkey Studies of Harry Harlow***
How does one choose monkeys as one's research subjects rather than rats or people? What significant event shapes the future research of a beginning psychologist? In Harry Harlow's case, his research path began when his graduate assistantship required him to take care of the monkeys in his college's primate laboratory. This unglamorous job included cleaning monkey cages. It seems that each infant monkey had a soft diaper in its cage to use as a bed, so Harlow had to launder lots of very dirty diapers. He noticed that during the couple of hours between the time he removed the dirty diapers and the time he returned them clean to the cages, the infant monkeys sat and rocked themselves back and forth. This rocking behavior led Harlow to wonder just how important it was for young monkeys to have contact with something soft. This idea led Harlow to a lifelong series of studies.

Harlow's most frequently cited work reports a study in which he found that monkeys preferred a cloth-covered surrogate mother to a wire surrogate mother that held a bottle. This finding led Harlow to propose that contact comfort is more basic than oral satisfaction. This idea was contrary to the psychoanalytic emphasis on oral satisfaction.

Harlow's monkey studies on separation and isolation, cited in this chapter, are also well known and were instrumental in furthering our knowledge about the protest-despair reaction. Harlow also paired some shy, isolated monkeys with outgoing, social monkeys who played the role of "peer therapist." He then monitored the healthier responses of the young isolates. In another study he forced male monkeys to be "househusbands." In the wild, male monkeys are notoriously poor fathers, but Harlow designed a cage that made male adult monkeys stay "home," and under these conditions the male monkeys became better dads.

Harry Harlow contributed a wealth of knowledge to psychology, but it is important to avoid anthropomorphism when we draw scientific conclusions from animal studies.

7. *Class activity.* Bring in crayons (or colored pencils, water paints, fingerpaints, colored chalk) and large sheets of paper and have students draw a picture that represents depression and one that represents mania. You can have each student show the two pictures and explain them. Or you can have them lightly write D or M on the back, shuffle the pictures, and see if the class can put them in the proper categories. Have the students discuss the ease or difficulty of the task, and by what aspects of the pictures they judged them. You could assign this activity as an outside project and not limit the materials that the students might use.

8. *Small-group discussion.* Assign one of the orientations (e.g., psychodynamic, behavioral, cognitive) to each group and have members suggest five ways to help a mildly depressed friend who fits the assigned orientation. Share the results with the whole class.

9. *Class project.* Ask each student to watch one network news program and one local news program and to read the front page of a newspaper. Each student, to the best of his or her ability, is to rate each news item as either negative or positive. Tally all the responses. Did the news receive more negative or more positive ratings? Did any news medium receive more negative or more positive ratings than the others? Why? In large classes you can compare the ratings for ABC, CBS, CNN, and NBC. Discuss the effects of various news media on one's personal mood. One study found that symptoms of mild depression abated when news coverage was avoided for a couple of weeks.

10. *Class activity.* As you discuss Beck's five common errors of thinking (arbitrary inference, selective abstraction, overgeneralization,

magnification and minimization, and personalization), list them on the chalkboard, leaving room to write in examples. Have class members give examples of each type of thinking error that is common among college students. For example, magnification and minimization are shown by "Oh, well, anybody could have gotten an A in that easy class" and "I'll never succeed in a career now that I've gotten a C in that course." Have the students discuss the effects of thinking errors on their emotional state. You might direct the discussion into ways to modify these common errors.

11. *Lecture additions.* You might add to your lecture on cognitive theory and depression some evidence of maladaptive automatic thoughts that you have noticed among students, such as muttering "Stupid jerk" to themselves when they see a C grade on a test. Students may not even realize they have made such comments but still feel depressed by them. Students who berate themselves for a C are also engaging in magnification, because a C indicates average rather than failure.

12. *Class demonstration.* Bring in Beck's Depression Inventory or some other depression inventory and share some of its items with the class. Discuss the usefulness of these inventories in both therapy and research.

13. *Small-group discussion.* Have students analyze and discuss the effects of learned helplessness and perceived lack of control in the lives of (1) college students; (2) children in foster homes; (3) terminally ill patients; (4) workers at a plant that is closing down; (5) political hostages; (6) a farmer facing foreclosure on a three-generation family farm. Try assigning a different situation to each group and then compare the groups' lists of effects. Are the lists similar? Why, or why not?

14. *Small-group activity.* Have each small group design a situation that would lead to an increase in learned helplessness and therefore depression. Have the students describe their situation to the other groups. What elements are common to the various situations? How do the elements differ?

15. *Class demonstration.* Have a pharmacist talk to your class about the effects of psychoactive drugs on depression (and other mental disorders). Discuss how other medication (e.g., hypertension medicines) can increase depression. Ask the speaker to evaluate the effectiveness of current medications, the advantages and disadvantages of drug therapy, and expectations for future medications.

16. *Lecture additions.* Choose literary passages that depict depression and manic states and read them to the class. Sylvia Plath's *The Bell Jar* provides good examples. Or use Saul Bellow's description of a person in a manic episode, an excerpt of which appears in the chapter.

17. *Class demonstration.* Bring to class a copy of the *Physician's Desk Reference* (PDR) and share the so-called side effects listed for lithium and some tricyclics and MAO inhibitors. Look up the adverse effects of more recent antidepressants such as Paxil, Proxac, and Zoloft.

18. *Class project.* Have students fill out a tally form to indicate the explanation they favor for gender differences in the incidence of depression. Rank each choice from 1 (most favored) to 5 (least favored). In large classes, tally men's and women's choices separately. Add up the number of first-place votes for each explanation. Eliminate the least popular option and add up the number of votes this option received for second place. In each round eliminate the least popular option and go in turn to the alternative third, fourth, and fifth choices. At the end you will have the choice that is the most popular. You can also print out a form such as the one offered here and have students survey other students (anonymously).
    A. Artifact hypothesis: Depression is underdiagnosed in men.
        1 2 3 4 5
    B. X-linkage hypothesis: Because depression is caused by a dominant mutation on the X chromosome, women are at higher risk for it than men.
        1 2 3 4 5
    C. Traditional psychoanalytic explanation: Women suffer from lifelong penis envy and are vulnerable to depression because they depend on relationships to maintain their self-esteem.
        1 2 3 4 5
    D. Sociocultural explanation: Society's devaluation of housewives and the stresses experienced by overburdened working wives make them prone to depression.
        1 2 3 4 5

E. Learned helplessness explanation: A perceived lack of control over one's life leaves one vulnerable to depression.
    1 2 3 4 5

19. *Lecture addition.* Write SIG E CAPS on the chalkboard and then show how students can remember the key symptoms of depression:
    S = sleep (much less or much more)
    I = interest (loss of; loss of pleasure)
    G = guilt (self-esteem low)
    E = energy (loss of)
    C = concentration (loss of)
    A = appetite changes (weight loss or gain)
    P = psychomotor activity (usually low, can be agitated; fatigue)
    S = suicide (thoughts of or plan for)

9

TREATMENTS
FOR MOOD DISORDERS

■

TOPIC OVERVIEW

This chapter discusses a wide range of treatments for unipolar depression: psychodynamic therapy, behavioral therapy, interpersonal psychotherapy, cognitive therapy, electroconvulsive therapy, and antidepressant drugs. Lithium therapy and adjunctive psychotherapy are the treatments discussed for bipolar disorders.

LECTURE OUTLINE

I. Treatments for Unipolar Patterns of Depression

A. About 10 percent of clients of mental health professionals have a unipolar disorder.

B. Psychodynamic therapy
    1. Grief over real or imagined losses must be brought to consciousness, understood, and resolved.
    2. Free association aids recall and interpretation of associations, dreams, resistance, and transference.
    3. Some therapists take a more active role early in therapy than is typical in psychoanalysis.
    4. Therapists need to take extra care in dealing with transference behaviors because depressed clients are extremely dependent on important people in their lives.
    5. Goals: less dependence on others, more effectiveness in coping with losses, changes in daily living.

   6. Depressed clients' passivity and fatigue make therapy difficult and their desire for quick relief may cause them to leave treatment prematurely in discouragement.
   7. Psychodynamic therapy may be somewhat useful for clients who have a history of childhood loss or trauma, a chronic sense of emptiness, or stringent self-expectations.

C. Behavioral therapy
   1. Lewinsohn starts by identifying reinforcing activities and then introduces several of them.
   2. Such therapists systematically ignore the depressive behavior and reinforce constructive statements and behavior.
   3. They teach or reteach social skills.
   4. Personal effectiveness training is a group technique by which members rehearse social roles, especially expressive behaviors.
   5. A combination of Lewinsohn's behavioral techniques can be effective with mildly or moderately depressed clients.
   6. Lewinsohn's two-hour group sessions over eight weeks, incorporating lectures, classroom activities. homework assignments, and a textbook, to reduce depression in 80 percent of clients.

D. Interpersonal psychotherapy (IPT)
   1. Klerman and Weissman's IPT emphasizes that regardless of the cause, all depression occurs in an interpersonal context.
   2. IPT incorporates concepts and techniques from psychodynamic, humanistic, and behavioral therapies.
   3. Therapists use 12 to 16 weekly sessions to rectify the interpersonal problems that accompany depressive functioning.
   4. If a grief reaction is involved, the client is encouraged to think about the loss and explore the lost relationship, including anger toward the departed person, then to develop new relationships to fill the empty space.
   5. Interpersonal role disputes, which occur when two people have different expectations about their relationship, lead to open conflict or hidden resentment and thus to depression; therapists help clients to resolve such disputes and develop appropriate problem-solving strategies.

6. Depressed people who are experiencing interpersonal role transition have difficulty coping with a significant life change because they experience it as a loss or as a threat to their self-esteem and sense of identity; IPT therapists help them review and evaluate their old roles, explore new opportunities, and develop a new social support system.

7. Clients whose depression is accompanied by such interpersonal deficits as extreme shyness, insensitivity to others' needs, and social awkwardness are helped to recognize their deficiencies and to learn social skills.

8. Research suggests that IPT can be effective in mild to severe cases of unipolar depression and that results are long-lasting.

9. IPT is recommended for depressed clients who are struggling with psychosocial conflicts in relationships or at work, or who are negotiating a transition in career or social roles.

E. Cognitive therapy
1. Beck suggests that depressed people have maladaptive attitudes, a cognitive triad of depression, and illogical ways of thinking.

2. Cognitive therapy usually requires 12 to 20 sessions.

3. Phase 1 is devoted to efforts to increase activities and elevate mood, and Beck works with clients to prepare a detailed schedule of activities for the coming week.

4. In phase 2 the client is helped to examine and invalidate automatic thoughts.

5. Phase 3 is devoted to identifying distorted thinking and negative biases.

6. Therapists who use the reattribution technique guide clients to identify possible causes of their problems other than themselves.

7. Phase 4 is devoted to altering primary attitudes.

8. Significant improvement has been demonstrated in mild to severe depressions; at least half of such clients have a total remission of depressive symptoms.

9. Cognitive therapy is probably less effective in groups than in individual sessions.

F. Electroconvulsive therapy (ECT)
1. ECT is one of the most controversial forms of treatment for depression.

2. It is one of the most effective and fastest-acting interventions for severe unipolar depression.

3. Unilateral ECT has largely replaced bilateral ECT because it is much safer and is thought to be as effective.
4. An electrical current causes a convulsion of a few minutes' duration.
5. Typically, six treatments are administered over two weeks.
6. Originally, camphor and its derivative metrazol were used to induce convulsions because it was believed that epileptic seizures removed psychotic symptoms; both were dangerous and sometimes fatal.
7. Insulin coma therapy was also dangerous.
8. Ugo Cerletti, the first person to administer ECT to humans, abandoned the practice because of the fractures, confusion, and neural damage it caused.
9. Today muscle relaxants and barbiturates reduce both the physical and mental traumas associated with this procedure.
10. The procedure has become more complex but less dangerous and less frightening.
11. Unilateral ECT has reduced the danger of brain impairment.
12. The procedure is most effective in severe cases characterized by delusions or melancholic symptoms (e.g., motor retardation, sleep disturbance, loss of appetite).
13. ECT increases neurotransmitter activity, probably correcting a deficit in norepinephrine and/or serotonin activity.
14. The number of patients receiving ECT each year has declined from 100,000 in the 1950s to between 30,000 and 50,000 now.
15. The decline is attributable to the adverse effects that still accompany ECT, its history of abuse, and the availability of alternatives in the form of medications.

G. Antidepressant drugs
   1. Before the 1950s, amphetamines were prescribed, but they increased activity without alleviating the depression; then monoamine oxidase (MAO) inhibitors and tricyclics were discovered.
   2. The ability of an inhibitor, iproniazid, to relieve depression was discovered accidentally during treatment of tubercular patients; however, it caused serious liver damage.
   3. Better MAO inhibitors (e.g., phenelzine (Nordil), isocarboxazid (Marplan), and tranylcypromine (Parnate) are now used to prevent the destruction of norepinephrine and serotonin.
   4. One problem is that the enzyme MAO is essential for certain normal body functions, such as control of blood pressure.

5. MAO inhibitors block MAO production in the liver and intestine and allow tyramine to accumulate, so patients must restrict their consumption of tyramine-containing foods (e.g., cheese, bananas, some wines).

6. Tricyclic antidepressants (e.g., imipramine (Tofranil), amitriptyline (Elavil), nortriptyline (Aventryl), and doxepin (Sinequan) are effective with unipolar patterns and are more commonly used than MAO inhibitors.

7. Studies show a 40 to 50 percent chance of relapse within six to twelve months, which drops to 20 percent if the drugs are taken for several months after the disappearance of depressive symptoms.

8. Tricyclics alleviate depression by acting on reuptake mechanisms and after several days alter the sensitivity of norepinephrine and serotonin receptors.

9. Tricyclics are used more than MAO inhibitors because they are less dangerous and more effective.

10. The adverse effects of tricyclics include dry mouth, dizziness, and blurred vision.

11. MAO inhibitors are most effective for depressed patients with such symptoms as overeating, oversleeping, and intense anxiety.

12. Tricyclics are most effective when the major symptoms are a slowing of movement, loss of appetite, and insomnia.

13. Rather than inhibiting MAO or affecting the reuptake process, second-generation antidepressants (e.g., maprotiline, amoxapine, traxodone) alter the sensitivity of norepinephrine and serotonin receptors.

14. Selective serotonin reuptake inhibitors, or SSRIs (e.g., fluoxetine, paroxetine, setraline), alter serotonin activity specifically.

15. Second-generation antidepressants and traditional tricyclics are equally effective; the second-generation drugs have fewer of the traditional adverse effects (but may produce nausea and headaches) and are less likely to be associated with suicidal overdoses.

16. ECT is more effective than tricyclic drugs and MAO inhibitors, but relapse is as likely after ECT if it is not followed by antidepressant medications.

17. ECT is reserved for severe depression that does not respond to other treatment or that is associated with high suicide risk (but studies have not shown that ECT actually thwarts suicide).

H. Trends in treatment
1. Unipolar depression can be effectively treated by cognitive, interpersonal, behavioral, and biological approaches.
2. Most effective are cognitive, interpersonal, and biological therapies, all of which completely eliminated depressive symptoms in 50 to 60 percent of subjects after 16 weeks of therapy.
3. Drug therapy reduces the symptoms of depression faster than cognitive and interpersonal therapies, but the three approaches are matched by the end of treatment.
4. The number of physician office visits in which an antidepressant was prescribed grew from 2.5 million in 1980 to 4.7 million in 1987.
5. Fluoxetine (Prozac), introduced in 1988, accounted for one-third of prescriptions in 1989.
6. Behavioral therapy is useful but less effective than other therapies.
7. Psychodynamic therapies are least effective.
8. The most useful approach is to combine cognitive therapy or IPT with drug therapy.

II. Treatments for Bipolar Disorders

A. Lithium therapy
1. Lithium is a mineral salt that has greatly improved treatment for bipolar disorders.
2. The correct dosage requires analysis of blood and urine samples.
3. A patient who is unresponsive to or unable to tolerate lithium may be helped by carbamaxepine (Tegretol), an anticonvulsive drug.
4. In 1949, having hypothesized that manic behavior is caused by a toxic level of uric acid, Gade injected guinea pigs with uric acid made soluble with lithium; where the animals became lethargic rather than manic, Cade researched lithium.
5. Research has supported the effectiveness of lithium in reducing manic episodes.
6. Lithium may be considered a prophylactic drug because it helps prevent symptoms from developing.
7. It also alleviates the depressive episodes of bipolar disorders.
8. Lithium also helped up to two-thirds of patients with tricyclic-resistant unipolar depression when it was added to their drug therapy.

9. Lithium appears to affect the "second messenger" systems that intervene between the reception of a message and the firing of a neuron.

B. Adjunctive psychotherapy
   1. Clinicians often use psychotherapy in conjunction with lithium to monitor and manage its effects.
   2. They help bipolar patients build better family and social relationships.
   3. They teach bipolar patients about their disorder.
   4. They help clients develop solutions for difficulties caused by the disorder.

III. The State of the Field: Treatments for Mood Disorders

A. Mood disorders are among the most treatable of all mental disorders.

B. The symptoms of unipolar depression can usually be reduced or eliminated in 2 to 20 weeks.

C. Lithium (often combined with counseling) is the treatment of choice for bipolar disorders.

D. A larger number of effective treatments are available for unipolar disorder, including combinations of psychotherapy and drug therapy.

E. Perhaps removal of any one factor that contributes to unipolar depression promotes improvements in other areas.

F. There may be various kinds of unipolar depression, each responsive to a different kind of therapy.

G. Though treatment helps the majority of people with mood disorders, as many as 40 percent do not improve under treatment and must wait until the mania or depression has run its course.

LEARNING OBJECTIVES

1. Describe the prognosis for persons in treatment for mood disorders.
2. Explain and evaluate the psychodynamic approach to clients with unipolar depression.

3. Describe and evaluate behavioral techniques to help depressed clients.
4. Describe and evaluate interpersonal therapy (IPT) for depressed clients.
5. List the four phases of cognitive treatment for depression and evaluate its effectiveness.
6. Describe electroconvulsive therapy and explain its effects on neurotransmitters.
7. Compare and contrast MAO inhibitors and tricyclics.
8. Distinguish between traditional tricyclics and second-generation antidepressants.
9. Summarize the effectiveness of the various treatments for unipolar depression.
10. Describe the roles of lithium and adjunctive psychotherapy in treating bipolar depression.

INSTRUCTION SUGGESTIONS

1. *Minilecture: Applying Karen Horney's Ideas to Depression*
Karen Horney considered the core of insecurities to be basic anxiety, which developed as a result of inadequacies in the parent-child relationship. The child might experience too little nurturance or too much rejection and hostility, be overwhelmed and smothered, or suffer from any of a number of other imbalances in the relationship.

Such people learn to protect their vulnerable and anxious selves by adopting one of three exaggerated styles in interpersonal relationships. Some people move toward people and become overdependent on them. These people are especially prone to depression because a real or imagined loss disturbs their basic way of coping with their insecurities. They cannot imagine how they will be able to cope without the person they have lost or fear they are about to lose. They are depressed about their own unworthiness and basic inadequacy and then doubly depressed because they are losing a person who helps them cope in spite of their shortcomings.

Others move away from people. They protect the vulnerable self by not allowing themselves to get close to others. As a result, they limit their own experience of many socially reinforcing situations. A lack of reinforcers is one cause of depression.

Still others move against people. Like the preceding group, they may become depressed because reinforcers in their lives are few. Their general pattern is to be hostile toward others. If they apply this hostile alienation to themselves, their depression deepens. One way to define depression is "anger turned inward."

In different ways, perhaps, both cognitive therapy and IPT address some of Horney's ideas during treatment. Can you find some of these parallels?

2. *Classroom discussion.* A good topic to discuss is the parallel that Freud and Abraham recognized between depression and grief. Have students describe personal situations that fit this model.

Point out that both depression and grief involve a sense of loss. Then have them compare the similarities and differences between the losses of a divorced person and those of a widowed person. What emotional and behavioral reactions do they share? How do they differ? Do students admit that they have grieved over grades or college admissions? Do people grieve for a lost job as well as for a lost person? If your students were to erect tombstones for lost dreams, situations, opportunities, and other such "deaths," what would they be burying? What rituals could help them deal with these "deaths"?

3. *Classroom discussion.* Introduce students to ideas from Moreno's psychodrama. Ask the class to compare personal effectiveness training and psychodrama.

4. *Class activity.* As a class or in small groups, brainstorm a list of things that students experiencing mild depression could do (in the context of this college) to reduce it (e.g., take a walk, do some good deed for another person, meditate, listen to up-tempo music, start feeding birds each day).

5. *Lecture additions.* Introduce students to O. H. Mowrer's "You Are Your Secrets from The New Group Therapy. The basic idea is that when people are alone, they often think about their secrets. Since most people keep "bad things" secret, when they think about these things they get depressed. Therefore, Mowrer suggests that we should learn to be open and honest about our negative characteristics and behaviors so they cannot haunt us when we are alone. In addition, we should anonymously do small, affordable good deeds for others. These good

deeds then become our secrets, and when we are alone we can feel good about them. Mowrer got this idea from Lloyd Douglas's novel, *The Magnificent Obsession.*

6. *Classroom discussion.* Try to show one or more ECT scenes from a fictional film (such as *One Flew Over the Cuckoo's Nest*) and from a documentary. Discuss the similarities and differences in the ECT treatments shown in the two films. Discuss students' reactions to the treatments.

7. *Classroom discussion.* Ask a pharmacist or psychiatrist to speak about psychoactive drugs for depression, and to explain how some medicines can contribute to depression.

8. *Classroom discussion.* Share some of the controversy over Prozac's unintended effects. Explain that all drugs have some adverse effects, and that depression is an effect of some medications.

9. *Classroom discussion.* Have a counselor come to class to discuss how therapists cope with the stress produced by hearing and dealing with other people's problems. Are they affected by another person's depression? How do they work through these feelings? What counseling techniques do they think are most effective with depressed clients? Do they incorporate any strategies in their own lives? You might have students write questions on file cards and give them to your speaker to address. You might want to invite a campus counselor who can specifically address the issue of depression among students.

10. *Classroom discussion.* Research your state's laws about ECT and get an ECT consent form from a local hospital. You might call local hospitals and find out how frequently they administer ECT. Use this demonstration in conjunction with Box 9-3, on ECT and the law. Have students discuss whether they would consent to ECT if they were severely depressed.

11. *Classroom discussion.* Bring a copy of the Physician's Desk Reference (PDR) to class and look up information on the antidepressant drugs discussed in this chapter, with particular attention to their so-called side effects. Ask students for their reactions to this material.

CHAPTER

10

SUICIDE

■

TOPIC OVERVIEW

This chapter discusses suicide and elaborates on the factors that precipitate it. The primary factors are stressful events and situations, changes in mood and thought, alcohol use, mental disorders, and modeling. The psychodynamic, biological, and sociocultural views of suicide are presented. The chapter also explores suicide among the various age groups. Both treatment after a suicide attempt and suicide prevention are discussed.

LECTURE OUTLINE

I. Suicide Statistics

    A. Only humans knowingly end their own lives, and suicide has been observed throughout history.

    B. Prevalence
        1. Suicide is one of the top ten causes of death in Western society.
        2. Suicide accounts for 120,000 deaths annually, 30,000 in the United States (more than 60 a day).
        3. Parasuicides, or people who make unsuccessful attempts to kill themselves, number more than 2 million each year, 600,000 in the United States.
        4. Over 5 million living Americans have survived a suicide attempt.
        5. Because suicide is stigmatizing, some suicides are probably classified as accidents.
        6. Suicide is not a DSM-IV mental disorder, but at least half of all suicides are associated with mental disorders, especially mood disorders, alcohol dependence, and schizophrenia.

    C. Misconceptions about suicide are common.

II. What Is Suicide?

    A. Defining Suicide
       1. Suicide is an intentional, direct, and conscious effort to end one's life.
       2. Death seekers have clear intentions of ending their lives at the time of their attempts, and therefore are likely to use the more lethal means.
       3. Death initiators want to end their lives because they believe they are already dying and are just hastening the process.
       4. Death ignorers believe they are not ending their existence but are going to a better life; this belief is typical of children and religious adults.
       5. Death darers are ambivalent in their intention to die and are most likely to take actions that do not guarantee death.
       6. Subintentional deaths are deaths occasioned by indirect, covert, partial, or unconscious acts, as when a sick person consistently mismanages medicines.
       7. The four categories just reviewed are proposed by Edwin Schneidman; Karl Menninger has added a fifth category, chronic suicide, to encompass life-endangering behavior over an extended period of time.

    B. The study of suicide
       1. Suicide is hard to study because all the subjects are now dead.
       2. One strategy is retrospective analysis, or a psychological autopsy.
       3. Material for retrospective analysis is scanty because less than a quarter of all suicide victims have been in counseling and fewer than 15 percent leave suicide notes.
       4. Another strategy is to study people who have survived suicide attempts.

    C. Patterns and statistics
       1. Among countries with high suicide rates are Hungary, Germany, Austria, Denmark, Finland, Belgium, Switzerland, and France (all over 20 per 100,000).
       2. Suicide rates are low in Egypt, Mexico, Italy, Greece, Spain, and Ireland (fewer than 9 per 100,000).
       3. The United States and Canada have between 12 and 13 suicides per 100,000.

4. Religious affiliation and belief partially account for national differences: rates tend to be low in predominantly Catholic, Jewish, and Muslim countries (Roman Catholic Austria is an exception).
5. The Shinto and Buddhist traditions of Japan partially explain why suicide is considered a normal, reasonable behavior there; pervasive sexism, academic pressures, and work stress are factors in suicide among Japanese (Box 10-2).
6. Women make three times as many attempts at suicide as men but more than three times as many men die by suicide.
7. Men use more violent methods (e.g., shooting, stabbing, hanging) than women (who favor such means as barbiturates), perhaps because they have a clearer intent to die.
8. Male and female college students perceive completed suicide as more powerful and more "masculine" than attempted suicide.
9. The suicide rate is relatively low among married persons, especially those with children, and highest among divorced people.
10. White Americans have a much higher suicide rate than members of other racial groups with the exception of Native Americans.

III. Precipitating Factors in Suicide

A. Stressful events and situations
1. Researchers find more undesirable events in the recent lives of suicide attempters than in those of other people.
2. A suicide attempt may be precipitated by a single recent event or by a series of events.
3. A common precipitating event is the loss of a loved one by death, divorce, breakup, or rejection.
4. Another such factor is the loss of a job.
5. Four long-term stresses that are factors in suicide are serious illness, an abusive environment, occupational stress, and role conflict.
6. A painful or disabling illness is often linked to suicide, especially now that physicians' ability to sustain life exceeds their ability to maintain its quality; some people argue for the right to commit suicide in these circumstances (Box 10-3).
7. People whose suicide is precipitated by an abusive or repressive environment have little or no hope of escape by other means.

8. Suicide rates are high among psychiatrists, psychologists, physicians, dentists, lawyers, and unskilled laborers.
9. Women in professional positions, who experience considerable role conflict, display the highest suicide rate of women in the workforce.

B. Mood and thought changes
1. Many suicide attempts are preceded by a shift in mood, especially an increase in sadness, anxiety, anger, or shame.
2. The single most sensitive indicator of suicidal intent is a sense of hopelessness.
3. Many people on the verge of suicide develop dichotomous thinking, viewing suicide as the only possible solution to their problems.

C. Alcohol use
1. At least 20 percent of people who commit suicide consume alcohol just before the act.
2. Alcohol's disinhibiting effect may allow them to overcome their fear of suicide and lower their inhibitions against violence.

D. Mental disorders
1. Between 30 and 70 percent of people who attempt suicide display a mental disorder.
2. The disorders most commonly linked with suicide are mood disorders, substance use disorders (especially alcoholism), and schizophrenia; about 10 to 15 percent of people with each of these disorders attempt suicide.
3. Panic disorder is also linked to suicide but usually in conjunction with another condition.
4. Because more people have mood disorders, more people with these disorders attempt suicide than people with other disorders.
5. Most people with a major depressive disorder experience suicidal thoughts.
6. Among the severely depressed, the risk of suicide increases as their mood improves and they have enough energy to act on their wish to die.
7. Severely or terminally ill patients are most likely to consider suicide if they are also suffering from depression.
8. Most suicides by alcoholic people occur in the late stages of the disorder, when cirrhosis and other medical complications begin.

9. Suicide is the leading cause of death among young and unemployed schizophrenics who have come to believe that the disorder will always disrupt their lives.

E. Modeling: the contagion of suicide
   1. Many people try to commit suicide after they observe or read about a suicide.
   2. Three kinds of models trigger suicides: suicides by celebrities, highly publicized suicides, and suicides by co-workers or colleagues.
   3. Highly publicized accounts may trigger suicides that are similar in method or circumstances (e.g., a self-immolation in England was followed by 82 similar suicides within a year).

IV. Views on Suicide

A. The psychodynamic view
   1. Psychodynamic theorists believe that suicide usually results from depression and self-directed anger and hatred.
   2. Wilhelm Stekel said in 1910: "No one kills himself who has not wanted to kill another or at least wished the death of another."
   3. Suicidal people are thought to have failed to learn to redirect Thanatos (the death wish) toward other people.
   4. Researchers have found a relationship between childhood losses and later suicidal behavior.
   5. National suicide rates drop significantly in times of war, when people presumably redirect their self-destructive energy to destruction of the enemy.

B. The biological view
   1. Pedigree studies show higher rates of suicidal behavior among the parents and close relatives of suicidal persons.
   2. Many people who attempt or commit suicide are found to have low levels of a by-product of serotonin.
   3. Low levels of 5-HIAA have been found among suicidal subjects who have had no history of depression.
   4. Low serotonin levels are associated with strong aggressive impulses and thus may lead to self-destructive behavior in the absence of depression.

C. The sociocultural view
   1. In 1897 Emile Durkheim developed the first comprehensive theory of suicidal behavior.

2. Egoistic suicides are committed by people over whom society has little or no control; i.e., by isolated, alienated, and nonreligious loners.
3. Altruistic suicides are committed by well-intentioned persons who sacrifice their lives for the good of society.
4. Anomic suicides are committed by persons whose social environment is unstable and who feel let down by society.
5. When societies go through periods of anomie, they have correspondingly high suicide rates.
6. A radical change in a person's immediate surroundings can also lead to anomic suicide.
7. Durkheim's theory does not explain why some but not a majority of people who experience anomie commit suicide.

V. Suicide in Different Age Groups

A. The likelihood of committing suicide generally increases with age, but individuals of all ages attempt suicide.

B. Children
   1. Suicide among children is relatively infrequent but is increasing.
   2. About 250 children under 15 years of age kill themselves each year in the United States.
   3. Boys are three times as likely as girls to kill themselves.
   4. The most typical method used by children is a drug overdose.
   5. Half of the children who attempt suicide are living with one parent and a quarter have made at least one previous attempt.
   6. Children's suicide attempts are often preceded by such behavior patterns as running away, accidents, temper tantrums, self-deprecation, loneliness, psychophysiological disorders, extreme sensitivity to criticism, low tolerance of frustration, and morbid fantasies and daydreams.
   7. Suicide attempts are also linked to recent or anticipated loss of a loved one, family stress and parental unemployment, abuse by parents, and depression.
   8. Because of their cognitive limitations, some children who attempt suicide are death ignorers.
   9. Suicidal thinking among children is more common than it was once thought to be.

C. Adolescents and young adults 15-24

1. Suicidal actions are much more common after the age of 14 than earlier.

2. In the United States, more than 6,000 adolescents and young adults kill themselves each year (13 of every 100,000); over 2,000 are adolescents.

3. Suicide is the third leading cause of death (after accidents and homicides) among these age groups.

4. Boys account for 83 percent of suicides among adolescents.

5. The suicide rate in the 15-to-24 age group is highest among white Americans, but the rate is increasing very rapidly among African Americans.

6. As many as 250,000 American adolescents attempt suicide each year; one-third of teenagers have considered suicide.

7. Warning signs: tiredness, sleep loss, loss of appetite, mood changes, decline in school performance, increased substance use, withdrawal, increased letter writing, giving away possessions.

8. The most common technique used is drug overdose, but teenagers who shoot themselves are most likely to die.

9. Most suicide attempts occur at home and after school.

10. About half of such attempts are linked to clinical depression.

11. Many would-be suicides are under considerable stress from such long-term pressures as missing or poor relationships, inadequate peer relationships, and social isolation.

12. Many attempts are also triggered by such immediate stressors as a financial setback in the family and loss of a boyfriend or girlfriend.

13. Many suicidal teenagers experience stress at school as they strive either to keep up or to achieve perfection.

14. The high Japanese suicide rate in the late teenage years is attributed to *shiken jigoku*, "examination hell."

15. Many teenagers who try to kill themselves struggle with anger and impulsivity.

16. There are more incomplete attempts among teenagers than among older persons; up to 40 percent of attempters try again, and 14 percent eventually die by suicide.

17. Adolescents may react to events more sensitively, angrily, dramatically, and impulsively than other people do, and 93 percent of adolescent attempters know someone who has attempted suicide.

18. Among the factors in the suicides of college students are academic pressures, loss of social support, unresolved past problems that complicate efforts to deal with the college situations and the lack of familiar resources for dealing with problems.
19. The high and increasing suicide rate for adolescents and young adults has been attributed to increased competition for jobs, admission to college, and athletic honors; world politics and the possibility of nuclear war; and the availability and use of drugs.

D. The elderly
   1. In Western societies old people are more likely to commit suicide than people in other age groups (more than 21 per 100,000 in the United States, or 19 percent of all suicides).
   2. Some investigators believe that suicide is the leading cause of death among the elderly.
   3. Factors in suicide among the elderly include illness, loss of close friends and relatives, loss of control over one's life, loss of societal status, increased hopelessness, loneliness, and depression.
   4. The risk of suicide is high in the first year of mourning for a spouse.
   5. Because the elderly are more resolute in their intent to die than younger persons, more of their suicides are completed.
   6. The suicide rate is lower among minority groups, including Native Americans (who hold the elderly in high esteem) and African Americans (one-third that of elderly white Americans).

VI. Treatment and Suicide

A. Treatment after a suicide attempt
   1. The first need is medical care.
   2. Many survivors do not become involved in therapy.
   3. Most therapy is conducted on an outpatient basis.
   4. Extended inpatient treatment is more effective with schizophrenia and severe mood disorders.
   5. Behavior therapy leads to faster improvement but insight therapy also helps.

B. Suicide prevention
   1. The first suicide prevention program was Farberow and Schneidman's Los Angeles Suicide Prevention Center, opened in 1955.

2. Callers to a suicide hotline typically speak to a paraprofessional, a trained person without a formal degree in a counseling profession who provides services under the supervision of a mental health professional.
3. Suicide prevention centers define suicidal people as people in crisis.
4. The goals of suicide prevention centers are to establish a positive relationship, to understand and clarify the problem, to assess and mobilize the caller's resources, and to formulate a plan to deal with the crisis.

C. The effectiveness of suicide prevention
1. Studies have produced mixed results.
2. Only 2 percent of people who actually killed themselves in Los Angeles ever contacted the prevention center.
3. Prevention programs do seem to avert suicide for high-risk people who call.
4. The clergy should be better informed about suicide.

VII. The State of the Field: Suicide

A. Suicide is now a publicized topic.

B. Much is known about motivations, conditions, and risk factors.

C. We need better, more comprehensive explanations of causes.

D. We need better, more successful interventions.

LEARNING OBJECTIVES

1. Define suicide and know how common it is.
2. Describe each of the four kinds of people who intentionally end their lives: death seekers, death initiators, death ignorers, and death darers. Also describe the category of subintentional death.
3. Describe the research strategies of retrospective analysis and interviewing suicide survivors.
4. Know the effects of cultural factors, race, and sex on suicide rates.
5. Be familiar with common precipitating factors in suicide.
6. List four long-term stresses that increase the frequency of suicide.
7. Discuss how mood changes, hopelessness, and dichotomous thinking are related to suicide.
8. Know which mental disorders are linked most strongly to suicide.

9. Describe the kinds of models that trigger suicide.
10. Give the psychodynamic explanation for suicide, including the role of Thanatos.
11. Explain the role of biological factors in suicide, including the role of serotonin.
12. Compare and contrast Durkheim's three categories of suicide: egoistic, altruistic, anomic.
13. Discuss age differences in suicidal thought and action.
14. Discuss the reasons for the rise in the rate of suicide among adolescents and young adults.
15. Explain the high suicide rate among the elderly.
16. Describe therapy for suicide survivors.
17. Discuss the characteristics of suicide prevention programs.

INSTRUCTION SUGGESTIONS

1. *Classroom activity.* Write on the chalkboard: "Suicide is _____." Ask students to write down five ways to complete this sentence and collect their answers. Read some of them aloud. Students may write such things as "a permanent solution to a temporary crisis"; "saying no thanks, world"; "a waste of humanity"; a way to get on with karma"; "a mess left for one's heirs"; "something to do when you don't want to be"; "something I once tried to do." Discuss what the responses say about values and societal beliefs.

2. *Classroom discussion.* Edwin Schneidman tells us that "at least 60 Americans will have taken their own lives by this time tomorrow." An effective way to start a lecture on suicide is to translate such statistics into the number of people who will kill themselves during the time of this lecture. If your class time is one hour, write 2.5 and 68.7 on the board. Then say, "By the time this class period is over, two or three Americans will have killed themselves and at least sixty-eight will have made attempts on their lives."

3. *Classroom discussion.* When you discuss Schneidman's categories of suicides, speculate on the primary values held by people whose suicide attempts fit each of these categories. This discussion can also be introduced in conjunction with Durkheim's classification of suicides.

4. ***Classroom discussion.*** Discuss the accuracy of statistics on suicide. For example, might some national statistics be adjusted to accord with cultural beliefs and values? How often are deaths listed as accidents instead of suicides to spare mourners? May accidents sometimes be intentionally called suicides? For an example, might family members want accidental death from hanging for masturbatory purposes listed as suicide? Might opponents of abortion want to overestimate the number of suicides caused by distress over having an abortion?

5. ***Minilecture: Gender Roles and Suicide Attempts***
   Do gender roles influence suicide attempts? The text suggests that more men than women are familiar with guns and willing to use this violent method against themselves. Do gender roles influence other aspects of suicide? It has been proposed that men get more negative responses from a failed suicide attempt ("Gee, he isn't even man enough to kill himself"), while women are more likely to get sympathy and help. This may be one reason why women make so many more attempts than men.

   Women are more likely to be in charge of cleaning, and police officers have noted that women who kill themselves are more likely to have considered what survivors will have to deal with in the aftermath of suicide. One officer related an incident in which a women who shot herself apparently first cleaned the entire house, did her family's laundry, laid out directions for how the kids should dress themselves the next week, and spread newspapers on the kitchen floor so that it would be easier to clean up her blood.

   Other professionals who have found bodies have also commented that women place more attention on how the body will look. Many choose their clothing carefully, or even choose to die nude. They may be more likely to use pills because they will die without disfigurement and will look as though they died peacefully—often with carefully applied makeup.

   In what other ways may men and women take their gender roles to the grave?

6. *Minilecture: Women at Risk for Suicide*
   The chapter mentions that men are more likely than women to kill themselves, but that women make three to four times as many attempts. What factors are involved in the risk of suicide among women? Research has found some indicators:
   *A history of physical and/or sexual abuse.
   *Major depression.
   *Borderline personality disorder (all personality disorders increase the risk for men).
   *Loss of the father through death or desertion before age 20 (this factor is found in 50 percent of women who commit suicide, in only 20 percent of other women).
   *European ancestry (these women have twice the rate of African-Americans and other ethnic groups).
   *Age at the middle of the life span (the youngest and oldest groups have the lowest suicide rates; since 1950, however, the rate has increased for younger women and decreased for older women).
   *Unemployment.
   *Impulsiveness and emotionality, moodiness, unhappiness, and lack of self-confidence.
   *An IQ above 135 (the Terman Genetic Studies of Genius found that the rate of suicide among gifted women was nearly 250 times that of the general population of women).

   The following factors are not indicators:
   *Any particular phase of the menstrual cycle.
   *Pregnancy (actually associated with lower risk).
   *Loss of the mother through death or desertion before age 20.
   *Chronic stress in the family of origin, parental conflict, and the conflict in the woman's relationship with her parents.

7. *Class demonstration.* Many appropriate speakers are available to talk about what they have seen and experienced in their careers in relation to suicide. You could even compose a panel. Consider a medical examiner/coroner, a suicide hot-line worker, emergency room personnel, a counselor, a police officer, a member of the clergy, a funeral director, a suicide survivor. Have them describe their experiences or work, their values in respect to suicide, how they deal with survivors and family members, and how they come to terms with the emotional aspects of their work.

8. *Class discussion.* Have students describe examples of mass suicide and their reactions to them. You might wish to compare and contrast the mass suicide of Jim Jones' cult followers in Jonestown and the mass suicide of the Jewish schoolgirls who chose to die rather than be forced into prostitution.

9. *Class discussion.* Discuss reasons for the popularity of Derek Humphrey's book *Final Exit*, which describes the best ways to kill oneself. Discuss the virtues or nonvirtues of the Hemlock Society, which promotes safe "self-deliverance" for the terminally ill. You might want to bring in the book or the society's newsletter and share an excerpt. What do these materials and this group say about our societal values? You might also want to discuss legal euthanasia, as in Holland, where patient and family doctor can agree to a medically caused death. Discuss the behavior of Dr. Jack Kevorkian.

10. *Class discussion.* Ask your students to discuss the beliefs about suicide cults among teenagers. If they believe that such cults exist, ask them to describe their purpose, how they got started, how they might lower inhibitions against suicide while providing information about how to kill oneself. What could be done to counteract suicide cults?

11. *Class discussion.* Discuss the role of rock lyrics in suicides among teenagers. Do your students think that a rock group could be held responsible for a death that occurred after a young person had repeatedly listened to their morbid, suicide-praising lyrics? What role might games such as Dungeons and Dragons play in suicides among children and adolescents? Movie plots? Would you censor these cultural phenomena?

12. *Class activity.* Design a one-day workshop for college students to inform them about suicide and related factors. What topics would you cover? What resources would you point out? What kinds of handouts would you like to have?

13. *Lecture additions.* Discuss specific cases of altruistic suicide, such as the deaths of three young people after the Soviet coup in 1991. What motivated these three? How was history affected? What was the

society's response? Other examples are the Vietnamese Buddhist monks who immolated themselves to protest the Vietnam War. For what causes would students be willing to die?

14. *Class activity.* Design a grief counseling treatment program for survivors of suicide. What elements would you include, and why?

15. *Lecture addition.* Both lesbians and gays are more likely to attempt suicide than a comparable group of heterosexuals. The most typical context of a suicide attempt among homosexual men is an intrapersonal conflict with family members over the man's homosexual identity. For homosexual women, the most typical context of a suicide attempt is an end of a relationship with a significant other.

16. *Class discussion.* Have students discuss couples who die together in a suicide pact. They will probably be able to describe a variety of cases, including elderly couples who commit suicide because of declining health and other couples who die together in the climax to a history of domestic violence. Discuss their reactions to the cases, and also provide the following facts during the course of the discussion: (1) The instigator of 95 percent of suicide pacts is the man. (2) The instigator is more likely to die and the cooperator is more likely to survive. (3) The instigator is more likely to be depressed (75%) and to have a history of suicidal behavior; the cooperator is more likely to have no psychiatric diagnosis and not to have been previously suicidal.

CHAPTER

11

PSYCHOLOGICAL FACTORS AND PHYSICAL DISORDERS

■

TOPIC OVERVIEW

This chapter describes the relationships between psychological factors and physical disorders. First it discusses factitious disorders. Next, the chapter covers the various somatoform disorders: conversion disorders, somatization disorders, pain disorder, hpyochondriasis, and body dysmorphic disorders. Finally, the chapter looks at traditional and new psychophysiological disorders and the field of psychoneuroimmunology.

LECTURE OVERVIEW

I. Factitious Disorders

    A. Malingering: the intentional feigning of illness for external gains.

    B. Factitious disorder with predominantly physical signs and symptoms
        1. Though a factitious disorder involves feigning, it is not the same as malingering.
        2. These patients feign symptoms in order to assume the sick role.

    C. Munchausen syndrome
        1. The syndrome is named for an eighteenth-century baron who went from tavern to tavern telling of improbable adventures.
        2. Patients travel from hospital to hospital reciting symptoms to gain admission and treatment.

3. In Munchausen syndrome by proxy, parents fabricate or induce physical illness in their children to get attention from physicians.

D. General information
1. The prevalence of factitious disorders is unknown, but they are believed to be more common among men and to begin most often in early adulthood.
2. They are most common among people who (a) have had extensive medical treatment as children; (b) have a grudge against the medical profession; (c) have worked in the medical field; (d) have had a significant relationship with a physician in the past; (e) are dependent, exploitive, or self-defeating.

E. New categories recognized by DSM-IV
1. A person with a factitious disorder with predominantly psychological signs and symptoms feigns symptoms of a mental disorder.
2. A person with a factitious disorder with combined psychological and physical signs and symptoms feigns symptoms of both mental and physical illness.

II. Somatoform Disorders

A. Introduction
1. A somatoform disorder involves physical complaints rooted exclusively in psychological causes.
2. Unlike people with factitious disorders, these patients have no sense of willing their symptoms or having control over them.
3. Hysterical disorders involve actual loss or alteration of physical functioning; they include conversion, somatization, and pain disorders.
4. Preoccupation disorders involve minimal loss or alteration of physical functioning but great preoccupation with the belief that a serious physical problem exists; they include hypochondriasis and body dysmorphic disorders.

B. Conversion disorders
1. Conversion disorders are characterized by one or more physical symptoms or deficits that affect voluntary motor or sensory functioning.
2. Their symptoms express a psychological factor, such as a conflict or need, which is converted to a physical symptom.

3. These rare disorders are most common in late childhood and young adulthood.
4. They are diagnosed twice as often in women as in men.
5. They appear suddenly during extreme stress and last a matter of weeks.

C. Somatization disorders
   1. Somatization disorders are characterized by numerous physical complaints without organic basis.
   2. These disorders typically last for years; though symptoms may fluctuate.
   3. When this pattern was first described, in 1859, it was called Briquet's syndrome.
   4. The criteria for a diagnosis of somatization disorder are pain symptoms at four sites or functions of the body, two gastrointestinal symptoms, one sexual symptom, and one pseudoneurologic symptom.
   5. These patients usually seek relief from doctor after doctor, describing their symptoms dramatically; most are anxious and depressed.
   6. Up to 2 percent of American women and only two-tenths of 1 percent of men are diagnosed with these disorders, which tend to run in families.
   7. The disorders usually begin between adolescence and young adulthood.

D. Pain disorder
   1. The pain of which these patients complain may occur in any part of the body.
   2. Pain disorder may be associated with psychological factors or with both psychological factors and a general medical condition.
   3. The prevalence of pain disorder is not known, but it is believed to be fairly common and to affect more women than men.
   4. Pain disorder often develops after an accident or during an illness that involved genuine pain.

E. Identifying hysterical symptoms
   1. The symptoms often reveal neurological and anatomical inconsistencies (e.g., "glove anesthesia").

2. The disorders do not follow the expected course of development.
3. The physical symptoms operate selectively.

F. Hypochondriasis
   1. People with hypochondriasis unrealistically and fearfully interpret bodily signs or symptoms as a serious illness.
   2. Their symptoms are often normal fluctuations in physical functioning (e.g., occasional coughing, sweating).
   3. Repeated diagnostic tests do not reassure them and they tend to go to doctor after doctor.
   4. Hypochondriasis is characterized by more anxiety and fewer physical symptoms than a somatoform disorder.

G. Body dysmorphic disorders
   1. Body dysmorphic disorders are characterized by preoccupation with some imagined or exaggerated defect in one's appearance.
   2. The most common objects of these people's concern are wrinkles, skin spots, excessive facial hair, facial swelling, and a misshapen nose, feet, hands, breasts, or penis.
   3. Some of these people worry about bad odors.

III. Views on Somatoform Disorders

A. Preoccupation disorders and anxiety disorders are viewed similarly.

B. Hysterical somatoform disorders are considered unique and to require special explanations.

C. Historical background: Greeks
   1. Green physicians believed that hysterical disorders were experienced only by women.
   2. They believed that the unsatisfied uterus wandered through the body in search of fulfillment.
   3. They saw marriage as the cure.

D. They psychodynamic view
   1. The development of psychoanalysis is traced to the use of hypnosis in the treatment of Anna O., who had hysterical deafness.
   2. Freud viewed conversion symptoms as representing underlying emotional conflicts.

3. Freud emphasized the role of the Electra complex in the development of somatoform disorders.

4. People with hysterical disorders achieve primary gain when they keep internal conflicts out of awareness; they achieve secondary gain when they avoid unpleasant activities or get sympathy and assistance from others.

E. The cognitive view
   1. Cognitive theorists view hysterical disorders as forms of communication, or as means of expressing emotions.
   2. Emotions are converted into physical symptoms not to defend against anxiety but to communicate the distressing emotion.

F. The behavioral view
   1. Behavioral theorists believe that the physical symptoms of a hysterical disorder bring the sufferer rewards, such as keeping out of a work situation, changing a relationship, eliciting attention.
   2. Reinforcements operantly condition people into assuming the role of an invalid.

IV. Treatments for Somatoform Disorders

A. These patients, believing their problems to be physical, consult physicians and shun psychotherapists.

B. Preoccupation somatoform disorders benefit from treatments similar to those used for phobic and obsessive compulsive disorders; e.g., exposure and response-prevention interventions.

C. Hysterical somatoform disorders receive interventions emphasizing either insight, suggestion, reinforcement, or confrontation.

D. The effectiveness of the various forms of psychotherapy has not been established.

E. Conversion disorders and pain disorders respond to therapy better than somatization disorders do.

F. Physicians must be careful to establish that the disorder has no organic cause, such as hyperparathyroidism, multiple sclerosis, or lupus.

V. Phychophysiological Disorders

A. DSM labels
1. Psychophysiological disorders are those in which both psychological and physical factors play causal roles.
2. Early versions of the DSM called these disorders psychosomatic or psychophysiological disorders.
3. DSM-IV labels them psychological factors affecting medical condition.

B. "Traditional" psychophysiological disorders
1. Ulcers are caused by interaction of psychological factors (e.g., anxiety, anger, dependency) and physiological factors.
2. Roughly 70 percent of asthma cases are psychophysiological disorders.
3. There are two types of chronic headaches: muscle contraction headaches and migraine headaches.
4. Hypertension, or a state of chronic high blood pressure, affects about 25 million Americans.
5. "Coronary heart disease" refers to angina pectoris, coronary occlusion, and myocardial infarction.
6. The Type A personality style is characterized by impatience, frustration, competitiveness, hostility, and constant striving for control and success.

C. Explanations of psychophysiological disorders
1. Gary Schwartz proposes that disruption of negative feedback loops between brain and body leads to a traditional psychophysiological disorder.
2. An extraordinarily stressful environment—cataclysmic stressors, personal stressors, background stressors—can interfere with physiological functioning.
3. Idiosyncratic psychological reactions to environmental events can affect functioning; e.g., frustrated dependency needs have been linked to ulcers; people who believe they are left out of things may develop asthma.
4. There is some evidence that a "repressive" coping style has a harmful effect on physical health, as in hypertension.
5. The hostility typical of the Type A personality style seems to be related to heart disease.
6. The sympathetic and parasympathetic systems of the autonomic nervous system complement each other to achieve homeostasis.

7. Hans Selye's general adaptation syndrome has three stages: alarm, resistance, and exhaustion.
8. The pituitary-adrenal endocrine system is stimulated during stress, and it may malfunction.
9. Organ malfunction in response to stress is affected by individual response specificity; e.g., one person under stress gets a headache, another gets a stomachache.
10. Autonomic learning is inadvertent conditioning of elements of the autonomic nervous system.

D. "New" psychophysiological disorders
   1. Holmes and Rahe (1967) developed a scale of life change units (LCUs) to investigate the relationship of life stresses and physical health.
   2. Both retrospective studies and prospective studies indicate that life change is associated with physical illness.
   3. The Holmes and Rahe scale did not take into account the differences in reactions to life events among such groups as African Americans and college students.
   4. Bereavement can be fatal.

E. Psychoneuroimmunology
   1. Psychoneuroimmunologists investigate the links between stress, the immune system, and health.
   2. Lymphocytes, including T-cells, killer T-cells, and antibodies (or immunoglobulins) fight antigens as part of the immune system.
   3. Astronauts' T-cell reactions to antigens decrease a few hours after the stress of splashdown, and are back to normal within three days.
   5. Lymphocyte functioning is lowered in bereaved subjects.
   6. Specific receptors for norepinephrine and epinephrine are located on the membranes of lymphocytes; when the neurotransmitters bind to these receptors, the lymphocytes reduce their activity.
   7. Perceptions of control affect the functioning of the immune system.
   8. People with a "hardy" personality style are less likely to become ill after stress; people with an inhibited power motive style are susceptible to illness under stress.

hardiness concept

9. People with a Type C personality style, which seems to be correlated with a poorer prognosis in cancer patients, deny negative emotions; do not express anger, fear, or sadness; and score high on social conformity and compliance.
10. Social support helps protect both humans and animals from stress, poor immune system functioning, and medical illness.

VI. Psychological Treatments for Psychophysiological Disorders

A. Behavioral medicine combines psychological and physical interventions.

B. Relaxation training is used to treat hypertension, headaches, insomnia, asthma, effects of cancer treatment, and Raynaud's disease.

C. Biofeedback training helps in the treatment of anxiety disorders, facial pain, tension headaches, muscular disabilities.

D. Medication has helped patients with cancer pain, hypertension, cardiovascular problems, asthma, diabetes, psoriasis, and viral infections.

E. Hypnosis has been effective in the control of surgical and dental pain and in the treatment of pain disorders, skin diseases, asthma, insomnia, hypertension, warts, and bacterial and viral infections.

F. Cognitive interventions, such as stress inoculation training, helps people cope with the pain of headaches, ulcers, and multiple sclerosis.

G. Insight therapy can reduce general levels of anxiety and has improved the adjustment of children.

H. Psychological techniques are often used in combination with medical treatment.

VII. The State of the Field: Psychological Factors and Physical Disorders

A. Physical disorders with psychological factors have moved from the fringe of psychology to a place within its borders.

B. Some health professionals now believe that psychological factors contribute to all physical disorders.

C. Much research in this area is being conducted.

LEARNING OBJECTIVES

1. Distinguish between malingering and factitious disorder.
2. Describe the Munchausen syndrome and the Munchausen syndrome by proxy.
3. Define somatoform disorders and distinguish between hysterical disorders and preoccupation disorders.
4. Describe conversion disorders.
5. Describe somatization disorders.
6. Describe pain disorders.
7. Explain how physicians distinguish between hysterical somatoform disorders and true medical problems.
8. Describe hypochondriasis, and distinguish between hypochondriasis and somatoform disorder.
9. Compare and contrast hypochondriasis and body dysmorphic disorders.
10. Compare and contrast the psychodynamic, cognitive, and behavioral views of somatoform disorders.
11. Distinguish between primary gain and secondary gain.
12. Discuss typical treatments for somatoform disorders.
13. Explain the label "psychological factors affecting medical condition."
14. Describe the "traditional" psychophysiological disorders: ulcers, asthma, hypertension, coronary heart disease.
15. Discuss chronic headaches and distinguish between muscle contraction (tension) headaches and migraine headaches.
16. Describe the Type A personality style.
17. Explain Schwartz's disregulation model of traditional psychophysiological disorders.
18. Discuss the factors that, according to Schwartz, interfere with the proper functioning of negative feedback loops: extraordinary environmental pressures, idiosyncratic psychological reactions, and physiological dysfunctioning.
19. List and describe the three stages of Selye's general adaptation syndrome.
20. Discuss research findings in regard to the relationship of stress and susceptibility to illness.
21. Describe the body's immune system and discuss psychoneuroimmunology.

22. Discuss how perceptions of control, personality and mood, and social support affect immune system functioning.
23. Discuss typical psychological treatments for psychophysiological disorders.
24. Summarize the state of the field in respect to psychological factors and physical disorders.
25. Define psychoneuroimmunology.

INSTRUCTION SUGGESTIONS

1. *Class discussion.* Should children with a serious (perhaps terminal) illness be told directly and honestly about their condition? Are there situations in which you would not tell children that they were seriously sick? A study of 117 childhood cancer survivors and their families found that the families thought children should be told early, in honest language that they can comprehend, and helped to achieve mastery over the disease.

2. *Lecture addition.* Type A behaviors are displayed by some children as well as by many adults. Researchers suggest that children as young as 3 can exhibit a marked pattern of impatience and restlessness (e.g., much squirming and sighing), expectation of meeting high standards, and above-average competitiveness. Children may carry these behaviors, with their potential impact on health, with them into adulthood. Little is known about the role of genetic factors and temperament on early Type A behaviors, but research suggests that parent-child interactions influence the Type A level of children. One study found that mothers of Type A boys provided fewer positive evaluations of their sons' performances than did other mothers. Therefore, these sons may make themselves work harder, more competitively, and more anxiously in an effort to receive their mothers' approval.

3. *Minilecture: A Close Look at Asthma*
Asthma, a common respiratory illness involving obstruction of the airway by degranulation of mast cells in the lung's lining, is underdiagnosed and therefore undertreated. It is sometimes misdiagnosed as recurrent bronchitis or pneumonia. About 10 percent of all children have asthma—about 3.2 million American children.

Asthma is also prevalent among adults (there are nearly 10 million asthmatic Americans), but 80 percent of them experienced their first symptoms before they were 5 years old.

Asthma can be affected by many factors—an inherited genetic predisposition, viral infections, food allergens, inhaled allergens, exercise, climatic changes, cigarette smoke, pets, and emotional stress. Research has shown that passive smoking also increases problems with asthma.

Three common misconceptions about asthma are these: (1) A child with asthma is fragile and cannot participate in gym class. In fact, 11 percent of the athletes on U.S. Olympic teams have asthma. (2) Children outgrow asthma. Actually, only half experience a remission of symptoms during puberty. (3) Emotions cause asthma. Stress affects asthma but is not its primary cause.

4. *Class activity.* Have your students create a list of the advantages of being sick. What messages about getting sick did they receive from their parents? From their teachers? (Did it get them excused for missing a test?) What messages did they receive about good health? About their own role in controlling their health?

5. *Class project.* If there is a pain clinic nearby, arrange for your class to visit it.

6. *Class demonstration.* Invite a professional who works with pain—an acupuncturist, a chiropractor, an osteopath, a neurologist, a behavioral counselor who does pain management—to speak to the class.

7. *Class discussion.* Many mental disorders are accompanied by physical symptoms—somatoform disorders, psychophysiological disorders, and so forth. Why is there no category for people who are overly concerned with good health—the "health nuts"? Aren't their concerns the flip-side of hypochondriasis?

8. *Lecture addition.* Some psychologists are much less concerned than they used to be about the effects of Type A personality on health.

Although Type A's have a high rate of coronary heart disease, their personality style also helps them to survive their heart attacks at a higher rate than other people who have heart attacks.

9. *Class activity.* Have class members take the Holmes and Rahe scale and turn in the number of their LCUs. Provide statistical information about the class' LCUs—the range, mean, median, and mode. Do they form a normal curve? You may wish to collect more specific data anonymously and relate the most common and least common stressors experienced by students in the class. You can suggest additional life changes that students face and assign an appropriate number of LCUs to each. Also discuss common student hassles and uplifts.

10. *Class discussion.* Have the class discuss the relationship between health and academic stress. Do health problems fit a semester pattern?

11. *Class demonstration.* Invite an AIDS patient, an AIDS health worker, or some other relevant speaker to address the class on the psychological effects of HIV and AIDS.

12. *Class discussion.* Discuss students' beliefs about their own role in health and sickness. Can they affect the course of a disease? Can they do things that prevent diseases? Is the patient to blame for being ill?

13. *Minilecture: Sleep Problems of the Elderly (also suitable for Chapter 20)* *Insomnia* involves difficulty in initiating and maintaining sleep or feeling that sleep does not restore energy. Problems with insomnia increase with age, and half of all individuals over the age of 80 complain of not sleeping well. Research has found that 15 percent of people over 65 sleep fewer than 5 hours a night; twice as many elderly women as elderly men get this little sleep. About 25 percent of men and 40 percent of women over 65 report that their sleep is light. In addition, about 10 percent of the elderly use sleeping pills at times. *Hypersomnia*, or excessive daytime sleepiness or prolonged periods of sleep, is not a common problem among the elderly.

Some older adults have *sleep-wake schedule disorders*: they switch from a normal sleep-wake schedule to a different pattern determined by their internal biological clock. A person with *delayed sleep-wake disorder* does not go to sleep until 2 or 3 a.m. and then awakens in late morning. A person with *advanced sleep-wake disorder* may go to bed early in the evening, say 6 or 7 p.m., and then awakens at 2 or 3 a.m. The elderly are especially at risk for developing sleep-wake schedule problems because they are less constrained by schedules. Some elderly people experience *disorganized sleep disorder:* they sleep for brief periods throughout the day and night; bedridden persons are especially prone to this disorder.

Sleep apnea, in which breathing stops for a few seconds, may be experienced by as many as one in four elderly persons. Sleep apnea is one prominent cause of excessive daytime drowsiness. During most apnea episodes, the oxygen level is lowered less than 5 percent and the heart rate increases fewer than 10 beats per minute. Sleep apnea becomes severe when multiple episodes—perhaps hundreds—occur in a night and are of longer duration. In some cases, severe apnea disrupts the rhythm of the heart, increases blood pressure (and thus the risk of a heart attack), and causes difficulty with cognitive processes.

Sleep apnea can occur when the respiratory center in the brain briefly ceases to function. Another type, obstructive sleep apnea, is accompanied by loud snoring. In obstructive sleep apnea, the soft tissue in the pharynx and throat relaxes so that the tissue obstructs the flow of air into the lungs.

Another sleep problem for many elderly persons, *periodic leg movements*, is more disturbing than apnea. Twitching of the legs during stage 1 and 2 sleep may last only a few minutes or may continue for a few hours. These uncomfortable movements usually keep the person from falling asleep or awaken the sleeper; some walk around in an effort to get the sensation to stop. When this problem occurs several times in a night, the elderly person may never achieve the stage of deep sleep and will experience excessive daytime sleepiness and increased difficulty in functioning. Some antianxiety medications, some antidepressant medications, caffeine, and alcohol can increase the likelihood of periodic leg movements.

14. *Minilecture: Hypochondriasis and Older Adults (also suitable for Chapter 20)*
The most common somatoform disorder in late life is hypochondriasis. These people misinterpret physical sensations and become convinced that they have a serious disease, even though physical examination

reveals nothing wrong. Moreover, the physician's reassurance does nothing to reduce their concern.

To be diagnosed as hypochondriacal, such behavior must be present for at least 6 months, during which the elderly person becomes increasingly perturbed about body functioning. For the person with hypochondriasis, every cough, cramp, pain, or change in heartbeat increases anxiety and concern about serious illness.

Some elderly persons engage in "doctor shopping," or shifting from doctor to doctor to find the answers to their problems. In addition to a primary care physician, these individuals tend to see a variety of medical specialists. Some elderly people with this disorder have engaged in this behavior all their adult years, but it is likely to be more severe from midlife on. Some have retired early for "health reasons."

It is important for the medical profession to attend to these individuals because real physical illnesses can develop in the midst of continual complaining about symptoms, especially as patients advance in age, and some medical problems are hard to diagnose initially (e.g., multiple sclerosis, thyroid disorders, Cushing's disease, lupus).

Busse has suggested four mechanisms that contribute to hypochondriasis in older adults. (1) Hypochondriacal symptoms can be used to excuse failure to meet personal or social expectations. (2) The older adult who becomes increasingly isolated may focus more intently on the body, and any physical discomfort becomes more noticeable. (3) The older adult may find it easier to be concerned with physical complaints than with anxiety-provoking psychological discomforts, such as the approach of death or declining cognitive abilities. (4) Hypochondriacal symptoms may represent self-punishment or atonement for hostility toward another person.

Another possibility is that this disorder results in secondary gain, in that friends, relatives, and professionals typically give more attention to the older adult who experiences multiple physical problems. Also, the sick in our society have a special role, in which they are not expected to keep up with the usual social obligations and are excused for depending on others for help.

Lesse, on the other hand, emphasizes that hypochondriacal symptoms can hide depressive symptoms for a long time. Depressed hypochondriacs suffer more than other hypochondriacs because they are also likely to experience anxiety, insomnia, loss of appetite, fatigue, poor memory, and difficulty in concentrating.

CHAPTER

12

EATING DISORDERS

■

TOPIC OVERVIEW

This chapter describes anorexia nervosa and bulimia nervosa. Several explanations of eating disorders are presented and the most useful treatments are discussed.

LECTURE OUTLINE

I. Introduction

    A. Western culture's preoccupation with thinness

    B. Two common eating disorders
        1. People with anorexia nervosa pursue extreme thinness and weight loss through starvation, sometimes to death.
        2. People with bulimia nervosa go on frequent eating binges during which they uncontrollably eat large quantities of food and then induce vomiting or take other steps to keep from gaining weight.
        3. Anorexia and bulimia used to be viewed as distinct disorders, but the similarities between the two are as important as the differences.

    C. Disproportionate prevalence among adolescent girls and young women

II. Anorexia Nervosa

    A. Characteristic symptoms recognized by DSM-IV
        1. Refusal to maintain body weight at or above minimally normal weight for one's age and height.
        2. Intense fear of gaining weight or becoming fat.

3. Disturbance in perception of body weight or image.
4. Amenorrhea for at least three consecutive menstrual cycles.
5. A preoccupation with food.
6. Cognitive disturbances as well as personality and mood problems.
7. Characteristic medical consequences.

B. Types
1. People with restricting type anorexia nervosa (about half of all cases) gradually and continuously cut back their food intake until their daily caloric intake levels off at 600 to 800 calories; they take little pleasure in eating and often do not vary their diet.
2. Others lose weight by forcing themselves to vomit after meals or by using laxatives or diuretics, a pattern called binge eating/purging type anorexia nervosa.
3. Individuals who meet all but one of the diagnostic criteria for anorexia nervosa receive a diagnosis of eating disorder not otherwise specified.

C. Incidence
1. Roughly 95 percent of cases occur in women and girls.
2. The peak age of onset is between 14 and 18 years, but the disorder can occur at any age.
3. One of every 100 females develops the disorder.
4. It typically begins after a slightly overweight person decides to lose a few pounds.
5. It often follows a stressful event, such as separation of the parents, moving away from home, or a personal failure.
6. Between 5 and 18 percent die from this disorder.
7. The incidence of the disorder is on the increase.

D. The pursuit of thinness and fear of obesity
1. Being thin is life's central goal.
2. Anorexia has also been called "weight phobia."
3. The anorexic person's preoccupation with food may be the result of food deprivation rather than its cause.

E. Cognitive dysfunction
1. Anorexic persons have a low opinion of their body shape and physical attractiveness and have a distorted body image.
2. More than half of anorexic persons overestimate their body size; most control subjects underestimate their body size.

3. Anorexic persons become perfectionistic in their striving for self-control and believe that their weight and shape determine their worth.

F. Personality and mood problems
   1. Anorexic persons tend to be at least mildly depressed and to have low self-esteem.
   2. They exhibit anxiety, general indecisiveness, and poor concentration.
   3. Some have such sleep disorders as insomnia.
   4. They commonly display obsessive compulsive patterns of behavior.
   5. Normal subjects on semistarvation diets report changes in mood and behavior.

G. Medical problems
   1. Anorexic women develop amenorrhea.
   2. Their body temperature and blood pressure fall, their bodies swell and their heart rate slows.
   3. Metabolic and electrolyte imbalances can lead to cardiac arrest, congestive heart failure, or circulatory collapse.
   4. Severe nutritional deficiencies can result in changes in the skin, brittle nails, and cold, blue hands and feet; hair may fall out of the scalp and lanugo may cover the rest of the body.
   5. Anxiety, depression, obsessive rigidity, and medical dysfunctioning increase.

III. Bulimia Nervosa

A. Characteristic symptoms recognized by DSM-IV
   1. Persons with bulimia nervosa—also called binge-purge syndrome, gorge-purge syndrome, and dietary chaos syndrome—engage in recurrent episodes of binge eating.
   2. To keep from gaining weight they then induce vomiting, misuse laxatives or diuretics, or exercise excessively.
   3. Binge eating and disappropriate compensatory behaviors occur an average of twice a week for 3 months.
   4. Their self-evaluation is unduly influenced by body shape and weight.
   5. The disturbance is not part of a larger pattern of anorexia nervosa.

B. Types and incidence
   1. The person with purging type bulimia nervosa regularly induces vomiting or misuses laxatives or diuretics.
   2. The person with nonpurging type bulimia nervosa fasts or exercises frantically.
   3. If binges are less frequent or are not followed by purging, the diagnosis is eating disorder not otherwise specified.
   4. Half of the college students surveyed reported periodic binges, 6 percent had tried vomiting, and 8 percent had experimented with laxatives at least once.
   5. Surveys in several countries suggest that between 2 an 6 percent of females develop the full syndrome.
   6. The pattern is most likely to begin in adolescence or young adulthood, especially after a period of intense dieting; 90 to 95 percent of the victims are females.
   7. The pattern often lasts for several years, with intermittent letup.

C. The clinical picture
   1. The weight of most people with bulimia is within the normal range but fluctuates within that range; some are underweight (and qualify for a diagnosis of anorexia nervosa instead) and some are overweight.
   2. As many as a third of obese people may be binge eaters.
   3. Binge eating, usually in secret, is the central feature of bulimia nervosa.
   4. The foods these people prefer usually have a sweet taste, high caloric content, and a soft texture.
   5. They hardly taste or think about the food while they are binging.
   6. The first binges are usually triggered by an upsetting event, hunger, or a depressed mood.
   7. Later binges become carefully planned events, almost rituals.
   8. Binges begin with feelings of unbearable tension.
   9. During a binge, the person feels unable to stop eating.
   10. A binge is followed by extreme self-reproach, guilt, depression, and fear of gaining weight.
   11. After a binge the person tries to undo its effects and to feel in control again by purging.
   12. Vomiting fails to prevent the absorption of at least one-third of the calories consumed, and laxatives are even less effective.
   13. Repeated vomiting disrupts the body's satiety mechanism and leads to more frequent and intense binges.

14. Most bingers recognize that they have an eating disorder, but their anxiety over gaining weight prevents them from interrupting the cycle.

D. Obesity (Box 12-1)
   1. At least 15 percent of adults in the United States between the ages of 30 and 62 are obese.
   2. Overweight is not a mental disorder, nor is it usually the result of abnormal psychological processes.
   3. Obese people often suffer discrimination in their efforts to get into college, to get jobs and promotions, and to gain satisfaction in relationships.
   4. Obesity results from multiple physiological and social factors.
   5. Children of obese parents are more likely to be obese, even if the parents did not raise them.
   6. People eat more in the company of others.
   7. People of low socioeconomic environments are more likely to be obese; but in developing countries where food is scarce, overweight is a sign of prosperity.
   8. Mildly to moderately obese people are not at increased risk of coronary disease, cancer, or any other disease.
   9. No diet has been shown to ensure long-term weight loss; the battle against one's weight set point leads to a rebound effect.
   10. Many obese people have lower metabolic rates than thin people and two to three times as many fat cells.
   11. Most mildly and moderately obese people do not consume more calories than thin people.
   12. Some researchers believe the focus should shift from weight loss to improved eating habits, self-concept, and body image.

E. Bulimia nervosa vs. anorexia nervosa
   1. Both bulimia and anorexia develop after a period of intense dieting.
   2. Both the bulimic and the anorexic person fear becoming obese and feel driven to be thin.
   3. Both are preoccupied with food, weight, and appearance.
   4. Both experience depression and anxiety and feel the need to be perfect.
   5. Both believe they weight too much.
   6. Both have difficulty identifying and differentiating internal states.
   7. People with bulimia are more likely to recognize that their behavior is pathological.

8. They are more inclined to want to please other people.
9. People with anorexia are less interested in sex and less sexually experienced.
10. They are more obsessive.
11. Bulimic people experience more dramatic mood swings.
12. They are less able to control their impulses.
13. Amenorrhea is characteristic of almost all people with anorexia nervosa but only half of those with bulimia nervosa.
14. Medical complications of bulimia nervosa include dental problems; hyposkalemia, which leads to weakness, gastrointestinal disorders, paralysis, kidney disease, irregular heart rhythms, or heart damage; and damage to the esophagus wall.

IV. Explanations of Eating Disorders

   A. Psychodynamic explanations
      1. Unresolved oral conflicts lead to anorexia nervosa.
      2. Children who become fixated at the oral stage become frightened as they approach adolescence and confront independence, separation from their parents, and the challenges of sexual maturity.
      3. Psychodynamic explanations have received little research support and have been replaced by a multidimensional risk perspective.

   B. Sociocultural pressures
      1. Western society currently emphasizes thinness.
      2. The pursuit of thinness is more prominent in the white upper socioeconomic classes and among women.
      3. The emphasis on thinness creates prejudice and hostility against overweight people.
      4. Physicians, insurance companies, and health organizations issue exaggerated warnings about the dangers of overweight.

   C. Family environment
      1. The families of half of the people with eating disorders emphasize thinness, physical appearance, and dieting.
      2. Abnormal and confusing family interactions and forms of communication can set the stage for eating disorders.
      3. An enmeshed family pattern, in which the members are overinvolved in one another's life and speaking about one's own ideas and feelings.

4. Enmeshed families are affectionate and loyal but they foster dependency and clinging.
5. Research results on enmeshed families are mixed.

D. Ego deficiencies and cognitive disturbances
1. Hilda Bruch argued that disturbed mother-child interactions led to serious ego deficiencies.
2. Effective parents provide discriminating attention to their children's biological and emotional needs but ineffective parents impose their own definitions of those needs on their children.
3. Unable to rely on internal standards, the children turn to external guides and fail to develop genuine self-reliance.
4. Unable to establish autonomy as adolescence approaches, they try to overcome their sense of helplessness by extreme self-control.
5. People with eating disorders perceive and distinguish internal cues inaccurately.

E. Biological factors
1. Bulimia nervosa bas been associated with a heightened physiological need for carbohydrates.
2. The lateral hypothalamus produces hunger and the ventromedial hypothalamus depresses hunger.
3. One's weight set point influences the body's metabolic rate.
4. One's weight set point reflects the range of body weight (or percent of body fat) that is normal in view of one's genetic inheritance and early eating practices and the body's need for internal equilibrium.
5. A strict diet modifies the set point and sets hyperlipogenesis in motion.

F. Mood disorders
1. People with eating disorders have high rates of depression, sadness, low self-esteem, pessimism, and errors in logic.
2. Mood disorders predispose some people to eating disorders.
3. Close relatives of people with eating disorders have high rates of mood disorders.
4. Serotonin activity is low in many people with eating disorders.
5. Some antidepressants are useful in altering dysfunctional eating patterns.

G. Multidimensional perspective
1. An interaction of sociocultural, family, biological, and psychological factors causes eating disorders.
2. The factors that protect some vulnerable people have not been identified.

V. Treatments for Eating Disorders

A. Treatments for anorexia nervosa
1. The immediate aim is to increase caloric intake and achieve quick weight gain.
2. In life-threatening cases, tube and intravenous feedings are used.
3. Antipsychotic drugs have been used (without much success) to reverse starvation habits; antidepressant medications are useful in relieving depression and obsessions.
4. Operant conditioning is often used but other interventions are also necessary for long-term success.
5. Supportive nursing care combined with a high-calorie diet is currently the most widely used approach.
6. Anorexic people used to address their underlying problems and alter their maladaptive thinking patterns.
7. Therapists help anorexic patients to become aware of autonomy issues.
8. Anorexic patients must change their misconceptions about eating and weight.
9. They must also correct their distorted body image.
10. Family therapists seek to change interactions in the anorexic patient's family.
11. Most therapists use a combination of approaches.
12. Weight may be restored quickly but complete recovery may take years.
13. The death rate seems to be declining.
14. Some patients remain amenorrheic for a while.
15. Depression, social anxiety, obsessiveness, and family problems can persist for years.
16. Adolescents recover better than older patients and females better than males.

B. Treatments for bulimia nervosa
1. Psychodynamic and cognitive approaches are the most commonly used insight therapies

2. Group therapy is often used, including the technique of the group meal.
3. Behavioral therapy may include monitoring and keeping a diary of eating behavior and emotions.
4. Many behaviorists use the technique of exposure and response prevention.
5. Antidepressant medications can be useful.
6. Untreated, the disorder usually lasts for years, but 40 percent of clients respond to treatment immediately; another 40 percent show a moderate improvement.
7. A binge-purge pattern of long duration or a daily routine that centers primarily on binging and purging is more difficult to change.

VI. The State of the Field: Eating Disorders

A. The prevalence of eating disorders is increasing.

B. Sociocultural pressures play a big role in the development of both disorders.

C. The disorders are brought about by a host of intersecting factors, are maintained by dieting, starvation, and biological factors, and are best corrected by multiple intervention programs.

D. Bulimia nervosa was not formally identified as a clinical disorder until the 1980s.

E. Patient-initiated national organizations educate and support people with eating disorders and their families.

LEARNING OBJECTIVES

1. Explain the relationship between the prevalence of eating disorders and Western culture's obsession with thinness.
2. Know in which age groups anorexia and bulimia are most common.
3. List the central features of anorexia nervosa.
4. Compare and contrast the various behavioral patterns of anorexia and bulimia.
5. Explain why bulimic people find purging behavior to be reinforcing.
6. Describe how eating disorders tend to be initiated.
7. Compare and contrast the ways in which bulimics and anorexics perceive their eating disorders.

8. Describe medical problems that can be caused by eating disorders.
9. Explain how each of the following factors can place a person at risk for an eating disorder: sociocultural pressures, family environment, ego deficiencies and cognitive disturbances, biological factors, and mood disturbances.
10. Describe the enmeshed family pattern.
11. Explain the concept of weight set point.
12. Know the goals of treatments for eating disorders.
13. Describe treatments for anorexia nervosa.
14. Describe treatments for bulimia nervosa.
15. Discuss the success rate of treatment for eating disorders.

INSTRUCTION SUGGESTIONS

1. *Minilecture: Twin Studies and Weight*
   Do you think your weight is determined more by your ancestry or by your lifestyle? A 1990 study analyzed weight and height records from the well-known Swedish study of 247 identical twin pairs and 426 fraternal twin pairs. The investigators found that twin siblings ended up with similar body weights whether or not they were raised in the same home. The correlation in body-mass index for the identical twins reared apart was nearly the same as that of identical twins reared together. Correlations were higher with biological parents than with adoptive parents. When both biological parents were obese, 80 percent of the offspring were also overweight. This study found that childhood environment did not strongly affect body weight.

   In another study, Canadian researchers had twelve pairs of identical twins consume 1,000 extra calories a day for 84 days. Weight gains ranged from only 9 pounds to nearly 30 pounds. Twin pairs tended to gain about the same amount of weight. The twins' weight gain were more similar than those of other siblings. According to an article in the May 1990 New England Journal of Medicine, "it seems genes have something to do with the amount you gain when you are overfed."

2. *Class demonstration.* Try to find case studies of people whose eating disorders do not fit the usual age pattern. Here are a couple of excerpts from former students that might be adaptable.
   *P.'s eating disorder started in her 30s, about the time her last child began going to school and her husband was busy at work. She simply started walking with friends and noticed she felt a lot better. Soon she walked much farther than they did, and

eventually was walking all over the city in a daily ritual that began as soon as the kids left for school and ended just minutes before they got home. She went for the same walk even in snowy, below-zero weather and during thunderstorms. She denied herself food all day long; then, after the family was asleep, she hitchhiked to an all-night store, bought cookie ingredients, and made the cookies in an electric frying pay in the bathroom with the exhaust fan going so that her family wouldn't smell them. She would gobble down a double batch of soft cookies each night and then walk all the following day. Doctors had trouble diagnosing P.'s eating disorder because of her age.

*N. initially used her drinking problem to control her weight. She would drink so much that she would vomit, and that would keep her from gaining weight. When she was sober, she was very upset by any weight gain. In a college class on eating disorders she learned about the behaviors of people with bulimia nervosa and started to induce herself to vomit even though she was hearing all about the negative effects of the pattern in her class. She finally had found a way to control her weight. Working through this pattern required an intensive in-patient treatment program when she was in her 30s; all the other patients at that time were under 18.

*H. had been featured in a newspaper article on noted cooks. Her obsession with good cooking was her way of dealing with her preoccupation with food, brought on by self-starvation. She rarely tasted any of the great dishes she made. Within a year of her appearance in the newspaper feature as a noted cook, she died of medical complications of anorexia. She was in her 30s at the time of her death.

3. *Minilecture: The Fat Mouse Research*
Researchers have bred mice that weigh ten times as much as normal mice. These mice enable experimenters to compare obesity with normal weight and to determine the differences between overweight attributable to genetic factors and caused by overeating.

The genetically fat mice have been found to be deficient in a protein made by fat cells (adipocytes). This protein, adipsin, is as much as ten times lower in genetically fat mice fed potato chips, candy bars, bologna, cookies, and marshmallows. It is speculated that adipsin may be a fat regulator for mice. As such, it circulates in the bloodstream and responds to changes in diet. When food intake is restricted, for example, adipsin levels rise. Researchers inject genetically fat mice with adipsin to see if their weight decreases.

It is still not known whether human beings have a factor equivalent to adipsin. Researchers are investigating complement factor D, which typically is used by the immune system to combat infections. This disease protector just might play a major role in the regulation of fat. Research on the fat-immune connection has identified cachectin, a protein that causes emaciation in many cancer patients while actually fighting cancer.

4. *Class activity.* Develop a list of cultural attitudes (and contradictions) in respect to food. Discuss these various values and how they may influence eating disorders.

5. *Class project.* Assign students to analyze television messages about food. Have them contrast food ads on prime-time TV and on children's TV shows. Is food sold as a biological necessity or as a reward, status object, and psychological need fulfiller ("You've got the right one, baby"; "You deserve a break today"; "We do it all for you")?

6. *Small-group discussion.* Have small groups of students discuss how food was used in their families. What messages did they get about food and eating? How and where was food used? Did families eat together? Were mealtimes pleasant? Was eating punished? Was food seen as the enemy of fat? Have each group summarize what they have discovered.

7. *Class demonstration.* Emphasize the changes in the ideal female body image by bringing in pictures of the women considered to embody the ideal in various eras (e.g., a painting by Reubens; Lillian Russell, a soprano who was popular around the turn of the century; any screen goddess of the 1950s, whose bust and hips swelled from a tiny waist; the emaciated models Twiggy of the 1960s and Kate Moss today; and the exercise guru Jane Fonda, at one time bulimic.

8. *Class project.* Have students find diet articles in popular magazines. Ideally find some very old ones too. Analyze their advice, their quality, and their emotional tone.

9. *Class discussion.* Have students evaluate self-help groups such as Overeaters Anonymous and various commercial enterprises such as Weight Watchers and NutriSystem. What do they have in common? What are their differences? What do they emphasize? How do students evaluate them?

10. *Class discussion.* Discuss the relationship between food and emotions from the psychodynamic, behavioral, biological, and cultural perspectives.

11. *Lecture addition.* Develop a brief lecture on what is known about good nutrition such as the advice that the diet should include little sugar and fat, only a little meat, and lots of fruits, vegetables, and grains; discuss the value of fiber; the value of the vegetable group consisting of cabbage, broccoli, and cauliflower.

12. *Class activity.* Have students address the similarities and differences between eating disorders and obsessive compulsive disorders, depression, drug addiction, phobic disorder, codependency, and workaholism.

13. *Class discussion.* What assumptions do you make when you see a thin person? A fat person?

CHAPTER

13

SUBSTANCE-RELATED DISORDERS

■

TOPIC OVERVIEW

This chapter describes disorders related to the use of depressants (alcohol, sedative-hypnotic drugs, and opioids); stimulants (cocaine and amphetamines) and hallucinogens. The chapter covers the effects of combinations of various substances, discusses explanations of substance abuse and dependence, and reviews typical treatments.

LECTURE OUTLINE

I. Substance Abuse and Dependence

   A. Definitions
      1. A drug is any substance other than food that changes bodily or mental functioning.
      2. "Drug" and "substance" are used interchangeably.
      3. A person is intoxicated when he exhibits impaired judgment, mood changes, irritability, slurred speech, and loss of coordination.
      4. Hallucinosis is a state of perceptual distortions and hallucinations.

   B. Substance use disorder
      1. Substance abuse is such excessive and chronic reliance on a drug that it occupies a central position in one's life.
      2. Substance dependence is a physical addiction as well as an abusive pattern.

3. "Tolerance" refers to the need for increasing doses to achieve the initial effect.

4. Withdrawal symptoms are unpleasant, sometimes dangerous reactions that occur when drug users suddenly stop taking or reduce their dosage of a drug.

5. Withdrawal symptoms can include muscle aches and cramps, anxiety attacks, sweating, and nausea.

C. Prevalence (in the United States)

1. Over the course of a year, about 9.5 percent of all adult Americans, or 15 million people, display substance-related disorder.

2. About 20 percent receive treatment.

3. More than 390,000 people die each year as a result of smoking.

4. About 29 percent of Americans over 12 years old are regular smokers.

5. Nearly 13 percent currently use marijuana, cocaine, heroin, or some other illegal substance.

6. Within the past year 27 percent of high school seniors have used an illicit drug.

II. Depressants

A. Depressants slow the activity of the central nervous system, causing a reduction in tension and inhibitions and impairing judgment, motor activity, and concentration.

B. Alcohol

1. Two-thirds of the U.S. population drink alcohol.

2. More than 5 percent of adults are heavy drinkers, consuming at least five drinks on at least five occasions during the past month.

3. Male heavy drinkers outnumber female heavy drinkers by more than 3 to 1 (8.6 percent to 2.4 percent).

4. Ethyl alcohol is rapidly absorbed into the blood through the stomach and intestinal lining.

5. Alcohol depresses or slows CNS functioning, affecting judgment and inhibition, impairing fine motor control, and increasing sensitivity to light.

6. When the blood alcohol content reaches 0.06 percent, one is relaxed and comfortable, but when it reaches 0.09 percent one is intoxicated, and at 0.55 percent death results (but most people pass out long before this level) is reached.

7. Most alcohol is metabolized by the liver into carbon dioxide and water.

8. Alcoholism (alcohol abuse or alcohol dependence) affects at least 7.4 percent of all American adults currently and at least 13 percent at some time in their lives.

9. Hispanic Americans have a slightly higher rate of alcoholism than African Americans and white Americans.

10. White American and Hispanic American men are at greatest risk in the young adult years; African American men are at greatest risk between the ages of 45 and 64.

11. Alcohol abusers regularly drink excessively and feel unable to change their drinking habits.

12. Some alcohol abusers drink large amounts of alcohol daily until they are intoxicated and plan their daily life around drinking.

13. Others drink to excess only on weekends or in the evenings.

14. Still others abstain for long periods and then go on periodic binges of heavy drinking.

15. Alcohol withdrawal delirium, or delirium tremens (DTs) is exhibited by alcohol-dependent persons within three days after they stop drinking.

16. A rare withdrawal reaction is alcohol psychotic disorder, which consists of delusions or auditory hallucinations.

17. Alcohol is one of society's most dangerous drugs, destroying millions of lives, families, relationships, and careers; it is a factor in up to half of all suicides and violent deaths.

18. Roughly 3.4 percent of high school seniors drink alcohol every day, and 5 million teenagers have experienced problems related to alcohol use.

19. Even 8 to 12 percent of elementary school children admit to some alcohol use.

20. Chronic and excessive alcohol consumption can seriously damage one's physical health.

21. Cirrhosis, an alcohol-induced disease that causes scarring of the liver, is the seventh most frequent cause of death in the United States, accounting for 28,000 deaths yearly.

22. Nutritional problems associated with excessive drinking of alcohol can lead to the organic mental disorder known as Wernicke's encephalopathy, which may develop into Korsakoff's syndrome.

C. Sedative-hypnotic drugs
   1. The benzodiazepine antianxiety drugs (e.g., Valium, Xanax, Librium) were discovered in the 1950s.

2. They have less impact on the brain's respiratory center than barbiturates, and therefore are safer.
3. However, large doses can cause intoxication and a pattern of abuse or dependence.
4. More than 1 percent of Americans misuse anxiety drugs at some time.
5. Barbiturates can relieve tension and insomnia but they can be dangerously misused.
6. Some other sedative-hypnotic drugs (e.g., methaqualone, or Quaalude) act on the brain in barbiturate-like ways.
7. In low doses the barbiturates and benzodiazepines reduce the excitement level by increasing the synaptic activity of the inhibitory neurotransmitter GABA, but they do so in different ways; only barbiturates affect the reception of messages in the reticular formation.
8. Some patients whose physicians prescribe barbiturates for their hypnotic effects learn to use them to cope with daily problems rather than to induce sleep, and develop a pattern of abuse.
9. Tolerance for barbiturates develops rapidly.
10. Withdrawal symptoms include nausea, vomiting, weakness, malaise, anxiety, depression, and in extreme cases delirium.
11. The lethal dose remains the same even while the body is building tolerance for the drug's effects.

D. Opioids
1. The opioids comprise opium and drugs derived from it, such as heroin, morphine, and codeine.
2. Morphine, (named for Morpheus, the Greek god of sleep,) was derived from opium in 1804 and was used as a pain reliever and sleep aid.
3. The use of morphine so greatly increased during the Civil War that morphine addiction became known as "soldiers' disease."
4. Morphine was converted into a new pain reliever, heroin, in 1898; it was believed not to be addictive but turned out to be more so.
5. The various opioid drugs, or narcotics, vary in potency, speed of action, and tolerance level.
6. Narcotics can be smoked, inhaled, injected beneath the skin, and injected into the bloodstream.
7. An injection of narcotics brings on a short rush followed by several hours of a pleasant, relaxed "high," or "nod."
8. Narcotics produce their effects by depressing the central nervous system and influencing endorphin receptor sites.

9. In addition to pain relief, sedation, and mood changes, opioids cause nausea, constriction of the pupils, and constipation.
10. It takes only a few weeks of repeated heroin use to be caught in a pattern of abuse.
11. Withdrawal symptoms, which set in immediately after the several-hour high, begin with anxious restlessness and a craving for heroin.
12. Heroin withdrawal distress peaks by the third day and gradually decreases over the next five days.
13. A heroin habit can cost several hundred dollars a day, so many addicted people turn to theft and prostitution to get money.
14. The most direct danger of heroin abuse is an overdose, which is most likely when a person resumes use after a period of abstaining.
15. Other risks are impure drugs and unclean needles, which can lead to AIDS, hepatitis, and skin abscesses.
16. Quinine is sometimes mixed with heroin to counteract the dangers of infection, but too much of it can cause flooding of the lungs and death.
17. Close to 1 percent of adult Americans become addicted to heroin or other opioids at some time.

III. Stimulants

A. The actions of stimulants
1. Stimulants increase the activity of the central nervous system.
2. The results are increased blood pressure and heart rate and intensified behavioral activity, thought processes, and alertness.

B. Cocaine
1. Cocaine, the most powerful natural stimulant known, was first isolated from the cocoa plant in 1865.
2. Only in the last few years have researchers understood how harmful cocaine is and how it produces its effects.

3. More than 23 million Americans have tried cocaine, and nearly 2 million use it at least once a month.
4. Cocaine induces a euphoric rush of well-being and confidence that make the user feel excited, talkative, and euphoric.
5. After a physical dependence develops, abstinence results in depression, fatigue, insomnia, bad dreams, deep sleep, irritability, tremulousness, and anxiety for weeks or even months.

6. One in five users falls into a pattern of abuse or dependence.
7. Crack is a powerful ready-to-smoke free-base cocaine with the ability to induce a more persistent and intense craving than most other drugs.
8. The dangers of cocaine include depression, paranoia, and death by overdose due to (a) its effects on the respiratory center; (b) an inability to sweat, so that the body temperature rises dangerously high; and (c) heart problems.
9. Cocaine crosses the placental barrier and penetrates fetal brain tissue; fetal cocaine syndrome is characterized by altered immune function, learning deficits, decreased activity in the brain's dopamine system, and abnormal thyroid size.

C. Amphetamines
1. The amphetamines—stimulant drugs that have been made in a laboratory since the 1930s—include amphetamine (Benzedrine), dextroamphetamine (Dexedrine), and methamphetamine (Methedrine).
2. They became popular as means to lose weight, to get a burst of energy, and to stay awake for work or study, but their dangers outweigh their benefits.
3. Amphetamines are usually taken as pills or capsules; they can also be injected and smoked.
4. Amphetamines increase energy and alertness and reduce appetite in low doses, but in high doses they cause intoxication, psychosis, and depression.
5. Users may acquire tolerance to amphetamines quickly.
6. As tolerance increases, users may expend more energy than they can afford and risk injuries and illnesses.
7. When regular abusers stop taking amphetamines, they become deeply depressed and may sleep for extended periods.

D. Caffeine
1. The most widely consumed stimulant drug is caffeine.
2. Americans consume an average of 200 mg (about 2 cups of coffee) per day; Europeans consume twice that amount.
3. Nearly all of the caffeine consumed is absorbed in the body, and reaches its peak of concentration in 30 to 60 minutes.
4. Caffeine releases dopamine, serotonin, and norepinephrine in the brain.
5. It increases vigilance, arousal, and general motor activity and reduces fatigue; it also disrupts the performance of complex motor tasks.

6. It can interfere with the quantity and quality of sleep, reduces heart rate, increases respiration, and increases the secretion of gastric acid by the stomach.
7. The symptoms of caffeine intoxication may include restlessness, nervousness, stomach disturbances, twitching, increased heart rate, and the symptoms of anxiety disorder.
8. Abrupt cessation of caffeine can result in significant withdrawal symptoms.
9. Caffeine seems to cause slight increases in blood pressure over time in regular users.

IV. Hallucinogens

A. Psychedelic drugs
1. Psychedelic drugs produce novel sensory experiences ("trips") that can be exciting or frightening.
2. Among the psychedelic drugs are LSD (lysergic acid diethylamide), mescaline, psilocybin, DOM, DMT, morning-glory seeds, bufotenine, and PCP.
3. LSD, developed in 1938 from the ergot alkaloids, became popular in the 1960s.
4. The hallucinosis produced by LSD is characterized by intensified perceptions (particularly visual perceptions), sensory distortions, and hallucinations.
5. LSD may cause synesthesia, a crossing of the senses.
6. It may cause time to slow.
7. Among its physical symptoms are dilation of the pupils, sweating, palpitations, blurred vision, tremors, and loss of coordination.
8. LSD affects neurons that use serotonin, which are involved in transmission of visual information and emotional experiences.
9. Users develop little tolerance and have no withdrawal symptoms when they stop taking LSD but they can develop hallucinogen-induced psychotic disorder or hallucinogen-induced mood disorder.
10. About a quarter of LSD users have flashbacks, sensory and emotional changes that occur unpredictably long after the LSD has left the body.

B. Cannabis
1. The main active ingredient of the hemp plant (cannabis sativa) is tetrahydrocannabinol (THC), found in the resin produced by the leaves and flowering tops; the more THC, the more powerful the cannabis.

2. The forms of cannabis range from strong (hashish) to weak (marijuana); ganja is among the forms of intermediate strength.
3. Low doses typically produce feelings of inner joy and relaxation; users feel either contemplative or talkative; a minority experience anxiety, paranoia, and apprehension, and some notice changes in perception and in their sense of time.
4. Physical changes induced by cannabis include reddened eyes, a fast heartbeat, an increase in appetite, a dry mouth, drowsiness, and dizziness.
5. High doses are associated with visual distortions, alterations in body image, hallucinations, confusion, impulsiveness, and panic.

C. Marijuana abuse and dependence

1. Until the 1970s, marijuana use rarely led to a pattern of abuse or dependence.
2. The marijuana now available is more potent, with a THC content of 10 to 15 percent compared to 1 to 5 percent in the 1960s.
3. Chronic users develop a tolerance and experience flulike withdrawal symptoms.

D. Dangers of marijuana
1. Marijuana occasionally causes a panic reaction, particularly but not exclusively in people with emotional problems.
2. Cannabis intoxication impairs performance of such complex sensorimotor tasks as driving a car.
3. It also interferes with cognitive functioning; memory and concentration are impaired.
4. One marijuana cigarette is equivalent to sixteen tobacco cigarettes in its effects on the lungs.
5. Chronic marijuana use lowers sperm counts and reduces spermatozoa activity in men and produces irregular and abnormal ovulation in women.
6. TCH has a mild and temporary suppressive effect on immune system functioning.
7. The incidence of daily marijuana use by high school seniors declined from 11 percent in 1978 to 2 percent in 1993.

V. Combinations of Substances

A. Cross-tolerance
1. Tolerance for one drug may create tolerance for a similar drug.

2. Cross-tolerance permits a drug abuser to reduce the symptoms of withdrawal from the abused drug by taking a similar drug.

B. Synergistic effects
1. Drugs used at the same time may potentiate, or enhance, each other's effects.
2. For example, alcohol, antianxiety drugs, barbiturates, and opioids are all depressants of the CNS, and in combination can lead to extreme intoxication, coma, and death.
3. Other synergistic effects result when drugs have opposite or antagonistic effects.
4. For example, cocaine and amphetamines used in conjunction with barbiturates or alcohol can build up toxic levels of the depressant drugs.

C. Polysubstance use
1. Synergistic effects may be produced by carelessness or ignorance.
2. Some people, especially teenagers and young adults, take multiple drugs deliberately.

VI. Explanations of Substance-Related Disorders

A. The genetic and biological view
1. Twin, adoption, and animal studies suggest that people can inherit a predisposition for substance abuse and dependence.
2. Researchers have found an alcohol-abuse concordance rate of 54 percent in a group of identical twins and only 28 percent in fraternal twins.
3. Gene mapping studies found the D2 receptor gene present in 69 percent of alcoholics but in less than 20 percent of nonalcoholics.
4. Drug use alters neurotransmitter activity: benzodiazepines lower the production of GABA; opioids reduce the brain's own production of endorphins; cocaine and amphetamines lower the production of dopamine and norepinephrine.
5. The discovery of anadamide, the body's own THC, suggests that excessive use of marijuana may reduce natural anadamide production.

B. The psychodynamic view
   1. Psychodynamic theorists link drug abuse to extraordinary dependency needs traceable to insufficient nurturance in childhood.
   2. Some theorists posit a "substance abuse personality," and researchers have found drug abusers to be more dependent, antisocial, impulsive, and depressive than other people.
   3. Researchers found that men who developed alcohol problems had been more impulsive as adolescents, and continued to be so in middle-age.

C. Behavioral view
   1. Reinforcement theorists believe that drug use is reinforced by the reduction of tension and sense of well-being that drugs induce.
   2. Many people use drugs to mediate themselves when they feel tense and upset, depressed, or angry.
   3. Richard Solomon's opponent-process theory suggests that the brain is structured in such a way that pleasurable emotions inevitably lead to opponent processes—negative aftereffects—that leave the person feeling worse than before.
   4. Classical conditioning may also contribute to drug abuse and dependence.

D. The sociocultural view
   1. Studies have found higher rates of alcoholism in regions where life is unusually stressful.
   2. Rates of alcoholism are higher in hunting societies than in agrarian societies, in cities than in small towns and rural areas, and in lower socioeconomic classes than in other classes.
   3. About 40 percent of American soldiers in Vietnam used heroin at least once, half of them so often that they had withdrawal symptoms when they stopped.
   4. Family attitudes and patterns of functioning may play a role in the development of substance abuse.
   5. Rates of alcohol abuse are lower among Jews and Protestants than among Catholics of Irish and Eastern European ancestry.

VII. Treatments for Substance Disorder

A. Problems for investigators of treatment programs
   1. Different substance use disorders often pose different treatment problems.

2. Some substance abusers recover without intervention, others recover and then relapse, others fail to recover after intensive treatment.

3. The different criteria and goals employed by different clinical researchers make it difficult to draw broad conclusions about a treatment's effectiveness.

B. Insight therapies
   1. Insight therapies address the psychological factors that contribute to substance abuse.
   2. Psychodynamic therapists help their patients to uncover their underlying conflicts and learn to accept their feelings.
   3. These approaches have not been found to be highly effective.
   4. They have been successfully combined with behavioral and biological therapies.

C. Behavioral and cognitive-behavioral therapies
   1. Aversive conditioning involves the repeated pairing of an unpleasant stimulus with a drug.
   2. The effectiveness of the paralyzing drug succinylcholine in conjunction with alcohol was short-lived.
   3. The alcoholic person who undergoes covert sensitization imagines upsetting, repulsive, or frightening scenes while drinking.
   4. Another approach is to teach alternatives to drug taking, such as relaxation, meditation, and biofeedback to reduce tension, or assertiveness training to enable clients to express anger directly.
   5. In contingency training, clients receive incentives contingent on submitting drug-free urine specimens.
   6. In behavioral self-control training (BSCT), clients learn to self-monitor their drinking behavior and become sensitive to the cues they associate with excessive drinking, then are taught to set appropriate limits on their drinking and to apply alternative coping behaviors; 70 percent show improvement.
   7. In relapse-prevention training, clients are taught to plan ahead of time how much drinking is appropriate, and they practice these strategies in either real or imagined high-risk situations.
   8. BSCT and relapse-prevention training are more effective for alcohol abusers than for people who are physically dependent on alcohol.

D. Biological treatments
  1. Detoxification is systematic and medically supervised withdrawal of a drug.
  2. Clients either gradually decrease the dose of the drug or take another drug that reduces withdrawal symptoms.
  3. Antagonistic drugs block or change the effects of the addictive drug.
  4. Disulfiram (Antabuse) or naltrexone may be used to treat alcoholism; narcotic antagonists (e.g., naloxone, cyclazocine, naltrexone, buprenorphine) may be used to treat opioid dependence.
  5. Antibodies are being investigated as an antagonist to cocaine.
  6. Drug maintenance therapy seeks to eliminate the destructive drug-related lifestyle.
  7. Legally administered methadone, at first hailed as a safe substitute for heroin, is itself addictive and can cause extensive withdrawal symptoms and long-lasting neurological effects in children exposed to it in utero.
  8. Still, methadone maintenance has enjoyed renewed interest as a way to decrease the rapid spread of HIV.

E. Self-help programs
  1. Alcoholics Anonymous (AA), started in 1935, now has more than 2 million members in 89,000 chapters.
  2. Members of AA find the peer support, spiritual features, and guidelines it provides helpful in efforts to overcome alcoholism.
  3. AlAnon helps people who live with and care about alcoholic persons.
  4. Such self-help programs as Narcotics Anonymous and Cocaine Anonymous are modeled on AA.

F. Controlled drug use vs. abstinence
  1. Cognitive-behavioral theorists believe problem drinkers can be restrained to drink moderately.
  2. AA says, "Once an alcoholic, always an alcoholic."
  3. Both controlled drinking and abstinence may be viable treatment goals, depending on the individual's personality and the nature of the drinking problem.
  4. Abstinence is the more appropriate goal for those who are physically dependent on alcohol.
  5. Both abstinence and controlled drinking are extremely difficult for alcoholic persons to achieve.

6. A longitudinal study found that 30 years after treatment, 20 percent of the subjects were moderate drinkers, 34 percent abstained, and the rest continued to have significant drinking problems.
7. Some studies suggest recovery rates of only 5 to 10 percent for alcoholism.
8. Twenty-five years after court-ordered treatment, 75 percent of heroin addicts were either dead, in jail, or still using heroin, and 25 percent were drug-free.

G. Sociocultural treatment programs
   1. Treatment programs are becoming increasingly sensitive to the problems of minorities, the poor, and the homeless.
   2. Therapists need to be aware of gender-specific issues.

H. Prevention
   1. Drug-prevention efforts have been expanding beyond the schools to target specific groups.
   2. Some programs advocate total abstinence from drugs and others responsible use.
   3. Programs may focus on the individual, the family, or the peer group.
   4. The Beginning Alcohol and Addiction Basic Education Studies (BABES) teaches preschool children to resist peer pressure.

VIII. The State of the Field: Substance-Related Disorders

A. Substance use is still rampant and causes many problems.

B. New drugs keep emerging.

C. Research is bringing better understanding of drugs' actions on the body.

D. Self-help groups and rehabilitation programs are flourishing.

E. Preventive education seems to be having an effect on teenagers.

LEARNING OBJECTIVES

1. Define the term "drug."
2. Compare and contrast the terms "substance abuse" and "substance dependence."

3. Explain the terms "tolerance" and "withdrawal symptoms."
4. Name some commonly used depressants and explain their effects on the central nervous system.
5. Describe typical patterns of alcohol abuse and know the signs of physical dependence.
6. Discuss possible physical disorders caused by excessive alcohol intake.
7. Distinguish between antianxiety drugs and barbiturates and explain why barbiturate abuse is dangerous.
8. Know which drugs are opioids and be able to explain the effects of these narcotics on the brain.
9. Describe the typical physical, emotional, and behavioral effects of cocaine.
10. Describe the typical effects of amphetamine use.
11. Know the general effects of hallucinogens, such as hallucinogenic hallucinosis and synesthesia, as well as unpleasant effects, such as hallucinogen delusional disorder, hallucinogen mood disorder, and flashbacks.
12. Know the short-term and long-term effects of cannabis use.
13. Explain cross-tolerance and a synergistic effect.
14. Discuss the biological view of substance misuse.
15. Explain the psychodynamic view of substance abuse.
16. Describing the behavioral view of substance abuse and how opponent process theory is applied to the paradoxical effects of drugs.
17. Discuss the sociocultural view of substance abuse.
18. Compare and contrast insight therapies and behavioral techniques in treatments for substance abuse.
19. Describe biological treatments of substance abuse and be able to define "detoxification," "antagonistic drugs," and "drug maintenance therapy."
20. Explain the role of self-help groups in efforts to combat substance abuse.

INSTRUCTION SUGGESTIONS

1. *Class discussion.* Discuss the practices of drug searches and drug testing in schools and workplaces. How can individual rights and the war on drugs be reconciled? Should your college conduct random drug tests for marijuana and cocaine? Arkansas has used blood tests, breathalyzer tests, and polygraph tests on high school students. New Jersey conducts spot searches of lockers, gym bags, and purses, even though the Fourth Amendment outlaws "searches and seizures" without a warrant issued upon "probable cause."

2. ***Class activity.*** The following quiz on fetal alcohol syndrome is based on magazine articles current in 1989. Have your students take the quiz, either orally or in written format. Discuss their answers. Did they have a tendency to under- or overestimate FAS? What strategies would they use to reduce the number of infants affected by FAS?

1. About _____ American babies are born each year with alcohol-related defects.
   A. 5,000
   B. 15,000
   C. 25,000
   D. 40,000
   E. 50,000

2. Of babies affected by alcohol _____ are severely enough affected to be called FAS babies.
   A. 2,000
   B. 6,500
   C. 12,500
   D. 18,000
   E. 25,000

3. FAS is responsible for _____ percent of all cases of mental retardation in this country.
   A. 5
   B. 10
   C. 15
   D. 20
   E. 35

4. Which group has the biggest risk for having a child with FAS?
   A. African Americans
   B. Anglo Americans
   C. Native Americans
   D. There are no differences in FAS rates among ethnic groups.

5. Drinking during the first trimester does not lead to FAS.
   A. True
   B. False

6. The motor development of breast-fed babies whose mothers drink alcohol can be impaired.
   A. True
   B. False

7. Studies suggest that some alcohol-induced injuries to the fetus may be corrected in the womb if a mother gives up alcohol before the end of the third trimester of pregnancy.
   A. True
   B. False

8. Barbiturates, opiates, and alcohol have similar effects on developing fetuses.
   A. True
   B. False

Answers:
1. E. Actually, this number is conservative.
2. C. Damage includes facial deformities, mental retardation, and heart abnormalities.
3. D. FAS is the primary threat to children's mental health, much greater than either Down syndrome or spina bifida.
4. C. The risk for African Americans is 6.7 times that of Anglo Americans; for Native Americans it is 33 times more likely than for Anglo Americans.
5. B. Although risk may be minimal during the first two weeks, during the rest of the first trimester the organs are developing and much damage can result.
6. A. Alcohol can be ingested in the breast milk.
7. A. Scandinavian, Boston, and Atlanta studies all indicate that some correction may occur. At least size and healthiness improve, but there is no evidence that intelligence is repaired.
8. B. Barbiturates and opiates affect the nervous system; alcohol can affect any cell.

3. *Class discussion.* Do you think that pregnant women who use drugs should face criminal prosecution? Do you think it would cut down on their drug abuse, or would it keep women away from professionals who provide prenatal care because they might get arrested? Is fetal abuse the equivalent of child abuse? Can you think of alternatives to criminal charges? Since parents who smoke increase their young children's risk of asthma, should smokers also be liable? Since a man's sperm count

can remain low for more than two years after he stops using cocaine, should a wife who is unable to become pregnant be able to sue her husband if he used to use cocaine? This is not just an abstract discussion. In August 1989, 23-year-old Jennifer Johnson was found guilty of delivering a controlled substance to a minor—her baby, who was born addicted to cocaine. She could have spent thirty years in prison but was sentenced to one year of "house arrest" in a drug rehabilitation center and fourteen years of probation.

4. *Minilecture: Athletes and Steroids*
What do you know about anabolic steroids? Some of you probably know someone who has used steroids to improve their athletic skills. After all, between 6 and 15 percent of high school boys have used or are using steroids. About 5 percent of college athletes use steroids. Anabolic steroids were the reason the Canadian track star Ben Johnson lost his Olympic gold medal. Although our primary image of the anabolic steroid user is an athlete, the first major use of steroids was by Hitler's SS troops in World War II. They took steroids to increase their aggressiveness. The first mention of the use of steroids by athletes was in a 1954 report on Russian athletes. Two years later American athletes were choosing methandrostenolone, or Dianabol.

One technique used by athletes is to follow the "stacking principle," or the simultaneous use of different anabolic steroid preparations to saturate many receptor sites. A second procedure, called the cycling method, involves the cycling of different steroids over six to twelve weeks in an effort to minimize negative effects and to schedule specific drugs for specific competitive events.

Why do athletes use anabolic steroids? They use them to increase strength, achieve a lean body mass, increase aggressiveness, and speed recovery from physical injury. Among the effects they do not anticipate are dramatic mood swings, sleep disturbance, male pattern baldness, acne, and altered libido. Men can experience impotence, lowered sperm count, and gynecomastia (breast development). Women can experience masculinization, hirsutism (male pattern of body hair), and cliteromegaly (enlarged clitoris). Teenagers may experience precocious puberty. More serious effects are possible: impeded growth, early heart attack or stroke, liver failure, liver cancer, and psychological addiction.

Abnormal aggression, mood swings, and psychiatric dysfunctions also seem to increase with the use of anabolic steroids. A study of forty one steroid-using football players and body builders found that nine had affective syndrome and five had psychotic symptoms. In a separate study of health club members who used steroids, 90 percent reported episodes of aggressive and violent behaviors.

5. *Lecture additions.* You can add the following facts to your lecture on marijuana use and abuse.

*A 1897 study of employed persons between 20 and 40 years old found that 16 percent had used marijuana within the last month.

* A 1988 Baltimore study found detectable levels of marijuana in the blood of one-third of over 1000 patients treated for shock/trauma after they were involved in accidents.

*Cannabis contains more than 400 chemicals, including 61 cannabinoids, 11 steroids, 20 nitrogenous compounds, 50 hydrocarbons, 103 terpenes, and benxoprene. Little is known about how these various components affect the body.

*THC is soluble in fat and binds tightly to blood proteins. Thus it can be taken in by tissues well supplied with blood: ovaries, testes, liver, spleen, lungs, and kidneys.

*THC reaches the brain within 14 seconds of being smoked.

*THC may remain in body tissues for 30 days or more and can be found in urine for a month after use.

*High doses or chronic use of marijuana are found to have medical consequences for the pulmonary, central nervous, and reproductive systems. Possible complications: tachycardia, laryngitis, bronchitis, decreased REM sleep, panic attacks, paranoia, memory impairment, and an altered menstrual cycle or a lowered sperm count. Fetal organ development can be negatively altered. Marijuana use also makes it harder to learn new information.

6. *Lecture additions.* Material that you might want to add to your lecture about cocaine:

*Cocaine bought on the streets has usually been "cut" (mixed) with other substances from four to eight times. "Cuts" include mannitol, lactose, sucrose, caffeine, phenylpropanolamine, ephedrine, amphetamine, procaine, lidocaine, and benzocaine. "Cuts" add volume and allow bigger profits but increase medical risks.

*The street value of cocaine in 1986 was six times the price of gold.

*Cocaine-related strokes climbed in the 1980s, especially among adults in their 20s, and cocaine is now one of the leading causes of strokes in young adults.

*Other serious medical complications are myocardial ischemia, hypertension, angina, hypothermia, renal failure, and seizure. Seizures are more likely after intravenous or freebase cocaine use than after snorting.

7. *Class activity.* The following quiz, designed by Lakeside Pharmaceutical Company, allows smokers to determine how dependent they are on nicotine. A score of 7 or higher indicates strong dependence. A answers receive no points, B answers receive 1 point, and C responses score 2 points.

1. How soon do you smoke after you wake up in the morning?
   A. after 30 minutes
   B. within 30 minutes

2. Do you find it hard to refrain from smoking in places where it's forbidden?
   A. no
   B. yes

3. Which of all the cigarettes you smoke in the day is the most satisfying?
   A. not the first
   B. first one in the morning

4. How many cigarettes a day do you smoke?
   A. 1 to 15
   B. 16 to 25
   C. 26 or more

5. Do you smoke more in the morning than during the rest of the day?
   A. no
   B. yes

6. Do you smoke when you are so ill that you're in bed most of the day?
   A. no
   B. yes

7. How high is the nicotine content of the brand you smoke?
    A. low
    B. medium
    C. high

8. How often do you inhale the smoke from your cigarettes?
    A. never
    B. sometimes
    C. always

8. ***Class demonstration.*** Ask someone from Alcoholics Anonymous, Narcotics Anonymous, AlAnon, or other self-help support group for recovering substance abusers to visit your class. As the speaker to explain the twelve steps, what typical meetings are like, and the general benefits of peer support. Another good speaker would be a worker in a detoxification treatment center or an inpatient treatment program.

9. ***Class activity.*** Have students generate a list of possible ways to reduce the numbers of persons who drink alcohol and develop alcoholism. After brainstorming as many ideas as possible, have students decide what changes could be made that would have an impact on society. Possibilities include a change in the legal drinking age; education of schoolchildren about the dangers of alcohol, with note taken of the effects of the sweetness of available drinks (young people tend to drink wine coolers rather than scotch); changes in the images displayed on TV (a banning of commercials that glorify beer drinking; substitution of coffee for alcoholic drinks in soap opera scenes).

10. ***Lecture addition.*** Review material about the think-drink effect and add this material to your lecture. Basically, subjects who thought they had drunk a moderate amount of alcohol but had actually drunk only tonic water made the behavioral changes associated with moderate drinking. Other subjects who had drunk alcohol but thought they had had none did not make such changes.

11. ***Minilecture: Classical Conditioning and Needle Freaks***
    Most people hate needles. We hate getting shots at the doctor's office and we dread a needle in the jaw at the dentist's office. How, then, do

some people get to be "needle freaks"? Needle freaks use needles to inject themselves with the drug of their choice, such as cocaine or heroin; but if they have no drug, they may inject some water just to go through the ritual of shooting up. And the needle freak is in no hurry; every part of the process is lovingly drawn out. Tying a tourniquet around the arm, filling the needle and making sure it contains no air bubble, thumping the lower arm to raise a much-used vein—all these actions are performed in slow motion. Each tiny detail is part of the high. Needle freaks may even take longer to find a usable vein than they need to because delay heightens the anticipation of the rush.

The classical conditioning model can explain the needle freak's behavior. Initially the drug (US) is what brings about the desired emotional effect (UR) and the needle is just a necessary vehicle. But since the needle always precedes the drug, it begins to acquire pleasant associations, with the added benefit of increasing the length of time that the desired emotion is experienced. Eventually the needle (CS) itself is able to produce pleasure (CR) even when water is injected rather than the drug. Can your students suggest classical conditioning parallels for drinking alcohol and smoking pot?

12. *Class discussion.* Discuss how drug use is portrayed in movies and on television. Have your students noticed any changes lately? You might be able to make a short videotape of some excerpts to advance the discussion. Many students will be able to offer examples, such as *Days of Wine and Roses, Arthur, Clean and Sober, The Lost Weekend, The Rose.*

13. *Class demonstration.* Since some substance abusers are treated as criminals rather than as people with a disorder that calls for medical and psychological treatment, you might have a narcotics officer or a probation officer address this issue. You can create a panel discussion by presenting those who treat vs. those who punish during the same class period.

14. *Minilecture: Dual Diagnosis Clients*
Some researchers estimate that 80 percent of people who abuse some substance have at least one other mental disorder. About 40 percent of those being treated for alcoholism have an affective disorder; the

lifetime risk of major depression among people addicted to opiates has been estimated to be as high as 75 percent.

A survey of inpatient substance abuse patients found more than half to have a personality disorder (most commonly antisocial personality disorder; the second most common disorder was borderline type). This group was more likely to use illegal drugs, to be less satisfied with their lives, and to be impulsive.

Researchers have also found high rates of agoraphobia, and other phobias and panic disorders among substance abusers.

15. *Minilecture: Geriatric Alcoholism*
   It is estimated that 10 to 15 percent of the elderly—more men than women—are addicted to alcohol. They display three distinct types of alcoholism: early-onset, late-onset, and intermittent alcoholism.

   Early-onset alcoholism is characterized by drinking that begins before the age of 40 and continues into old age. Typically, these people display a life-long addictive pattern and have weak family affiliations. Family alcoholism is common. This group has many medical problems, such as high rates of cirrhosis of the liver, peripheral neuropathy, and cerebellum degeneration.

   Late-onset alcoholism is characterized by an absence of previous drinking problems and little family history of alcoholism. On the average, these people have greater psychological stability and higher occupational and socioeconomic status than the early-onset group. Drinking increases as life stressors accumulate—isolation, physical problems, cognitive impairment, loss of family support.

   Intermittent alcoholism among the elderly is characterized by alternating periods of heavy drinking and sobriety. Relapses may be due to the stressors that accompany aging.

16. *Class demonstration.* The appendixes of *Cognitive Therapy of Substance Abuse* by Aaron Beck Fred Wright, Cory Newman, and Bruce Liese include several scales that can form the basis of a lecture on the cognitive approach to substance abuse. The scale called "Beliefs about Substance Use" comprises twenty beliefs about the use of drugs ("I'm not a strong enough person to stop"; "I can't function

without it"; "Having this drug problem means I am fundamentally a bad person"; "Using is the only way to increase my creativity and productivity"). The person who takes the Relapse Prediction Scale predicts the strength of the urges and the likelihood of using cocaine in fifty circumstances ("I am in a place where I used cocaine or crack before"; "I just got paid"; "My friend is offering me some cocaine or crack"; "I am under pressure at work"; "I had a fight with my family"). Beck and his colleagues also list advantages and disadvantages of using an illegal substance and advantages and disadvantages of not using one.

17. *Class discussion.* Have students discuss ethnic differences in adolescent drug use. First, have them estimate which ethnic group has the lowest incidence of drug use during adolescence. Which one has a lower incidence now than it did two decades ago? According to an article in the February 14, 1994, *Newsweek*, the correct answer to both questions is African-Americans. At least 20 percent fewer of these teenagers than of European-American adolescents use cocaine or marijuana.

What explains these changes? More inner-city schools are beginning drug education in kindergarten, more minority churches are involved in the effort, and urban TV commercials feature the message "Don't do drugs. Don't die and go away."

Ask students to discuss their beliefs about the upward or downward trend in drug use among teenagers. The use of cocaine and crack is down substantially and alcohol use is down a bit, but after several years of decline, the use of marijuana, amphetamines, and LSD is gradually growing. Among high school seniors, according to a University of Michigan study, the use of LSD rose 1.2 percent, the use of marijuana rose 4.1 percent, and the use of "uppers" rose 1.3 percent from 1992 to 1993.

CHAPTER

14

SEXUAL DISORDERS AND GENDER IDENTITY DISORDERS

∎

TOPIC OVERVIEW

This chapter describes sexual desire disorders, sexual arousal disorders, orgasm disorders, and sexual pain disorders. The chapter explains several paraphilias: fetishism, transvestic fetishism, pedophilia, exhibitionism, voyeurism, frotteurism, sexual masochism, and sexual sadism. The chapter also discusses gender identity disorders.

LECTURE OUTLINE

I. Sexual Dysfunctions

   A. Introduction
      1. Problems in sexual functioning are very common.
      2. Psychological effects include sexual frustration, guilt about failure, loss of self-esteem, and emotional problems with the sex partner.
      3. Most dysfunctions can be treated successfully in relatively brief therapy.
      4. Heterosexual and homosexual couples are subject to the same dysfunctions.

   B. Types of sexual dysfunctions
      1. DSM-IV defines sexual dysfunctions as "psychophysiological disorders which make it impossible for the individual to have and/or enjoy coitus."
      2. They are classified according to the phase of the sexual response cycle that is primarily affected.

3. The sexual response cycle has four stages: desire, arousal, orgasm, and resolution; dysfunctions can affect any of the first three stages.
4. Associated with the desire phase are hypoactive sexual desire, or lack of interest in sex, and sexual aversion, or avoidance of sex as unpleasant.
5. The arousal phase is marked by increases in heart rate, muscle tension, blood pressure, and respiration; pelvic vasocongestion leads to erection of the penis in men and to swelling of the clitoris and labia and vaginal lubrication in women.
6. Dysfunctions of the arousal phase include male erectile disorder (impotence) and female arousal disorder (frigidity).
7. The most common male sexual dysfunction of the orgasm phase is premature ejaculation; much rarer is inhibited male orgasm.
8. The female disorder of the orgasm phase is inhibited female orgasm.
9. Sexual pain disorders—vaginismus, or spastic contractions of the muscles around the outer third of the vagina that prevent entry of the penis, and dyspareunia, or painful intercourse—do not fit any of the specific phases well.
10. Sexual dysfunctions are described as lifelong or not lifelong (depending on whether the person has ever experienced minimal sexual functioning) and as global or specific.

C. Prevalence of sexual dsyfunctions
1. Accurate statistics are difficult to come by.
2. Sex surveys typically have 25 percent refusal rates and participants are more liberal, experienced, and unconventional than the norm.
3. Probably 24 percent of people suffer from some type of sexual dysfunction; only substance abuse disorders are more common.
4. Hypoactive sexual desire is found in about 15 percent of men.
5. Only recently would a woman whose male partner had hypoactive sexual desire suggest sex therapy.
6. Erectile disorder and premature ejaculation vary by age; erectile disorder is most common among older men and premature ejaculation among men under age 30.
7. Inhibited male orgasm occurs in 1 to 3 percent of the general population.
8. Hypoactive sexual desire is found in 20 to 35 percent of women.

9. Up to 48 percent of women have had arousal disorders, 10 to 15 percent only rarely experience orgasm.
10. Lack of orgasm during intercourse is not itself a dysfunction.
11. While 20 percent of women may occasionally experience pain during intercourse, vaginismus probably occurs in less than 1 percent of the population.

D. Causes of sexual dysfunctions
   1. Sexual dysfunctions have been traced to the influences of childhood learning, problematic attitudes and beliefs, biological factors, individual psychodynamic factors, and relationship issues.
   2. Hypoactive sexual desire is defined as persistent, recurrent deficiency or absence of sexual fantasies and desire for sexual activity.
   3. The diagnosis is not warranted unless the patient desires sex less frequently than once every two weeks.
   4. Most people who seek therapy for this disorder have virtually no desire for sex.
   5. The negative reactions experienced by people with sexual aversion disorder include panic attacks, nausea, and vomiting.
   6. The sex drive can be affected by the levels of testosterone, luteinizing hormone, estrogen, and prolactin.
   7. Some prescription and illicit drugs, including drugs used to treat high blood pressure, ulcers, glaucoma, allergies, and heart disease, can suppress the sex drive.
   8. A chronic physical illness can also suppress the sex drive.
   9. A stressful situation can cause hypoactive sex drive.
   10. Being raised in an antisexual religion or culture is associated with hypoactive sexual desire and sexual aversion.
   11. These disorders can also affect people who are exaggeratedly hardworking and serious, who view sex as frivolous or self-indulgent, who are mildly obsessive compulsive, or who are homosexual in a heterosexual marriage.
   12. Adopting their culture's double standard, some men cannot feel sexual desire for a woman they love and respect or for a wife after she becomes a mother.
   13. The experience of being molested or assaulted often leads to sexual aversion.
   14. Vascular abnormalities may play a role in erectile failure.
   15. Many medications that lower the sex drive also interfere with erection.

16. Doppler ultrasound recording measures blood flow in the penis to help detect vascular abnormalities.
17. Nocturnal penile tumescence (NPT) can be used to assess neurological damage.
18. Performance anxiety and the spectator role play a part in both erectile failure and premature ejaculation.
19. As a man ages, more intense, direct, and lengthy physical stimulation of the penis may be needed for an erection.
20. Inhibited ejaculation is associated with neurological disease, multiple sclerosis, diabetes, and drugs that inhibit arousal of the sympathetic nervous system.
21. From 50 to 75 percent of women molested as children or raped as adults have arousal and orgasm dysfunctions.
22. Such physiological conditions as multiple sclerosis and diabetes can affect women's arousal and orgasm.
23. Vaginismus has no physiological cause; it is a conditioned fear response.
24. Dyspareunia usually has a physical cause, such as injury during childbirth, undiagnosed vaginal infection, or endometriosis.

E. Treatment of sexual dysfunctions
1. In the 1950s and 1960s, behavioral therapists began to develop procedures to treat sexual dysfunctions.
2. The anxiety-reduction approach is not effective when dysfunctions are caused by misinformation, negative attitudes, and lack of effective sexual techniques.
3. The publication of Masters and Johnson's *Human Sexual Inadequacy* in 1970 revolutionized the treatment of sexual dysfunction.
4. The first component of sex therapy is assessment and conceptualization of the problem, with emphasis on the principle of mutual responsibility.
5. Sex therapists then provide accurate information about sexuality.
6. They then work to change problematic attitudes, cognitions, and beliefs.
7. Their next task is to eliminate performance anxiety and the spectator role through sensate focus and nondemand pleasuring.
8. They then work to increase communication and the effectiveness of sexual technique.
9. Finally, they work to change destructive lifestyles and marital interactions.

10. A four-element sequential model has been developed for the treatment of hypoactive drive and aversion: affectual awareness, insight, cognitive and emotional change, and behavioral interventions.
11. A patient with erectile failure is taught to reduce performance anxiety and increase stimulation with the "tease" and "stuffing" techniques.
12. Major physical problems may call for a penile prosthesis, a vacuum erection device, or vascular surgery.
13. Premature ejaculation is treated by direct behavioral retraining procedures, such as the "stop–start" and "squeeze" procedures.
14. Inhibited male orgasm is treated by reducing performance anxiety and ensuring adequate stimulation.
15. Techniques used to treat female arousal and orgasm dysfunctions include self-exploration, body awareness, and directed masturbation training.
16. Vaginismic patients practice contracting and relaxing the pubococcygeal muscle.

II. Paraphilias

  A. Introduction
    1. Paraphilias are characterized by recurrent and intense sexual urges and sexually arousing fantasies involving nonhuman objects, children, nonconsenting adults, or suffering and humiliation.
    2. Only people who repeatedly act on these urges or feel extreme guilt and shame over them receive this diagnosis.
    3. Though these disorders seem to be quite prevalent, few people are treated for them, and almost all are men.

  B. Fetishism
    1. People with fetishism use an inanimate object or body part to achieve sexual arousal, often exclusively.
    2. The disorder usually begins in adolescence.
    3. Some persons commit petty thievery to get the objects that arouse their desire.
    4. Psychodynamic theorists see fetishes as defense mechanisms.
    5. Behaviorists sometimes treat fetishism with aversion therapy or covert sensitization.
    6. They also may use masturbatory satiation.

C. Transvestic fetishism
1. Transvestism, or cross-dressing, involves the need to dress in clothes of the opposite sex to achieve sexual arousal.
2. The typical person with this disorder is a heterosexual male.
3. Many transvestites are hostile and self-centered, with limited capacity for intimacy; their marriages tend to be discordant.

D. Pedophilia
1. People with pedophilia achieve sexual gratification with children.
2. Some (exclusive type) are attracted only to children; others (nonexclusive type) are attracted to both adults and children.
3. About 4 percent of pedophile victims are 3 years old or younger; 18 percent are from 4 to 7; and 40 percent are from 8 to 11.
4. The victim usually knows the molester; 15 to 30 percent of molesters are related to their victims.
5. Both girls and boys can be victims, but most victims are girls.
6. Pedophilia usually develops in adolescence.
7. Many pedophiles are married and have other sexual difficulties and frustrations.
8. Alcohol abuse is involved in many cases.
9. Some clinicians attribute pedophilia to immaturity.
10. Pedophilia is treated with aversion therapy, orgasmic reorientation, and relapse-prevention training.

E. Exhibitionism
1. The "flasher" acts out sexually arousing fantasies of exposing his genitals to a woman to produce a reaction of shock.
2. These urges typically intensify when the person is under stress or underoccupied.
3. Most exhibitionists are married but have unsatisfactory sexual relationships with their wives.
4. Exhibitionism is treated with aversion therapy, covert sensitization, arousal reorientation, social skills training, and psychodynamic intervention.

F. Voyeurism
1. Voyeurs have recurrent and intense desires to observe people secretly as they undress or have sex.
2. They may masturbate while they watch.
3. The disorder usually begins before age 15 and tends to be chronic.

    4. Voyeurism has been seen as a way to exercise power over others, possibly motivated by feelings of inadequacy or social inhibition.

    5. Psychodynamic theorists view voyeurism as an attempt to reduce fear of castration.

    6. Behaviorists see it as learned behavior, traceable to a chance and secret observation of a sexually arousing scene.

G. Frotteurism
    1. The frotteur acts on recurrent and intense sexual urges to touch and rub against a nonconsenting person.

    2. Typically he fantasizes that he has a caring relationship with his victim.

    3. Frotteurism usually begins in adolescence or earlier and diminishes after age 25.

H. Sexual masochism
    1. Sexual masochism is a pattern of sexual urges to be humiliated, beaten, bound, or otherwise made to suffer.

    2. The masochistic person acts on these urges in relationships or in autoeroticism.

    3. Most masochistic sexual fantasies begin in childhood and are acted out in adulthood.

    4. A pattern of sexual masochism is often developed through classical conditioning.

    5. Victims of autoerotic asphyxia inadvertently cause a fatal cerebral anoxia by hanging, suffocating, or strangling themselves while masturbating.

I. Sexual sadism
    1. Sadists, nearly always men, are sexually aroused by the infliction of physical of psychological suffering.

    2. They fantasize about having total control over another person.

    3. Behaviorists believe that sexual masochism develops through classical conditioning when a person comes to associate inflicting pain with being sexually aroused.

    4. Psychodynamic and cognitive theorists trace the pattern to underlying feelings of sexual inadequacy.

J. Societal norms and sexual labels
    1. The definition of any paraphilia depends on the society's norms.

2. It has been argued that many behaviors are disorders only when someone is hurt by them.
3. Homosexuality used to be considered a paraphilia, and that judgment shaped laws and justified prejudice.

III. Gender Identity Disorder

A. Description
1. The person with a gender identity disorder, or transsexualism, feels that a vast mistake has been made in the assignment of his or her sex.
2. These people want to have the primary and secondary sex characteristics of the other sex; they feel uncomfortable wearing the clothes of their own sex and often engage in activities that are traditionally associated with the other sex.
3. For transsexuals cross-dressing is not a means to sexual arousal, as it is for transvestites; it is a matter of sexual identity.

B. Incidence and explanation
1. Male transsexuals outnumber female transsexuals by more than 3 to 1.
2. Biological causes have been suspected, but studies find no hormonal or EEG differences.
3. Many transsexuals have a gender identity disorder in childhood; in others it develops in mid-adulthood.

C. Treatment
1. Many transsexuals seek hormone treatments: estrogen causes breast development, loss of body and facial hair, and change in the distribution of body fat in men; testosterone produces male secondary sex characteristics in women.
2. Drug therapy and psychotherapy enable many transsexuals to lead satisfactory lives as members of the opposite sex.
3. Others, after a year or two of hormone therapy, undergo sex-change surgery, a procedure that was first performed in 1931 but gained acceptance only in the 1950s.
4. By 1980, sex-reassignment surgery was routine in at least forty medical centers in the western hemisphere.
5. For men, the procedure involves amputation of the penis, creation of an artificial vagina, and face-altering plastic surgery.
6. For women, surgery includes bilateral mastectomy, hysterectomy, and creation of a penis by either phalloplasty (not yet perfected) or insertion of a silicone prosthesis.

7. Some people consider sex-change surgery a humane solution; others liken it to lobotomy as a drastic physical invasion to treat a purely psychological problem.

IV. The State of the Field: Sexual Disorders and Gender Identity Disorders

A. Mental health professionals have only recently begun to understand the causes of sexual dysfunctions and to develop effective treatments for them.

B. They have made only limited progress in explaining and treating paraphilias and gender identity disorders.

C. Much research has been conducted since 1970.

D. Sex therapy is a complex process with multiple components tailored to the particular problems and personality of an individual and couple.

LEARNING OBJECTIVES

1. Distinguish between sexual dysfunctions and paraphilias.
2. Describe each of the four phases of the sexual response cycle: desire, arousal, orgasm, and resolution.
3. Explain the two most common dysfunctions of the desire phase: hypoactive sexual desire and sexual aversion.
4. Describe the dysfunctions of the arousal phase: male erectile disorder and female arousal disorder.
5. Discuss the orgasmic sexual dysfunctions of premature ejaculation and inhibited male or female orgasm.
6. Define vaginismus and dyspareunia.
7. Describe the incidence of sexual dysfunctions in men and women.
8. Explain the role of sex hormones in sexual desire and activity.
9. Discuss the effects of some drugs and medications on sexuality.
10. Know the possible etiologies of erectile failure and how the diagnosis is made.
11. Discuss the etiology of premature ejaculation, female arousal and orgasmic dysfunctions, vaginismus, and dyspareunia.
12. Describe and evaluate typical sex therapy techniques.
13. Define paraphilias and fetishism and describe behavioral treatment for them.
14. Define transvestism, pedophilia, exhibitionism, voyeurism, and frotteursim.

15. Compare and contrast sexual masochism and sexual sadism.
16. Define gender identity disorder, or transsexualism, and explain how it differs from transvestism.
17. Discuss treatments used for gender identity disorder.

INSTRUCTION SUGGESTIONS

1. *Class demonstration.* Bring in an assortment of respected sex therapy manuals to show to your students and discuss with them. You might want to find some old sex education books and address some of the outmoded information in them.

2. *Class discussion.* Have the class (possibly in small groups) discuss what aspects of sexuality should be considered criminal acts. How would they define these crimes and what punishment would they prescribe? Have them address issues of sexual orientation (homosexuality, bisexuality), sex acts with nonconsenting partners (pedophilia, incest, bestiality, rape, voyeurism, exhibitionism, date rape), and other topics discussed in the text. You might bring up highly publicized incidents such as Pee Wee Herman's arrest for masturbating in an adult movie theater.

3. *Class demonstration.* Have a speaker from Planned Parenthood or a sex therapist address issues of sexuality.

4. *Lecture additions.* You can point out how cultural norms, beliefs, and values influence what is considered healthy sexuality by discussing outmoded terms such as "nymphomania" (which in the Victorian era might be applied to any woman who was regularly orgasmic and enjoyed sex) and "masturbatory insanity." Point out that into the 1930s physicians believed that masturbation could cause fatigue, physical illness, and mental illness. These beliefs led parents to punish children for "playing with themselves" and to tell them that "if you play with that, it will fall off."

5. *Class discussion.* Discuss the idea that sexual orientation can be classically conditioned after presenting some of Storms's ideas. In general, research has shown that objects that are repeatedly paired with erotic stimuli come to acquire arousing properties on their own.

In a 1981 article in *Psychological Review*, Storms suggested that classical conditioning determines one's erotic orientation. The initial US-UR connection is between masturbation (US) and pleasurable arousal (UR). Any fantasized images of tangible stimuli that are repeatedly paired with initial masturbatory experiences influence sexual orientation. Storms suggests that early sexual maturation and early masturbation can be associated with a homosexual orientation because under these circumstances the classical conditioning occurs at an age before heterosexual activities usually develop. To support his view, Storms suggests that homosexuals have more same-gender siblings than heterosexuals do, and that college athletes, who tend to mature early, have a higher incidence of homosexuality than other college students.

How convincing are Storms's ideas? What do you like and dislike about his explanation of sexual orientation? Can you think of information inconsistent with his view? How would you conduct research on his hypothesis? If his model were correct, would sexual orientation be modifiable? How? Does his model suggest that families could learn how to control the sexual orientation of their children? What problems might result from attempts to modify or control the development of sexual orientation? In view of societal changes, including the publicizing of sexual issues by the media, if Storms is correct, would you expect the incidence of homosexuality to change? Why? Does classical conditioning explain the development of some of the paraphilias better than it does sexual orientation?

6. *Minilecture: Sexual Addiction*
   Working with a model similar to the one developed to describe a pattern of substance abuse, Patrick Carnes has described a four-step sexual addiction cycle. As a person's sexual addiction progresses through the four-step cycle, the addiction intensifies with each repetition. The first step is preoccupation: the person is completely engrossed in thoughts of sex. This mental state leads to an obsessive search for sexual stimulation. In the second step, the person engages in rituals that move him or her toward sexual behavior. These special rituals serve to intensify the preoccupation and to add to the sexual arousal and excitement. The third step is the compulsive sexual behavior itself. The sexual addict is unable to stop this sexual act, which represents the culmination of the preoccupation and ritualization. The final step is despair: the person feels powerlessness to break the cycle.

Carnes suggests that the sexual addict has four central or core beliefs: (1) I am basically a bad, unworthy person. (2) No one would love me as I am. (3) My needs are never going to be met if I have to depend on others. (4) Sex is my most important need.

Finally, there are four main signs of compulsive sexuality. (1) The compulsive sexuality is a secret. (2) The sexuality is degrading, exploitive, or harmful to the addict and others. (3) Sex is used to avoid painful feelings or it is the source of painful feelings. (4) The person in the grip of compulsive sexuality is incapable of a caring, committed relationship. Carnes has published material appropriate for both professionals and nonprofessionals who want to learn more about sexual addiction.

7. *Small-group discussion.* Have the class generate a list of childhood sexual messages and misconceptions. Have class members evaluate common errors and prohibitions, and consider how these early beliefs have affected their lives.

8. *Class discussion.* Why are transvestites overwhelmingly male? Why aren't homosexual drag queens considered transvestites? Are there women who dress in male clothes for sexual gratification?

9. *Class discussion.* Have your students decide on the criteria for exhibitionism. Are career-minded nude dancers and strippers exhibitionists? Are their customers voyeurs? Are nudists exhibitionists? Are sculptors and artists who create nude statues and paintings symbolic exhibitionists? Are some rock stars who appear in fairly explicit videos exhibitionists? Are "dirty jokes" funny because of the exhibitionistic/voyeuristic satisfaction they provide?

10. *Minilecture: Healing after Child Sexual Abuse*
In her book *Healing Your Sexual Self*, Janet Woititz describes several coping mechanisms that many victims of sexual abuse use—resistance (compliance of the body but not of the spirit in a situation from which one cannot escape), emotional shutdown, dissociative behavior, amnesia, blocking out of the experience, identifying with others, and returning memories. Painful as it is, gaining an awareness of what happened seems to be the key to resolution.

The effects of sexual abuse on children can include a sense of being damaged, low self-esteem, guilt and shame, fear and lack of trust, depression and anger, confused role boundaries, uneven development (or no childhood), and a sense of powerlessness. All of these experiences can become more generalized in adulthood if sufficient help is not available. The victim may engage in compulsive behavior, suffer from posttraumatic stress disorder, and have unhealthy intimate relationships. Childhood sexual abuse does not cause homosexuality; more adult heterosexuals than homosexuals were sexually abused as children. It does contribute to compulsive overeating, anorexia nervosa, bulimia, self-mutilation, substance abuse, sexual addiction, and co-dependency, but all of these disorders can have other causes.

Woititz believes that the victim must take three steps before sexual healing can begin: (1) express what happened; (2) admit that life is unmanageable; (3) admit to being victimized and to needing help.

If someone else confides his or her sexual abuse (or other form of childhood abuse) to you, the following are helpful ways to respond, according to J. Patrick Gannon: (1) believe what you are told about the abuse; (2) accept what the person says are the consequences of having been abused; (3) reinforce the judgment that the abuse was the parents' responsibility; (4) accept the person's feelings about family members; (5) provide empathy, support, compassion, encouragement, and hope; (6) encourage attempts to get good help.

11. *Class discussion.* Introduce students to some of the controversies surrounding the evaluation of possible victims of sexual ritual abuse (some of whom are evaluated as adults). Have them discuss the controversies and suggest solutions. Four of the difficulties are presented here.

A. Discrepancies.
   Discrepancies are often noted between the stories told by children and those told by their accused offenders. Although denial or minimization can be playing a role in the offender's account, differences are also found in the types of sexual behavior described in events and their sequences, and in timing. One big problem is that young children's sequencing ability is not adequate to enable them to encode some facts accurately. The feelings they express are likely to reflect their experiences more accurately than the details of the events they describe.

B. Leading questions.

Leading questions, such as "Did he touch your private parts?" can influence what children say and come to believe. Such questions are inadmissible as evidence in the courtroom, and they are ill advised in therapy, too.

C. Anatomically correct dolls.

Some clinicians believe that anatomically correct dolls are leading questions in another form. Indeed, they increase the probability of a sexual response, whether or not it is accurate (nonvictimized children also may play at pseudosexual behavior with these dolls). They are more useful as a facilitative tool in therapy than as an investigative tool.

D. False memory syndrome.

Some people believe that therapists working with adult survivors of childhood abuse have helped clients create false memories. Critics suggest that the consistency of the stories is suspect and complain that the stories cannot be substantiated by hard physical evidence. We do know that many people have been sexually abused as children, and we are just beginning to understand the false memory syndrome.

12. *Minilecture: Remembering Childhood Sexual Abuse*

There is much controversy about the incidence of childhood sexual abuse and even more about the remembering and forgetting of such abuse. Studies find that anywhere from one in four to one in two adults have been sexually abused as children.

How often are memories of childhood sexual abuse repressed? Many investigators claim that "half of all incest survivors do not remember that the abuse occurred," and that "total repression of memories of abuse is common." In 1989 Briere and Conte asked subjects who had been sexually abused: "During the period of time between when the first forced sexual experience happened and your 18th birthday was there even a time when you could not remember the forced sexual experience?" The researchers reported that 59 percent answered yes, and this reply was more likely when there had been violent abuse, multiple perpetrators, and fear of harm if the abuse was disclosed. Although some investigators interpret a yes response as evidence of repressed memories, Loftus claims that it can also mean "I found the memories too unpleasant to remember, so I tried not to," or "I didn't want to feel terrible, so I refused to think about it."

In 1992 Williams interviewed 100 women, the majority of African-American background, who seventeen years earlier, when their ages had ranged from infancy to twelve years, had been brought to a city hospital's emergency room for treatment after sexual abuse. About a third of the cases had involved sexual intercourse, a third fondling. Williams found that 38 percent were either amnesic for the abuse or chose not to report it. For those under 5 years old at the time of the abuse, childhood amnesia plays a role. We can retrieve few memories before the age of 5—for example, we usually don't remember moving to a new home or the birth of a younger sibling during those years. Of the remaining forgotten abuse cases, some may be due to repression, but some may be routine failures of memory. Loftus reports on a study that showed that one in four adults who had been discharged from a hospital during the previous year did not remember the hospitalization, and more than one in ten who had been in a car accident during the past year did not remember it. In other words, it is quite common to forget significant life events.

An article by Loftus and her colleagues in the March 1994 issue of *Psychology of Women Quarterly* looks at the incidents of recollections of childhood sexual abuse among 105 women undergoing treatment for substance abuse. They found that 54 percent reported a history of childhood sexual abuse. Four of five remembered all or part of the abuse through all of their lives; the other one in five reported that she forgot the abuse for a period of time and then later remembered it. Women without a period of forgetting reported greater intensity of feelings at the time of the abuse and clearer memories of it, but they did not differ from the others in respect to the violence of the abuse or to whether incest was involved. When the women were asked about the frequency of abuse, 35 percent reported that abuse occurred once, 49 percent said it occurred several times, and 16 percent said it occurred many times. The taking of photographs and anal intercourse were not frequently reported (9 and 5 percent, respectively). Most common were attempted sex, the exposure of private parts, and sexual touching. About one in three experienced intercourse, and about one in eight experienced fellatio.

13. *Class discussion.* Have students discuss the definition of rape. What are the differences between a rape script and a seduction script? Some

rape scripts feature violent, stranger, and blitz rape. People with these scripts may not define acquaintance rape (date rape) as rape. A 1994 study found that nearly half of college-aged women who experienced, forced, nonconsensual sexual intercourse do not label their experience as rape. In 1991 Parrot suggested four reasons why victims do not identify their rape as rape: (1) concern for the rapist, (2) self-blame, (3) the social stereotype of "real" rape, and (4) the victim's attempt to repress the memory of the rape.

CHAPTER

15

SCHIZOPHRENIA

■

TOPIC OVERVIEW

This chapter describes typical symptoms of schizophrenia, the course of the disorder, and its diagnosis. The sociocultural view, the genetic and biological views, and the psychological views of schizophrenia are explored.

LECTURE OUTLINE

I. Introduction

A. Psychosis
   1. The preceptual and thought processes of people with a psychosis become so impaired that they lose touch with reality.
   2. Schizophrenia is the most common form of psychosis.

B. Incidence
   1. Schizophrenia strikes about one in every 100 people.
   2. More than 2 million Americans have been or will be diagnosed as schizophrenic.
   3. Between 200,000 and 400,000 new cases are reported each year.
   4. The financial costs run to tens of billions of dollars annually.
   5. Schizophrenia is associated with increased risk for physical illness and suicide (about 15 percent commit suicide).
   6. Schizophrenia is more common in the lower socioeconomic classes.
   7. The age of onset is earlier for men.
   8. About 3 percent of divorced of separated persons have the disorder, vs. 1 percent of married persons and 2 percent of single persons.

C. Historical information
1. The Bible calls schizophrenia "madness," and King Saul seems to have suffered from it.
2. Hippocrates thought it was caused by an imbalance of humors.
3. Galen called it "dementia" and attributed it to a reduction in "animal spirits," and on coldness and excess humidity in the brain.
4. In 1899 Emil Kraeplin called it "dementia praecox."
5. In 1911 Eugen Bleuler called it "schizophrenia," from the Greek for "split mind," and defined it as fragmentation of thought processes, a split between thoughts and emotions, and withdrawal from reality.

II. The Clinical Picture of Schizophrenia

A. Diversity
1. The symptoms and course of the disorder vary considerably.
2. Responsiveness to treatment also varies.
3. Schizophrenia may be a group of distinct disorders with some common features, but this possibility is not reflected in DSM-IV.

B. Types of symptoms
1. Positive symptoms are bizarre additions to normal behaviors, such as delusions and hallucinations.
2. Negative symptoms, such as flat emotions and lack of volition, reflect pathological deficits.
3. Patients also exhibit psychomotor abnormalities.
4. Men have more negative symptoms than women; positive symptoms are found equally in men and women.

C. Positive symptoms
1. Delusions are unfounded ideas that are fervently believed and often absurd.
2. Persons with schizophrenia are subject to delusions of persecution, of reference, of grandeur, and of control.
3. Some display positive formal thought disorders in peculiar excesses of verbal expression.
4. People who reveal loose associations, or derailment (the most common thought disorder), shift rapidly from one topic to another in incoherent ways.
5. Neologisms are made-up words with meanings known only to the person who uses them.

6. Schizophrenic people also perseverate—repeat words and statements again and again.
7. They also clang, that is, rhyme their thoughts and statements.
8. Loose associations and perseverations are common in severe mania as well as schizophrenia.
9. Some degree of disorganized speech or thinking may appear long before a full pattern of schizophrenic symptoms unfolds.
10. Many people with schizophrenia report heightened sensitivity to sounds and sights, a sense of being flooded with stimuli.
11. Hallucinations are perceptions without external stimuli; auditory hallucinations are most common, but hallucinations can be tactile, somatic, visual, gustatory, and olfactory as well.
12. Schizophrenic persons display inappropriate affect, or emotions unsuited to the situation.

D. Negative symptoms
1. Manic schizophrenic persons display alogia, or poverty of speech; their brief and empty replies reveal decreased command and productivity of speech.
2. Some people with alogia experience blocking: their thoughts disappear from memory even as they are trying to express themselves.
3. Other schizophrenic people may speak fluently but their speech reveals poverty of content.
4. Many schizophrenic persons display blunted or flat affect: they manifest little or no emotion.
5. Many display avolition, or apathy, and ambivalence.
6. Many withdraw emotionally and socially from their environment.

E. Psychomotor symptoms
1. Many patients display loss of spontaneity in movement and make odd gestures and often grimace ritualistically.
2. Extreme psychomotor symptoms—catatonic stupor, catatonic rigidity, catatonic posturing, waxy flexibility, catatonic excitement—are known collectively as catatonia.

III. The Course of Schizophrenia

    A. Onset typically emerges between late teens and mid-30s.
        1. Symptoms are not prominent in the prodromal phase, but deterioration has begun; the person may withdraw socially, have trouble completing tasks, develop peculiar habits, display emotional blunting, have difficulty in communication.
        2. Symptoms, often triggered by stress, are prominent in the active phase.
        3. In the residual phase florid symptoms recede but the person does not return to normal functioning.
        4. Each phase may last days or years, and the active phase may recur.

    B. Recovery
        1. Some persons recover completely but most continue to be impaired.
        2. Recovery is more complete and more likely in persons whose premorbid functioning was good.

IV. Diagnosing Schizophrenia

    A. Main DSM-IV criteria
        1. The person must have shown continuous signs of schizophrenia for at least six months, with at least one month of an active phase that includes at least two major symptoms.
        2. Deterioration from a previous level of functioning must be noted.
        3. Any depressive or manic episode must have preceded or followed the symptoms of psychosis or been briefer than those symptoms.
        4. The symptoms must not be due to substance use or a medical condition.

    B. Disorganized type
        1. The central symptoms of disorganized schizophrenia are confusion, incoherence, and flat or inappropriate affect.
        2. Any delusions or hallucinations are fragmentary.
        3. Formal thought disturbances and perceptual problems make for difficult communication.
        4. "Silliness" is a common feature.

C. Catatonic type
1. The central feature of catatonic schizophrenia is a psychomotor disturbance.
2. These people either fall into a stupor, are seized with uncontrollable excitement, or alternate between the two.

D. Paranoid type
1. The central feature of paranoid schizophrenia is an organized system of delusions and auditory hallucinations.
2. Anxiety or anger may accompany these symptoms.
3. Persons with delusions of grandeur remain cool and aloof, confidant in their special knowledge.

E. Undifferentiated type
1. Persons whose schizophrenia is diagnosed as undifferentiated do not fit neatly into one category.
2. The category has often been misused.

F. Residual type
1. When florid symptoms have receded but some symptoms remain, the psychosis is diagnosed as residual.
2. These persons may display blunted or inappropriate affect, social withdrawal, eccentric behavior, and some illogical thinking.

G. Other categorizations of schizophrenia
1. Type I schizophrenia is characterized by positive symptoms, such as delusions and hallucinations.
2. Type II schizophrenia is characterized by negative symptoms, such as flat affect and poverty of speech.
3. People with Type I schizophrenia have better premorbid adjustment, greater likelihood of improvement, and better responsiveness to antipsychotic drugs.

V. Views on Schizophrenia

A. The sociocultural view
1. Sociocultural theorists believe that many features of schizophrenia are caused by the diagnosis itself; the label becomes a self-fulfilling prophecy.
2. David Rosenhan's study with pseudopatients supports this view.

3. But symptoms produced by a society's expectations should vary from culture to culture, and in fact they seem to be universal (e.g., ***nuthkavihak*** among the Eskimos and ***were*** among the Egba Yorubas of Nigeria).

B. The genetic view
1. Genetic researchers believe that some people inherit a biological predisposition to schizophrenia.
2. Schizophrenia is more common among relatives of schizophrenic people than among relatives of nonschizophrenic people.
3. Schizophrenia appears in 1 percent of the world population but in 10 percent of first-order relatives.
4. Identical twins have a higher concordance rate (40 to 60 percent) than fraternal twins (17 percent).
5. Biological relatives of schizophrenic adoptees are more likely than adoptive relatives to develop schizophrenia.
6. Many researchers believe that the genetic factor in schizophrenia is as great as that found in diabetes, hypertension, coronary artery disease, and ulcers; but few believe it is the only factor.
7. Chromosomal mapping researchers hope to identify more precisely the genetic factors involved in schizophrenia.

C. Biological views
1. Biological research focuses on biochemical abnormalities and abnormal brain structures.
2. According to the dopamine hypothesis—developed after the accidental discovery that phenothiazines, which are dopamine antagonists, relieve the symptoms of schizophrenia—the neurons that use the neurotransmitter dopamine fire too often and transmit too many messages, thus producing the symptoms.
3. Phenothiazines also produce the muscular tremors seen in Parkinson's disease, which are relieved when L-dopa is taken to raise the dopamine level; and an excess of L-dopa produces schizophrenic symptoms.
4. Research on amphetamines also supports the hypothesis.
5. Certain dopamine synapses in schizophrenic people are overactive; these people may have an unusually large number of D-2 receptors (which are blocked by typical antipsychotic drugs).

6. The dopamine hypothesis is not a definitive explanation, as such atypical antipsychotic drugs as clozapine use a different mechanism (they bind to D-1 receptors and to receptors for serotonin) and are often more effective than the dopamine suppressors.

7. Some investigators believe that excess dopamine is a factor only in Type I cases, and that Type II is caused by abnormal brain structure.

8. Patients with enlarged ventricles tend to display more negative than positive symptoms, have poorer premorbid social adjustment, greater cognitive disturbances, and poorer responses to traditional antipsychotic drugs.

9. Other structural abnormalities linked to Type II schizophrenia are smaller or damaged frontal lobes, cerebrum, and cranium, and reduced blood flow.

10. The flow of blood in Broca's area, the speech region of the brain, has been found to increase when a person experiences auditory hallucinations.

11. Some researchers speculate that the brain abnormalities associated with schizophrenia are due to pre-birth exposure to viruses that remain latent until puberty, when they are reactivated by hormonal changes.

12. The viral theory is supported by evidence that more schizophrenic persons are born during winter.

D. The psychological view
1. Freud believed that schizophrenia involved regression to a pre-ego state and restitutive efforts to reestablish ego control; eventually these people regress to a state of primary narcissism.

2. Behaviorists explain schizophrenia as resulting from operant conditioning; many people regard this view as only a partial explanation.

3. Frieda Fromm-Reichmann used the term "schizophrenogenic mother" to describe a cold, domineering mother who is impervious to her children's needs, simultaneously overprotective and rejecting.

4. According to Gregory Bateson's double-bind hypothesis, some parents repeatedly deliver pairs of messages that are mutually contradictory, so that any response the child makes is bound to be wrong; the child may then adopt a special life strategy of ignoring messages, interpreting them literally, or looking for hidden clues; any of which may develop into symptoms of schizophrenia.

5. Theodora Lidz thought that marital schism and marital skew can push offspring toward schizophrenic functioning.

6. The families of schizophrenics have been found to display more conflict, to have greater difficulty communicating with one another, and to be more critical of and overinvolved with their children than other parents.

7. R. D. Laing suggested that families who communicate in confusing ways and convey contradictory expectations prevent their children from discovering their true selves, even from developing a false self that would manage to meet other people's demands; the children therefore withdraw and seek cues to meaning and purpose within themselves.

8. The cognitive explanation suggests that biological problems cause the strange sensory experiences of schizophrenia and that further symptoms develop when other people deny the reality of these experiences; delusions are the explanation that schizophrenic people devise to account for other people's denial of their experiences.

VI. The State of the Field: Schizophrenia

A. Significant insight began with the discovery of antipsychotic drugs, which enabled investigators to work backward to identify biological factors in the development of schizophrenia.

B. Research suggests that different types of schizophrenia may represent entirely different disorders.

LEARNING OBJECTIVES

1. Distinguish between the terms "psychosis" and "schizophrenia."
2. Describe the incidence of schizophrenia.
3. Summarize historical views of schizophrenia.
4. Distinguish between positive symptoms and negative symptoms of schizophrenia.
5. Compare and describe delusions of persecution, reference, grandeur, and control.
6. Define the various types of positive formal thought disorders—loose associations or derailment, neologisms, perseveration, and clang—and discuss their role in the developmental course of schizophrenia.
7. Discuss the role of heightened perceptions and hallucinations in schizophrenia.

8. Describe the various types of hallucinations: auditory, tactile, somatic, visual, gustatory, and olfactory.
9. Define inappropriate affect.
10. Discuss the negative symptoms of schizophrenia; that is, poverty of speech, blunted and flat affect, and disturbed relationships with the external world.
11. Describe the psychomotor symptoms of schizophrenia, and define catatonic stupor, catatonic rigidity, catatonic posturing, waxy flexibility, and catatonic excitement.
12. Summarize the characteristics of the prodromal, active, and residual phases of schizophrenia.
13. List and explain the four main diagnostic criteria for schizophrenia.
14. Describe disorganized (hebephrenic) schizophrenia.
15. Describe catatonic schizophrenia.
16. Describe paranoid schizophrenia.
17. Describe undifferentiated schizophrenia.
18. Describe residual schizophrenia.
19. Distinguish between acute and chronic schizophrenia and between Type I and Type II schizophrenia.
20. Discuss the sociocultural view of schizophrenia.
21. Summarize Rosenhan's study in which eight normal people gained admittance to mental hospitals.
22. Summarize evidence from twin and adoption studies that supports the genetic view of schizophrenia.
23. Discuss chromosomal mapping and schizophrenia.
24. Discuss the dopamine hypothesis and evidence that both supports and fails to support it.
25. Describe the abnormal brain structures of schizophrenic people.
26. Discuss the psychodynamic view of schizophrenia and describe primary narcissism.
27. Discuss the behavioral view of schizophrenia.
28. Discuss hypotheses concerning the families of schizophrenic persons and describe the schizophrenogenic mother, double-bind communications, marital schism, and marital skew.
29. Discuss the existential view of schizophrenia.
30. Discuss the cognitive view of schizophrenia.
31. Summarize the state of the field of schizophrenia.

INSTRUCTION SUGGESTIONS

1. *Lecture additions.* You can use the historical information about schizophrenia to make the following points in your lecture: (1) schizophrenia was established as a mental disorder a long time ago; (2)

traditionally, professionals learned to make correct diagnoses before any effective treatment was available; and (3) workable treatments often have preceded the understanding of etiology.

2. *Lecture additions.* When you discuss Bleuler's views, you might compare the "split within the mind" definition with one schizophrenic man's description of his experience as "like agitated bits of hamburger distributed throughout the universe." When you note that Bleuler believed many people with schizophrenia stabilized or even improved, mention that for many years the standard was one-third, one-third, one-third—a third got well, a third improved, and a third couldn't be helped. Now, however, the last group has dropped to between a tenth and a fourth.

3. *Class activity.* Ask your students to respond to the items in the Magic Ideation Scale in M. Eckblad and L. J. Chapman's "Magic ideation as an indicator of schizotypy," Journal of Consulting and Clinical Psychology, 51 (1983), 216-217. Present the scale here or in conjunction with Chapter 17. You can also present a few items from the Sc (8) scale of the MMPI.

4. *Class discussion.* Lead a discussion comparing New Age beliefs and experiences with those of schizophrenia. Look at channeling, auras, and astral projections from both perspectives.

5. *Lecture additions.* In discussing thought broadcasting, Jan Larson of the Menninger Foundation has talked about a man who had schizophrenia for many years and she was the first to tell him what thought broadcasting meant. He asked, "You mean all along nobody has been able to hear my thoughts—that it's just part of that schizophrenia?" Larson said that was indeed the case, and then asked him how his belief that other people could hear everything he thought affected him. He replied, "Well, it sure makes for charitable thoughts."

6. *Class discussion.* Ask your students to propose reasons for the presence of so many contradictory symptoms in schizophrenia—sensory flooding and sensory blunting, loose associations and blocking,

flat affect and inappropriate affect, catatonic excitement and catatonic stupor, thought broadcasting and thought insertion.

7. *Class activity.* Help students to learn about schizophrenia by playing a Jeopardy-like game. You can use these categories and answers and have teams propose appropriate answers.

> DELUSIONS: persecution, thought broadcasting, thought withdrawal, thought insertion, reference
> THOUGHT SYMPTOMS: loose associations, neologisms, word salad, clang, blocking
> OTHER SYMPTOMS: hallucinations, inappropriate affect, flat affect, catatonic stupor, waxy flexibility
> TYPE: paranoid, catatonic, disorganized, undifferentiated, residual
> EXPLANATIONS: inheritance, dopamine hypothesis, schizophrenogenic mother, double bind, marital schism, paleologic thought

8. *Class activity.* Have groups of students develop scenarios of schizophrenia with hallucinations, developing delusions to fit. Share the scenarios with the whole class.

9. *Class discussion.* Have students discuss their own occasional experiences with schizophrenia-like symptoms, such as inappropriate affect (e.g., giggling during a sermon). What's the difference between their experiences and those of persons with schizophrenia? Also, share experiences of supposedly schizophrenia-creating behaviors, such as double-bind communications.

10. *Class demonstration.* Appropriate speakers on aspects of schizophrenia include a psychiatrist, a group home worker, a NAMI advocate, a person with schizophrenia, or a relative of one.

11. *Class discussion.* The text mentions that schizophrenia was once a "wastebasket category." Have students discuss what today's wastebasket categories might be. Possibilities include adjustment disorders, posttraumatic stress disorder, borderline personality disorder, multiple personality disorder, co-dependency, addictive personality.

12. *Class activity.* Assign students to small groups and ask each group to write a description of a patient with one of the various types of schizophrenia; then ask the other groups to determine the appropriate diagnosis.

13. *Class activity.* List the symptoms of schizophrenia and read them to the class. Respond quickly to students by raising the right hand for a Type I (positive) symptom and the left hand for a Type II (negative) symptom. Which ones did most students identify correctly? Which ones did they have difficulty identifying?

CHAPTER

16

TREATMENTS
FOR SCHIZOPHRENIA

∎

TOPIC OVERVIEW

This chapter describes the kinds of care available for patients with
schizophrenia, including institutionalization, antipsychotic drugs,
psychotherapy, and the community approach.

LECTURE OVERVIEW

I. Institutionalization

    A. Past institutional care
       1. Institutionalization was the main strategy for the first half of
          this century.
       2. Institutional care changed in 1793, when Philippe Pinel
          substituted "moral treatment" for chains.
       3. Large mental hospitals, located in isolated areas, were
          developed as havens from the stresses of life.
       4. States were required to establish public mental institutions.
       5. State hospitals became overcrowded in the mid-nineteenth
          century.
       6. Patients who failed to improve were sent to a "back ward" and
          subjected to mechanical restraints, hydrotherapy, and perhaps
          lobotomy.
       7. Such treatment often led to the social breakdown syndrome:
          extreme withdrawal, anger, physical aggressiveness, and loss of
          interest in personal appearance and functioning.

   B. Improved institutional care
      1. Milieu therapy is based on humanistic principles.
      2. Patients are referred to as "residents" of the therapeutic community and treated as persons capable of ordering their own lives.
      3. Milieu therapy may be a helpful adjunct to other hospital approaches.
      4. Token economy programs are based on behavioral principles.
      5. Patients receive tokens for selected appropriate behaviors, and can exchange them for various rewards.
      6. Some hospitals organize leveled programs, each representing a different order of difficulty.
      7. Research shows a token economy program can help change some schizophrenic patterns and related inappropriate behaviors.
      8. Token economy programs raise ethical and legal questions in respect to patients' rights.

II. Antipsychotic Drugs

   A. History
      1. Antipsychotic drugs are traced to the development of phenothiazine antihistamines in the 1940s.
      2. Chlorpromazine (Thorazine), a phenothiazine, reduced the symptoms of psychotic patients.
      3. Other antipsychotic drugs collectively called neuroleptic drugs, were soon developed: thioridazine (Mellaril), mesoridazine (Serentil), fluphenazine (Prolixin), and trifluoperazine (Stelazine), all phenothiazines; and haloperidol (Haldol) and thiothixene (Navene), which belong to different classes of drugs.
      4. These drugs reduce the symptoms of schizophrenia by reducing excessive activity of dopamine.

   B. The effectiveness of antipsychotic drugs
      1. More than three-fourths of patients given antipsychotic drugs were evaluated as much improved, compared to one-fourth of those given a placebo.
      2. Antipsychotic drugs are the most effective intervention for patients during hospitalization.
      3. Some patients' symptoms return if they stop taking antipsychotic drugs too soon.

4. The drugs relieve the positive symptoms of schizophrenia more completely, or at least more quickly, than the negative symptoms.

C. Adverse effects of antipsychotic drugs
   1. Disturbing "extrapyramidal" effects are caused by the drugs' actions on the extrapyramidal areas of the brain.
   2. DSM-IV lists these undesired effects as medication-induced movement disorders.
   3. From 20 to 40 percent of patients develop Parkinsonian symptoms: severe and continuous muscle tremors and muscle rigidity, very slow movement, shuffling of the feet, little facial expression.
   4. Parkinsonian symptoms can often be reduced or reversed by benztropine (Cogentin).
   5. Dystonia, characterized by involuntary muscle contractions that cause bizarre and uncontrollable movements of the face, neck, tongue, and back, is related to the blocking of dopamine receptors in the substantia nigra; it responds to anti-Parkinsonian drugs.
   6. Akathisia, marked by extreme restlessness and agitation, also seems to be related to reduced dopamine activity in the substantia nigra, but does not respond well to anti-Parkinsonian drugs; in that case the dose of the antipsychotic drug must be reduced.
   7. Neuroleptic malignant syndrome is a severe, potentially fatal reaction marked by muscle rigidity, fever, altered consciousness, and autonomic dysfunction; the only recourse is to withdraw antipsychotic drugs immediately and treat the symptoms.
   8. Tardive dyskinesia, which may occur after long-term use of antipsychotic drugs, consists of involuntary writhing or ticlike movements of the tongue, mouth, face, or whole body; about 10 to 20 percent of patients who take antipsychotic drugs for more than a year develop this disorder.
   9. The longer a person takes antipsychotic drugs, the less likely the symptoms of tardive dyskinesia are to disappear when medication is stopped.
   10. Patients who fail to respond to one neuroleptic drug rarely respond to a higher dose or to a different neuroleptic medication.

11. Most clinicians try to prescribe the lowest effective dose to which each patient responds and to halt medication after normal functioning has been well established.
12. Some patients relapse after their medications are withdrawn.

D. New antipsychotic drugs
1. Clozapine (Clozaril), an atypical antipsychotic medication, can help 80 to 85 percent of schizophrenic persons.
2. Clozapine produces extrapyramidal symptoms, and no cases of tardive dyskinesia have been traced to it.
3. Persons on clozapine have a 1 to 2 percent risk of developing agranulocytosis, a life-threatening drop in white blood cells; thus they need frequent blood tests.
4. Other unwanted effects of clozapine include drowsiness, dizziness, excessive salivation, weight gain, and seizures.
5. Other new drugs are risperidone (Risperdal) and remoxipride (Roxiam).

III. Psychotherapy

A. Successful psychotherapists work patiently to earn patients' trust and build an emotional bond so that they can begin to explore relevant issues.

B. Successful insight therapists take an active role in therapy, set limits, express opinions, challenge patients statements, and guide them in specific life adjustments.

C. Social therapy focuses on problem solving, decision making, and development of social skills, and symptom management.

D. Family therapy
1. Between 25 and 40 percent of recovering schizophrenic people live with family members, and their recovery is affected by those people's behavior and reactions.
2. A higher relapse rate is associated with families that have high levels of expressed overinvolvement, and hostility.
3. Family therapists provide family members with guidance, training, advice, and emotional support.
4. Family therapists also help the patient to cope with the pressures of family life, make use of family resources, and avoid disturbing interactions.

5. Family support groups and family psychoeducational programs enable family members to share their thoughts and emotions, receive and offer support, and learn more about schizophrenia.

IV. The Community Approach

A. The deinstitutional movement

B. Effective community care
    1. Recovering schizophrenic people need help in handling daily responsibilities, guidance in decision making, training in social skills, residential supervision, and vocational counseling and training.
    2. Community mental health centers are intended to provide medication, psychotherapy, and inpatient emergency care, and to coordinate the services provided by other community agencies.
    3. Coordination of services is especially important for MICAs, or patients with a dual diagnosis of schizophrenia and substance abuse.
    4. Short-term hospitalization in an emergency is followed by aftercare in the community.
    5. Some communities offer partial hospitalization in day centers or day hospitals.
    6. Halfway houses, staffed by paraprofessionals, offer a supportive environment where recovering patients are encouraged to be independent and responsible.
    7. Vocational rehabilitation agencies and sheltered workshops provide occupational training.

C. Inadequacies in community treatment
    1. Only 23 percent of patients received outpatient care in 1955; 94 percent do so now.
    2. Close to 40 percent of all people with schizophrenia fail to receive any form of treatment in any given year.
    3. The factors are primarily responsible for this situation: poor coordination of services and a shortage of services.
    4. Most mental health professional prefer to work with people whose problems are less disabling and who pose no cultural and language challenges.

5. Community residents often resist efforts to local halfway houses, day centers, and other such facilities in their neighborhoods (the NIMBY "Not in my back yard" syndrome).

6. Little federal and state money is allocated to community services, which cost more than local governments can afford.

7. Many patients are discharged prematurely from state hospitals without adequate follow-up treatment.

8. The result is the "revolving door" syndrome—70 percent of admissions to state hospitals are readmissions.

9. Many people discharged from state hospitals are among the homeless.

D. The promise of community treatment

1. Since 1977 the Community Support Program has provided funds to communities and states to develop coordinated support symptoms for chronic and severely disturbed mental patients.

2. The Task Force on Homelessness and Severe Mental Illness seeks to meet the needs of the homeless mentally ill for community services and low-cost, stable housing.

3. The National Alliance for the Mentally Ill is a powerful lobbying group, with more than 60,000 members in 900 chapters.

V. The State of the Field: Treatments for Schizophrenia

A. The initial treatment is usually given on an outpatient basis, starting with antipsychotic drugs.

B. Hospitalization, if necessary, is usually short-term.

C. A large number of patients respond reasonably well to treatment.

D. Between 10 and 30 percent of patients continue to require hospitalization for much of their lives.

E. Many schizophrenic persons are not receiving effective community intervention.

Learning Objectives

1. Summarize the changes in institutionalization since 1793.
2. Describe the social breakdown syndrome.
3. Compare and contrast milieu therapy and token economy programs.
4. Discuss the effectiveness of token economy programs.
5. Summarize the early development of neuroleptic drugs and give examples.
6. Discuss the effectiveness of antipsychotic drugs.
7. Discuss the extrapyramidal effects of antipsychotic drugs: dystonia, akathisia, neuroleptic malignant syndrome, and tardive dyskinesia.
8. Discuss current prescription practices.
9. Discuss new antipsychotic drugs, such as clozapine.
10. Discuss the effects of psychotherapy on schizophrenia.
11. Compare and contrast the effects of high expressed emotion and low expressed emotion on the course of schizophrenia.
12. Describe effective community care of schizophrenic patients.
13. Describe day hospitals and halfway houses.
14. Explain the shortcomings of community care.
15. Discuss the NIMBY syndrome.
16. Describe the Community Support Program.
17. Summarize the state of the field concerning schizophrenia.

Instruction Suggestions

1. *Lecture additions.* When you lecture on milieu therapy, introduce the concept of the narrow therapeutic corridor. According to this concept, each of us has a range of optimal sensory input, emotional experience, and general activity. Too little, and we become bored or depressed; too much, and we become stressed or inefficient. College students experience their own therapeutic corridor during the semester. When little is happening, they tend to feel underchallenged, lonely, bored, and depressed. But when term papers are due, and exam's loom, the level of stimulation exceeds the bounds of the healthy corridor and students freak out. For schizophrenics, the therapeutic corridor is narrower, and the optimal level of activity is lower. Because overactivity of dopamine receptors subjects them to sensory overload, a level of stimulation that is optimal for the rest of us is overwhelming for them and triggers symptoms. When they are hospitalized, however, so little may be happening that boredom triggers additional symptoms. The key is for professionals and caring family members to help schizophrenic patients structure activities so that the stimulation they receive fits their narrow therapeutic corridor.

2. *Lecture additions.* One of the ways in which behavioral therapists can help patients with schizophrenia is to teach them ways to appear normal despite the symptoms that remain after the optimal level of medication has been reached. Jan Larson of the Menninger Foundation tells of a patient whose primary symptom was the belief that his head was not attached to the rest of his body. The patient had coped with this unpleasant belief by covering his throat with a tie. This strategy made for an odd appearance, which kept him from being hired for simple jobs that he could have managed. His therapist solved this problem by switching him to turtleneck sweaters. Other patients are taught to control their auditory hallucinations by devoting several minutes in the morning and evening to listening to what the voices have to say and the rest of the time letting them fade into the background. On the few occasions when this strategy fails, patients are instructed to pick up a phone and dial an automated weather report and then speak to the voices so that they appear to others to be engaged in a normal telephone conversation.

3. *Class demonstration.* Ask a social worker, halfway house worker, or psychiatrist to come and address his or her role in the treatment of schizophrenic persons.

4. *Minilecture: HEE and LEE Families*
   High expressed emotion (HEE) families make frequent critical comments expressing disapproval, resentment, or dislike and inducing guilt; they direct their criticism at the person rather than at the person's behavior; and they display marked emotional overinvolvement by their overprotective attitudes, frequent intrusions, and constant worrying over small matters. They believe that their schizophrenic relative could control his or her behavior.

   Low expressed emotion (LEE) families are low-keyed and calm; they tend to believe that schizophrenia is an illness and not a willful display of unacceptable behavior.

   When schizophrenic patients return to their families, the family's expressed emotion style becomes one of the best predictors of relapse (along with medical compliance). The relapse rate for patients in HEE homes have a 58 percent relapse rate and those with LEE families have a 16 percent relapse rate. The good news is that HEE families can be taught LEE style, and the result is a much lower relapse rate.

How should relatives and friends of schizophrenic patients behave?

a.   Communicate briefly, concisely, and clearly.
b.   Do not make fun of a delusion to try to talk the patient out of it, but ask the patient to talk about it only in private.
c.   Expect the schizophrenic person to be emotionally aloof and often to avoid conversation.
d.   Provide a place where the person can withdraw and be alone.
e.   Minimize noise and the number of social events in the home.
f.   Help the person establish a predictable, simple daily routine.
g.   Help the person find leisure activities with low sensory input and usually without interaction with other people.
h.   Develop a quiet, calm, confident attitude.

5.   *Class discussion.* Discuss some of the controversies that surround neuroleptic drugs. Check news magazines and papers for the latest controversies. One current controversy involves the control and costs of the blood tests necessary to monitor patients who take Clozaril.

6.   *Class discussion.* Who would like to work with schizophrenic patients? Of students who wish to be professional counselors, who has the goal of working with people who have this mental disorder? Few, if any, will volunteer. Why? Some people claim that counselors want YAVIS clients—young, attractive, verbal, intelligent, and social. Schizophrenic patients don't fit this category. What would be the rewards of working with schizophrenic patients?

7.   *Class demonstration.* Have a speaker come from the National Association for the Mentally Ill, or share some of the association's literature with your class.

17

PERSONALITY DISORDERS

■

TOPIC OVERVIEW

This chapter describes paranoid personality disorder, schizoid personality disorder, and schizotypal personality disorder, which are the odd or eccentric personality disorders. Next the dramatic, emotional, or erratic personality disorders are discussed—antisocial, borderline, histrionic, and narcissistic personality disorders. The anxious or fearful personality disorders are the avoidant, dependent, and obsessive compulsive personality disorders. The categorizing of personality disorders is discussed.

LECTURE OVERVIEW

I. Introduction

   A. Definition
      1. Personality consists of the unique and enduring patterns of inner experience and behavior that each person displays.
      2. A personality disorder is a pervasive, enduring, and inflexible pattern of inner experience and behavior that deviates markedly from the expectations of one's culture and leads to distress or impairment.
      3. Personality disorders begin before adulthood and persist into adult life without much variation in intensity and without improvement.

B. Description
1. Whether mild or severe, a personality disorder affects every facet of a person's being.

2. Personality disorders are among the most difficult mental disorders to treat.
3. Many people with these disorders do not attribute their problems to their personal style of thinking and behaving.

C. Categorization
1. Personality disorders are Axis II disorders.
2. Axis I and Axis II disorders often coexist.
3. DSM-IV distinguishes ten personality disorders in three clusters.

II. Odd or Eccentric Personality Disorders (Cluster A), or Schizophrenia-spectrum Disorders

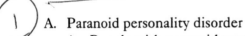

A. Paranoid personality disorder
1. People with paranoid personality disorder display a pattern of pervasive distrust and suspiciousness.
2. They suspect everyone of intending to harm them but have excessive trust in their own ideas and abilities.
3. They doubt other people's loyalty, are cold and distant, and are reluctant to confide in others.
4. They are critical of weakness and fault in others but are very sensitive to criticism of themselves.
5. They are argumentative and rigid.
6. Between 0.5 to 2.5 percent of adults—more men than women—display this personality disorder.
7. Psychodynamic theorists trace this disorder to demanding and rejecting parents; others look for genetic factors.
8. Few people with the disorder come to treatment willingly.
9. Treatment may focus on intrapsychic conflicts and deficits, relationships, or defensive anger.
10. Cognitive therapists work to reduce the vigilance and defensiveness and increase a sense of self-efficacy.
11. Whatever the therapeutic approach, progress is typically slow or nonexistent; drug therapy is not useful.

B. Schizoid personality disorder
1. People with schizoid personality disorder do not have close ties with others because they genuinely prefer to be alone.
2. They display a restricted range of emotional expression.

3. They seek occupations that require little or no contact with other people.
4. They are unaffected by praise or criticism and are unmoved by others' opinions.
5. Slightly more men than women are affected by this disorder.
6. Psychodynamic theorists describe schizoid personality disorder as a defensive reaction to an unsatisfied basic need for human contact.
7. Self theorists believe these people suffer from a diffuse identity: they cannot relate to others because they are unsure of who they are.
8. Cognitive theorists suggest a profound vagueness and poverty of thought, and an inability to scan the environment effectively.
9. People who shun personal contact, as these people do, are unlikely to seek therapy; if they do, it is usually for some other reason, such as a substance abuse disorder.
10. These people resist treatment because they feel threatened by the intimacy of the therapeutic relationship.
11. Cognitive-behavioral therapists try to increase these clients' positive emotions through role playing and to teach them social skills.
12. Neither drug therapy nor group therapy has proved very helpful to these people.

C. Schizotypal personality disorder
1. The pattern of interpersonal deficits displayed by these people is marked by acute discomfort in close relationships, cognitive or perceptual distortions, and behavioral eccentricities.
2. People with schizotypal personality disorder seek isolation, feel anxious around other people, and have few or no close friends.
3. They display ideas of reference, bodily illusions, magical thinking, and eccentricities of thought and behavior.
4. Many of these people have difficulty sustaining attention.
5. Some theorists see a relationship between this disorder and creativity.
6. The positive symptoms of the disorder are more common in women and the negative ones are more common among men.
7. Schizotypal persons are at greater risk of suicide than the general population.
8. Perhaps 3 percent of the population have this disorder.
9. Research with the backward masking task suggests that these people have defects in attention.

10. Higher levels of dopamine activity have been found in these people.
11. Therapists must work slowly and supportively to help these clients to "reconnect" with the world.
12. Cognitive therapists try to teach them to evaluate their unusual thoughts or perceptions according to objective evidence.
13. Both behavioral techniques and antipsychotic drugs have sometimes been helpful.

III. Dramatic, Emotional, or Erratic Personality Disorders (Cluster B)

A. Antisocial personality disorder
1. Persons with antisocial personality disorders (formerly called psychopaths, or sociopaths) consistently disregard other people's rights.
2. A person must be at least 18 years old to receive this diagnosis, but signs of it are usually seen before age 15.
3. These people are repeatedly deceitful, irresponsible, impulsive, and manipulative.
4. They are often arrested.
5. Alcoholism and other substance abuse are common among these people.
6. Children with conduct disorder or attention-deficit hyperactivity disorder have a heightened risk of developing the disorder.
7. The psychodynamic explanation stresses absence of parental love during infancy.
8. Some cognitive theorists suggest a delay in the development of moral reasoning.
9. Some behaviorists believe that antisocial characteristics may be acquired through modeling.
10. Research has linked the disorder to underactivity of the autonomic and central nervous systems.
11. No known specific intervention appears to be effective.
12. Cognitive-behavioral therapists try to move these people's thinking to a more abstract plane.

B. Borderline personality disorder
1. People with a borderline personality disorder display a pervasive pattern of instability in interpersonal relationships, self-image, and moods, and marked impulsivity.
2. Some theorists view these various personality types as midway between mood disorders and schizophrenia.

3. Some of these people swing in and out of intense depressive, anxious, and irritable states that last anywhere from a few hours to a few days.
4. Their anger can be directed outward in physical aggression or inward in self-destructive behavior.
5. Uncertain about their identity, they form intense, conflict-ridden relationships, alternating between overidealization and devaluation of the other person.
6. They frequently lose sight of the boundaries that distinguish their feelings and identities from those of the other person.
7. They become enraged when others fail to meet their expectations yet remain intensely attached to their relationships, paralyzed by fear of abandonment.
8. This disorder afflicts 2 percent of the population, more women than men.
9. Instability and risk of suicide usually peak in the young adult years; the best outcomes are associated with higher intelligence, shorter disability, and less severe symptoms.
10. Psychodynamic theorists trace borderline personality disorder to a relationship with unaccepting parents, which leads to loss of self-esteem, heightened dependence, and lowered capacity for coping with separation; and in fact the families of many such patients were disrupted by divorce or death in the patient's early childhood.
11. Some studies have found a high prevalence of childhood physical and sexual abuse among these people.
12. Biological factors associated with a borderline personality disorder include low serotonin activity and abnormalities in REM sleep and in dopamine activity.
13. The dependency and anger of these people make treatment very difficult.
14. Individual therapy leads to sustained improvement for some patients.
15. Some therapists combine cognitive-behavioral strategies with a psychodynamic approach, modeling alternative interpretations of situations to increase the patient's awareness of other people's perspectives.
16. Group therapy can be somewhat helpful.
17. Antidepressant, antibipolar, and antipsychotic drugs are sometimes helpful, alone or in combination with psychotherapy.

C. Histrionic personality disorder
   1. People with histrionic personality disorder (formerly called hysterical personality disorder) display excessive (shallow) emotionality and attention seeking.
   2. They are continually "on stage."
   3. Their opinions and beliefs, like their moods, are usually fleeting.
   4. They require the constant presence of others to witness their emotionality and to validate their being and their mood states.
   5. Approval and praise are their lifeline.
   6. They do not tolerate delays in gratification well, and are vain, self-indulgent, egocentric, and demanding.
   7. They commonly make an exaggerated display of physical illness and weakness, and may try to manipulate others by suicidal or seductive behavior.
   8. They are highly suggestible and responsive to fads.
   9. Their sense of the intensity and appropriateness of their relationships is distorted.
   10. From 2 to 3 percent of adults display this disorder, as many men as women.
   11. Psychodynamic theorists see these people as feeling an extraordinary need for love and nurturance; their overly emotional behavior is designed to encourage others to act protectively toward them.
   12. Cognitive theorists focus on these people's cognitive deficiencies.
   13. Sociocultural theorists trace this disorder to society's norms and expectations, which encourage dependency and childishness in women.
   14. These people tend to seek out treatment, but their unreasonable demands, tantrums, and seductiveness make progress difficult.

D. Narcissistic personality disorder
   1. People with a narcissistic personality disorder display a chronic and pervasive pattern of grandiosity, need for admiration, and lack of empathy.
   2. They exaggerate their achievements and talents, and often appear arrogant and haughty.
   3. They are unable or unwilling to recognize and identify with others' thoughts and needs, and are envious of others even as they expect other people to be envious of them.

4. Less than 1 percent of adults, most of them men, display this disorder.
5. Some psychodynamic theorists propose that negative treatment by rejecting parents may lead a child to develop a grandiose self-image to maintain illusions of self-sufficiency.
6. Self theorists argue that rejecting parents promote the dominance of their children's "grandiose selves" by failing to mirror their uniqueness.
7. Behavioral and cognitive theorists trace the disorder to doting parents who teach their children to overvalue themselves.
8. Sociocultural theorists trace narcissistic personality disorder to Western culture's encouragement of individualism and self-expression.
9. This is one of the most difficult conditions to treat.
10. The object relations therapist confronts the grandiose self and uncovers the pathological defense mechanisms that protect it.
11. Self therapists interpret narcissistic vulnerability and provide a safe haven in which the true self can emerge.
12. Cognitive therapists try to change narcissistic clients' ways of thinking and their grandiose self-image by challenging their all-or-none categorizations.

IV. Anxious or Fearful Personality Disorders (Cluster C)

A. Avoidant personality disorder
   1. Persons with avoidant personality disorder display a chronic and pervasive pattern of inhibition in social situations, feelings of inadequacy, and extreme sensitivity to disapproval.
   2. In social situations they are preoccupied by the way others perceive them, timid, and afraid to speak.
   3. They believe themselves to be personally unappealing or inferior to others.
   4. The withdrawal, low self-esteem, and fear of rejection displayed by these people are typical of depression.
   5. Up to 1 percent of adults have this disorder; it affects men and women equally.
   6. Both psychodynamic and cognitive theorists link the disorder to parental ridicule, criticism, and rejection.
   7. These clients come to therapy to find acceptance and affection, but tend to distrust the therapist's sincerity.
   8. Psychodynamic, behavioral, cognitive, drug, and group approaches are at least modestly helpful.

B. Dependent personality disorder
1. People with dependent personality disorder display a pattern of submissive and clinging behavior and fear of separation.
2. They want continual advice and reassurance and go to great lengths to avoid being alone.
3. They differ from people with avoidant personality disorder in that they experience difficulty with separation rather than with initiation of relationships.
4. Their distress, loneliness, depression, self-criticism, and low self-esteem are pathological.
5. Close relatives of male subjects have more depressive disorders than usual; those of female subjects have more panic disorders.
6. Freudian theorists trace the disorder to unresolved conflicts during the oral stage.
7. Other psychodynamic theorists and behaviorists point to parents who encourage dependent behavior and punish independent actions.
8. The therapist's goal is to get these clients to accept responsibility for themselves, through either insight, a change of assumptions, or assertiveness training.
9. Group therapy is beneficial to these clients.

C. Obsessive compulsive personality disorder
1. People with obsessive compulsive personality disorder display a preoccupation with orderliness, perfectionism, and mental and interpersonal control, at the expense of flexibility, openness, and efficiency.
2. They set unreasonably high standards for themselves, so are never satisfied with their performance.
3. They are rigid in matters of morals and ethics, and judge other people by their own personal code.
4. They are rarely generous with their time or money.
5. The disorder is found in 1 to 1.7 percent of the general population, and in twice as many men as women.
6. The symptoms of obsessive compulsive personality disorder are ego syntonic, whereas those of obsessive compulsive anxiety disorder are ego dystonic.
7. Some theorists link this personality disorder to the Type A personality pattern.
8. Freudian theorists trace the disorder to overly rigid and punitive toilet training, which causes the child to become fixated at the anal stage.

9. Other psychodynamic theorists point to overcontrolling parents who punish the child for autonomous behavior and thus inhibit development of a separate identity.

10. Cognitive therapists point to illogical thinking processes, such as dichotomous thinking, magnification, and catastrophizing.

11. These people tend to seek treatment only if they need help for an accompanying Axis I disorder, such as anxiety or depression.

V. Categorizing the Personality Disorder

A. Diagnostic difficulties
   1. Each diagnosis relies heavily on subjective judgment rather than on specific observable behaviors.
   2. The criteria for some of the personality disorders overlap.
   3. Many people seem to qualify for diagnosis in more than one cluster.
   4. People with very different personality profiles qualify for the same diagnosis.

B. Revisions in diagnosis criteria
   1. DSM-IV has dropped passive-aggressive personality disorder.
   2. Sadistic personality disorder and self-defeating personality disorder, targeted for further study in DSM-III-R, do not appear in DSM-IV.

C. Millon's reinforcement schema (Box 17-4)
   1. Theodore Millon distinguishes the various personality disorders on the basis of the kinds of reinforcements that sustain them.
   2. People may seek either primarily positive or primarily negative reinforcements.
   3. They may seek reinforcements in themselves or in other people, or may be ambivalent, or may have difficulty obtaining reinforcement from any source.
   4. They may pursue reinforcements by strategies that are either instrumental or passive.

VI. The State of the Field: Personality Disorders

A. The "character disorders" of earlier psychodynamic and humanistic theorists have given way to the personality disorders.

B. Theorists have proposed unifying principles and themes that distinguish the personality disorders, and diagnosticians have developed effective means to assess them.

C. Future research can be expected to produce further changes in categories.

LEARNING OBJECTIVES

1. Define personality disorder and explain Axis II disorders.
2. Discuss the concept of schizophrenia-spectrum disorders, or Cluster A personality disorders.
3. Describe and explain paranoid personality disorder and discuss treatment options.
4. Describe and explain schizoid personality disorder and discuss treatment options.
5. Describe and explain schizotypal personality disorder and discuss treatment options.
6. Define Cluster B personality disorders.
7. Describe and explain antisocial personality disorder and discuss treatment options.
8. Discuss possible relationships between personality disorder and conduct disorder or attention-deficit hyperactivity disorder.
9. Describe and explain borderline personality disorder and discuss treatment options.
10. Describe and explain histrionic personality disorder and discuss treatment options.
11. Describe and explain narcissistic personality disorder and discuss treatment options.
12. Define Cluster C personality disorders.
13. Describe and explain avoidant personality disorder and discuss treatment options.
14. Describe and explain dependent personality disorder and discuss treatment options.
15. Describe and explain obsessive compulsive personality disorder and discuss treatment options.
16. Discuss difficulties involved in the categorizing of personality disorders.
17. Explain why passive-aggressive personality disorder was dropped from DSM-IV.
18. Explain Millon's criteria for classifying various personality disorders.
19. Summarize the state of the field with respect to personality disorders.

INSTRUCTION SUGGESTIONS

1. *Class discussion.* Since this chapter deals with imbalanced personality patterns that develop early and persist throughout life, it might be a good place to discuss some of Carl Jung's ideas about personality in the second half of life. His basic assumption is that middle age is the time during which we balance our personality—learn to expand ourselves and become more complete. If introversion came most easily, then in middle age social settings become easier to handle. If one was naturally an extrovert, in middle age one better develops one's reflective, solitary side. Having managed either masculinity or femininity well, many individuals become more androgynous. How might Jung address the course of personality disorders in middle age?

2. *Class activity.* Either ask students to write a brief description (such as a possible patient profile) for various personality disorders or assign parts of this task to small groups, then have teams determine the personality disorders that fit these descriptions. Assign points for correct answers and award one team a "personality disorder detector award."

3. *Class activity.* Have students in small groups analyze the most typical reinforcement schemes (types, sources, strategies) in their lives. What are some typical examples in their roles as college students? As family members? What patterns are the most common in the small group? In the class?

4. *Class demonstration.* Get a copy of Robert Emmons's Narcissistic Personality Inventory, which appears in his article "Narcissism: Theory and measurement," Journal of Personality and Social Psychology, 52 (1987), 11-17. It measures narcissism in four areas: (1) leadership/authority, (2) self-absorption/self-admiration, (3) superiority/arrogance, and (4) exploitiveness/entitlement. Have students discuss these four aspects of narcissism and the level of narcissism that is characteristic of our culture today.

5. *Class discussion.* Is narcissism becoming more common in America? Why? What role does narcissism play in the lives of politicians? Rock and movie stars? Business executives? Is there both a narcissistic style

and a narcissistic personality disorder? What would the similarities and differences be?

6. ***Class activity.*** Have small groups list ways in which they think Nancy the Narcissist and her twin sister, Heloise the Histrionic, would differ from and resemble each other, especially in their interactions with other people, their behavior during classtime, and their perceptions of and reactions to a crisis. Have groups share their lists.

7. ***Class discussion.*** Do students find themselves in each of the personality disorders? If so, why does this happen? What criteria should be used to separate incidents in which the characteristics appear from a pervasive pattern of those characteristics?

8. ***Class activity.*** Ask small groups to role-play an employee going to the human resources office or an employee assistance program for help in dealing with a boss who is (1) narcissistic, (2) obsessive compulsive, (3) antisocial, or (4) histrionic. While two people play the helper and employee roles, others in the group can feed them appropriate lines. Do the groups make good suggestions for dealing with an employer who has a personality disorder?

9. ***Minilecture: The Personality Disordered Workplace***
Sometimes unhealthy personalities are fostered by our work environments. For example, many workplaces help to create unhealthy workaholic patterns and many people end up entering counseling to learn how to deal with the stresses caused by bosses whom workers label tyrants, connivers, and bad-mouthers. Best-selling books have been written to help employees deal with difficult bosses and companies.

In ***The Addictive Organization*** Schaef and Fassel suggest that workplaces can be addictive. Such organizations have characteristics similar to those found in the dysfunctional families that factor addictions and personality disorders. These workplaces have been described as confusing, self-centered, dishonest, demanding, perfectionist, denying, ethically deteriorated, spiritually bankrupt, chaotic, and crisis oriented. People who work in such places learn to cope by becoming workaholics, numbing and freezing all emotions, getting sick, drinking too much, or denying reality.

In these workplaces, communication patterns are unreliable and rumors and gossip reign. Chaos is magnified by changes in many personnel and in work processes. Some administrators may be belligerent, vindictive, arrogant, deceitful, manipulative, and exploitive. Sexual harassment and other inappropriate behavioral patterns tend to be tolerated.

When the workplace does not make a commitment to change, individuals must do the changing. Some choose to leave an unhealthy workplace and move on to a healthier one. Others change their strategies for working with the unhealthy components of the workplace. In *Working with Difficult People* Solomon describes many poor personal styles displayed by bosses, colleagues, and subordinates and suggests emotional and behavioral strategies for interacting with them. Solomon describes bullies, for example, as people who appear self-confident and strong but use belittlement and threats to keep control. She suggests standing up to them in a friendly and self-confident manner in order to avoid a clash of wills. If your boss is a bully, Solomon recommends that you (1) let the bully vent anger without venting your own; (2) deal with the problem without criticizing the bully; and (3) do not gang up with colleagues to make a complaint because this strategy usually backfires. Bullies lose their power, she says, if you don't cower.

Of course, other individual solutions are possible too. An individual can reduce work stress by relaxation training, exercise, assessing and correcting irrational cognitions about work, and limiting the number of hours that are spent on work.

10. *Class discussion.* Schizotypal symptoms may include magical thinking, such as mindreading and clairvoyance; odd perceptions, such as hallucinations of a dead friend; and other unusual thoughts. How are New Age/psychic persons similar to schizotypal persons? How do they differ? Do you think that most psychic experiences are due to schizotypal personality disorder? If not, how could you detect the differences between someone with schizotypal personality disorder and a person with psychic abilities?

11. *Class demonstration.* Share some items from Millon's assessment scales for the personality disorders.

12. *Class demonstration.* Invite a speaker from Gamblers Anonymous or use some of the organization's literature to address some of the issues involved in this impulsive disorder. The speaker may wish to address opinions about state government's involvement in lottery games, casinos, and other forms of betting.

13. *Minilecture: Cognitive Therapy and Personality Disorders*
Material for this minilecture comes from a 1990 book, *Cognitive Therapy of Personality Disorders*, by Aaron Beck and Arthur Freeman (Chapter 3 is especially useful). Students are familiar with a general assumption of cognitive therapy because of its acceptance in the area of depression—that cognitions about loss add to depression. Individuals with personality disorders, too, are susceptible to certain life experiences because of their cognitive errors and oversensitivity to one type of stress. The narcissist, for example, focuses on threats to self-esteem, and the dependent person is overly sensitive to loss of love and support.

Here, briefly, is a basic belief associated with each of the personality disorders as well as the major strategy in overt behavior. The dependent personality disorder believes "I am helpless" and so uses an attachment strategy. The avoidant personality disorder focuses on "I may get hurt" and uses an avoidance strategy. Paranoid personality disorder involves a wariness strategy because "people are potential adversaries." The narcissistic personality disorder is associated with the attitude "I am special," and this attitude is accompanied by a self-aggrandizement strategy. The belief of the histrionic personality disorder is "I need to impress" and therefore the strategy consists of dramatics. The basic belief of the person with obsessive compulsive personality disorder is that "Errors are bad—I must not err"; this person adopts the perfectionist strategy. The basic belief of the antisocial personality is that "people are there to be taken" and the central strategy is attack. "I need plenty of space" is the schizoid's basic belief and therefore the strategy of isolation is used. Borderline personality disorder is characterized by a wide range of typical beliefs and overt behavioral strategies and is better thought of in terms of ego deficit than of specific belief content. Schizotypal disorder is typified by peculiarities in thinking rather than by an idiosyncratic basic belief.

Persons with personality disorders tend to have both overdeveloped and underdeveloped patterns as a result of their chosen strategy. For example, since a person with obsessive compulsive personality disorder adopts the perfectionist strategy, the overdeveloped patterns are control, responsibility, and systematization, while the underdeveloped patterns are spontaneity and playfulness. The paranoid personality disorder leads to overdevelopment of vigilance, mistrust, and suspiciousness, and underdevelopment of serenity, trust, and acceptance. Each personality disorder expresses unique self-views and unique views about other people. For example, people with obsessive compulsive personality disorder view themselves as responsible for themselves and for others, fear being overwhelmed, and demand perfection of themselves. They view others as too casual, too self-indulgent, and too incompetent. People with paranoid personality disorder see themselves as righteous and mistreated by others and see others as devious, deceptive, treacherous, and manipulative.

The cognitive therapist knows that the core beliefs of clients with personality disorders are deeply ingrained and do not yield readily to cognitive techniques. Even when clients realize that their basic beliefs are dysfunctional, they find those beliefs difficult to modify. Treatment takes a long time but there are spurts of improvement.

CHAPTER

18

DISORDERS OF MEMORY
AND IDENTITY

■

TOPIC OVERVIEW

This chapter describes dissociative amnesia, dissociative fugue, and
dissociative identity disorder, or multiple personality disorder. The chapter
also describes amnesic disorders and dementias, that affect memory and
identity.

LECTURE OVERVIEW

I. Introduction

    A. Memory links past, present, and future.

    B. Memory provides us with an identity.

    C. Integration and self-recognition may break down.

    D. Some alterations in memory have no clear physical cause; others
        are organic.

    E. DSM-IV's listing of depersonalization disorder as a dissociative
        disorder is controversial because memories and identity seem to
        remain intact while the sense of self becomes altered; people with
        this disorder feel that they are observing themselves from outside
        their bodies.

II. Dissociative Disorders

A. Dissociative amnesia
1. A sudden inability to remember some or all of one's past life is directly precipitated by a specific upsetting event.
2. The person with localized, or circumscribed, amnesia, the most common form forgets all events that occurred over a limited period of time.
3. The person with selective amnesia remembers some, but not all, events occurring over a circumscribed period of time.
4. People with generalized amnesia do not remember events in their past life, and may not even recognize friends and relatives.
5. In continuous amnesia, forgetting continues into the present.
6. Amnesia disrupts episodic memory only; semantic memory remains intact.
7. War and natural disasters are typical triggers of amnesia; so is childhood sexual abuse.
8. Between 5 and 14 percent of all mental disorders that emerge during military combat are cases of dissociative amnesia.
9. Another trigger can be sudden loss of a loved one or guilt over an immoral act.

B. Dissociative fugue
1. A loss of memory accompanied by actual physical flight is called a dissociative fugue
2. These people forget their personal identity, flee to a new location, and establish a new identity.
3. A fugue may last only a few hours or days, and end suddenly; or it can be extensive.
4. Most people regain most or all of their memories and the fugue state does not recur.

C. Dissociative identity disorder (multiple personality disorder)
1. A person with dissociative identity disorder displays two or more distinct personalities, or subpersonalities, each with unique memories, behaviors, thoughts, and emotions, and usually its own name, vital statistics, abilities, preferences, and physiological responses.
2. The primary or host personality is the one that appears most often.
3. Transitions are usually sudden and often dramatic, and usually are precipitated by a stressful event.

4. There are three kinds of relationships among the subpersonalities: mutually amnesic, mutually cognizant, and one-way amnesic.

5. Mutually cognizant subpersonalities may be on good terms with one another or mutually hostile.

6. In the one-way amnesic relationship, some subpersonalities are aware of others that are not aware of them; those that are aware (the "co-conscious" subpersonalities) are "quiet observers" of the others.

7. The average number of subpersonalities is 15 for women and 8 for men.

8. Some researchers view the disorder as iatrogenic, but belief in its authenticity and willingness to diagnose it are growing.

D. Explanations of dissociative disorders
1. Psychodynamic theorists consider dissociative disorders to represent an extreme use of repression.

2. They see amnesia and fugue as concealing a single repressed event, multiple personality disorders as representing a lifetime of excessive repression.

3. They believe that subjection to brutal abuse in childhood can precipitate a dissociative identity disorder.

4. Behaviorists see the emergence of dissociative reactions as accidental and their development as the result of a subtle reinforcement process.

5. Investigators of state-dependent learning believe that changes in arousal are at the core of dissociative disorders.

6. Some theorists suggest that dissociative disorders represent a form of self-hypnosis, a purposeful forgetting of unpleasant events.

7. Some theorists see hypnosis as a special process or trance; others believe it can be explained by common processes such as attention and expectation.

E. Treatments for dissociative amnesia and fugue
1. Psychodynamic therapists strive to uncover repressed memories.

2. Hypnotherapy can recall forgotten memories.

3. Sodium amobarbital or sodium pentobarbital is sometimes used to help patients recall forgotten events.

4. Therapy for multiple personality disorder involves recognizing the disorder, recovering memories, and integrating the subpersonalities (which the client may view as a form of death).

III. Organic Disorders Affecting Memory and Identity

A. Memory
1. Short-term memory collects new information, evaluates it, and either stores or discards it.
2. Long-term memory holds all the information stored over the years.
3. Procedural memories are physical or cognitive skills performed without deliberate thought.
4. Declarative memory consists of information that can be recalled.
5. The temporal lobes and the nearby hippocampus and amygdala, along with the diencephalon, mediate short-term and long-term memory.
6. Long-term potentiation (LTP) and the receptor N-methyl-D-aspartate (NMDA) play roles in memory formation.
7. The cholinergic hypothesis suggests that increased sensitivity to acetylcholine is an important part of memory formation.

B. Amnesic disorders
1. Retrograde amnesia is disruption in the retrieval of memories; anterograde amnesia is inability to encode new information.
2. Korsakoff's syndrome, or alcohol-induced persisting amnesic disorder, results from a deficiency of thiamine caused by excessive drinking.
3. The early stage of Korsakoff's syndrome, called Wernicke's encephalopathy, is marked by extreme confusion, which yields to large doses of thiamine; untreated, the disorder progresses to profound anterograde and some retrograde amnesia, which patients may try to disguise by confabulation.
4. Brain surgery and head trauma can cause amnesia.
5. Vascular disease, heart attacks, and infectious diseases, such as herpes encephalitis, can cause amnesic disorders.

C. Dementias
1. Dementias, marked by memory loss and impairment of at least one other cognitive function, are usefully distinguished as either cortical or subcortical.

2. Alzheimer's disease, the most common cortical dementia, is marked by difficulty in immediate recall of new information and impaired memory of the past; procedural memory remains intact for some time; cognitive abilities eventually become so impaired that the patient's sense of identity is destroyed.
3. Pick's disease, a degenerative disease affecting the frontal and temporal lobe, usually strikes between the ages of 50 and 60.
4. Jakob-Creutzfeldt disease is a rapidly progressing pattern of dementia caused by a virus.
5. The speech disorder aphasia is common in cortical dementias but not in the subcortical dementias.
6. Huntington's disease is an inherited progressive degenerative disease marked by severe retrograde amnesia and impaired ability to learn procedural skills.
7. Parkinson's disease is a slowly progressive neurological condition marked by tremors, rigidity, unsteadiness, and often dementia.
8. Other subcortical dementias are supranuclear palsy, Wilson's disease, and multiple sclerosis.
9. Other dementias are caused by infectious disorders such as AIDS, meningitis, and advanced syphilis; by epilepsy; and by abused drugs or toxins.

D. Treatment of amnesic disorder and dementias
1. The most important step is to identify the type and cause of the disorder.
2. Extensive neuropsychological testing identifies specific cognitive impairment.
3. No reliable, effective treatments for amnesic disorders and dementias have yet been found.
4. Researchers seeking to develop drugs to combat degenerative dementias are focusing on neurotransmitters and neurologic pathways.

IV. The State of the Field: Disorders of Memory and Identity

A. Scientists' skepticism has given way to belief in the existence of dissociative disorders.

B. The growing number of reported cases of dissociative disorders, particularly of multiple personality disorder, has led to intensive research on state-dependent learning and self-hypnosis.

C. Some legal defenses based on multiple personality disorder may be contrived.

D. Researchers are investigating genetic and biochemical factors in these disorders.

LEARNING OBJECTIVES

1. Describe the general characteristics of dissociative disorders.
2. Explain why DSM-IV's listing of depersonalization disorder as a dissociative disorder is controversial.
3. Describe and explain dissociative amnesia.
4. Distinguish among localized or circumscribed amnesia, selective amnesia, generalized amnesia, and continuous amnesia.
5. Describe and explain dissociative fugue.
6. Describe and explain dissociative identity disorder, or multiple personality disorder.
7. Describe subpersonalities, the primary or host personality, mutually amnesic relationships, mutually cognizant patterns, one-way amnesic relationships, and co-conscious subpersonalities.
8. Discuss the assessment and prevalence of dissociative identity disorder.
9. Define state-dependent learning.
10. Discuss the possible role of self-hypnosis in dissociative identity disorder.
11. Describe treatments for dissociative amnesia and fugue.
12. Distinguish between short-term (or working) memory and long-term memory.
13. Compare and contrast procedural memory and declarative memory.
14. Summarize the anatomy and biology of memory.
15. Distinguish between retrograde amnesia and anterograde amnesia.
16. Describe and explain Korsakoff's syndrome, Wernicke's encephalopathy, and confabulation.
17. Discuss amnesia caused by brain surgery and head trauma.
18. Define dementias.
19. Discuss cortical dementias, including Alzheimer's disease, Pick's disease, and Jakob-Creutzfeldt disease.
20. Define aphasia.
21. Describe Huntington's disease
22. Describe Parkinson's disease.
23. Discuss dementia and supranuclear palsy, Wilson's disease, and multiple sclerosis.

24. Discuss treatments for amnesic disorders and dementias.
25. Summarize the state of the field with respect to dissociative disorders.

INSTRUCTION SUGGESTIONS

1. *Class discussion.* If you have any soap opera buffs in your class, you may be able to elicit examples of dissociative disorders from favored soap opera plots (if a current story line includes amnesia, fugue, or multiple personality, you may want to videotape a few pertinent scenes and show them to the class). On *The Bold and the Beautiful,* Stephanie lost her memory and went from riches to homelessness. Several years ago Dr. David Stewart on *As the World Turns* experienced a fugue state and went from being a medical researcher to a pharmacist. On the now-defunct *The Doctors*, Dr. Althea Davis experienced psychogenic amnesia on three separate occasions over the years. What examples can your students give? Any examples from prime-time television? You can point out that psychogenic fugues are rare—that is, except in daytime TV. If students (or you) can describe any programs that provide details of such disorders, discuss whether the details shown are accurate.

2. *Class demonstration.* Videotape and show to your class a few brief scenes from movies that deal with dissociative identity disorder, or multiple personality disorder. You can use *The Three Faces of Eve*, for example, or *Sybil.* You can contrast a specific movie scene with the scene as it is presented in the book.

3. *Class discussion.* Discuss why dissociative identity disorder, once dismissed as an illegitimate diagnosis, is increasingly being accepted as a real disorder. What factors do students think provide the best explanation?

4. *Class demonstration.* Compare some passages from *The Three Faces of Eve* with some from *I'm Eve.*

5. *Class demonstration.* Talk shows and TV news magazines often cover dramatic cases of amnesia, fugue, and multiple personality disorder. It might be worthwhile to tape and show a portion of one of these programs.

6. *Class discussion.* A man has been convicted of the rape of a woman
    with a multiple personality disorder after he knowingly seduces a
    subpersonality who was, the prosecutor argued, incapable of
    consenting to sexual intercourse. What do you think of this verdict? If
    you were on the jury, what criteria would you have used?

7. *Class discussion.* Schizophrenia was once called the "wastebasket"
    diagnostic category. Now that dissociative identity disorder (DID) or
    multiple personality disorder (MPD), posttraumatic stress disorder
    (PTSD), and borderline personality disorder (BPD) are increasingly
    being diagnosed, have any of these disorders become the new
    wastebasket category? One professional says, "Beware of any diagnosis
    becoming popular enough to be known by an acronym."

19

PROBLEMS OF CHILDHOOD AND ADOLESCENCE

■

TOPIC OVERVIEW

After describing the normal stages of development, this chapter looks at abnormal developments of childhood and adolescence: childhood anxiety disorders, childhood depression, disruptive behavior disorders, attention-deficit hyperactivity disorder, and elimination disorders; disorders of learning, coordination, and communication; and autistic disorder and mental retardation.

LECTURE OUTLINE

I. Normal Stages of Development (Erikson's stages)

   A. Stage 1: crisis of trust vs. mistrust in infancy

   B. Stage 2: crisis of autonomy vs. shame and doubt in second year

   C. Stage 3: crisis of initiative vs. guilt in preschool years

   D. Stage 4: crisis of industry vs. inferiority in the school years

   E. Stage 5: crisis of identity vs. role confusion in adolescence

   F. Stage 6: crisis of intimacy vs. isolation in early adulthood

   G. Stage 7: crisis of generativity vs. stagnation in middle adulthood

   H. Stage 8: crisis of integrity vs. despair in late adulthood

II. Abnormal Developments of Childhood and Adolescence

    A. Prevalence and history
        1. Most children experience at least some emotional and behavioral problems in the normal course of development.
        2. Worrying, bed-wetting, nightmares, temper tantrums, and restlessness are common, but these problems usually resolve themselves as children get older.
        3. Today's adolescents report less happiness, confidence, affection, and trust and more insecurity than those of earlier generations.
        4. From 17 to 22 percent of children and adolescents experience a diagnosable mental disorder.
        5. More boys than girls have mental disorders (whereas more women are affected by them than men).
        6. Adult and childhood disorders often differ significantly.
        7. Some developmental disorders (e.g., disturbances in the acquisition of cognitive, language, motor, or social skills) may persist in stable forms into adult life.

    B. Childhood anxiety disorders
        1. Close to half of all children have multiple fears.
        2. Children who have a social phobia usually become upset in the presence of strangers and withdraw from these situations.
        3. Children with generalized anxiety disorder are very self-conscious and tend to worry excessively.
        4. Separation anxiety disorder is marked by excessive anxiety, even panic, when the child is separated from a parent.
        5. Separation anxiety is often precipitated by a stressful situation and is somewhat more common among girls than among boys.
        6. School phobia, or school refusal, may be a form of separation anxiety disorder but it may also be caused by other fears or by depression.
        7. Childhood fears are caused by classically conditioned fear responses (according to behaviorists), by excessive repression and displacement (according to traditional psychoanalysts), by relationship confusion and self-fragmentation (according to contemporary psychodynamic theorists), and by physiological abnormalities (according to biological theorists).
        8. Because children are highly dependent on their parents, overprotection or rejection tends to have long-lasting effects on them.

9. Because children's capacity for analysis and reflection is limited, psychodynamic theorists typically use play therapy to explore their feelings and motives.
10. Family therapy, drug therapy, and behavioral and cognitive techniques are also used.

C. Childhood depression
1. Before the 1980s, few clinicians believed that young children could be severely depressed.
2. Depression symptoms are persistent crying, negative self-concept, decreased activity, social withdrawal, and suicidal thoughts.
3. No sex difference is found in the rates of depression before age 11; by age 16, twice as many girls as boys have the disorder.
4. The disorder has been attributed to such factors as loss, learned helplessness, negative cognitive bias, low norepinephrine activity, a negative life event, a major change, rejection, and ongoing abuse.
5. A relatively high rate of depression and other forms of mental dysfunctioning has been found among the parents of depressed children.
6. Childhood depression responds best to cognitive-behavioral therapy, social skills training, and family therapy.
7. Studies have not supported the use of antidepressants in treating childhood depression.

D. Disruptive behavior disorders
1. Children with oppositional defiant disorder argue repeatedly with adults, lose their tempers, swear, feel great anger and resentment, and blame others for their own mistakes.
2. Conduct disorder is more severe; these children violate others' basic rights by cruel and criminal behavior.
3. Conduct disorders usually begin before age 10 and are exhibited by 6 to 16 percent of boys and 2 to 9 percent of girls.
4. One-third of children seen at child guidance clinics are sent there for conduct disorders.
5. More than half of the juveniles who are arrested each year are recidivists.
6. Behavior disorders have been attributed to genetic and biological factors, antisocial traits, drug abuse, poverty, and family dysfunction.

7. Conduct disorders often emerge in an atmosphere of family conflict and hostility, and family interventions are the most effective approaches.

8. Treatments are generally more effective with children under 13 years old.

9. Community-based residential programs, school-based interventions, and skill-training techniques have had limited effectiveness.

10. Drug therapy.has recently been recommended.

11. Institutionalization in juvenile training centers has not been very successful and may solidify the delinquent culture.

E. Attention-Deficit Hyperactivity Disorder (ADHD)

1. Children with ADHD attend poorly to tasks or are overactive and impulsive.

2. The diagnosis may be ADHD, predominantly inattentive type; ADHD, predominantly hyperactive-impulsive type (also called hyperactivity); or ADHD, combined type.

3. The symptoms are usually highly visible at home, school, and work and in social situations; they are less apparent in a novel setting or a one-on-one situation, or when the child receives frequent reinforcement or strict control.

4. ADHD is found in 3 to 5 percent of schoolchildren, 80 percent of them boys, and may continue into adulthood.

5. Some researchers suggest biological dysfunctioning but have not determined its precise nature; others point to psychological factors.

6. Most clinicians today view ADHD as a disorder with multiple and interacting causes.

7. The most common treatment has consisted of stimulant drugs, such as methylphenidate (Ritalin), which is prescribed for 1 to 2 percent of schoolchildren.

8. The Feingold diet, which eliminates food additives, has not been supported by research.

9. Behaviorists teach parents and teachers to systematically reinforce proper attention and appropriate behavior.

10. A combination of operant conditioning and drug therapy has been relatively successful.

F. Elimination disorders

1. Enuresis, or involuntary urination, may be nocturnal (primarily at night) or, less commonly, diurnal (primarily in the day).

2. Its prevalence decreases from 7 percent of boys at age 5 to 3 percent at age 10, and from 3 percent of girls at age 5 to 2 percent at age 10.
3. It may continue from infancy or resume as a reaction to stress.
4. Psychodynamic theorists see it as a symbol of other conflicts; family systems theorists attribute it to anxiety or hostility aroused by disturbed family interactions; and behaviorists view it as a failure of toilet training.
5. Treatments based on behavioral principles have been successful.
6. Encopresis, or inappropriate and usually involuntary defecating, is less common than enuresis.
7. It usually starts after age 4 and affects about 1 percent of 5-year-olds, more boys than girls.
8. It occurs mainly during the day, usually late in the afternoon, and seldom at night.
9. Encopresis is considered more serious than enuresis and causes more shame and embarrassment.
10. The most successful treatments are behavioral and/or medical approaches; family therapy is also helpful.

G. Disorders of learning, coordination, and communication
  1. Grossly inadequate development and functioning in learning, coordination, or communication are more common in boys than in girls.
  2. Adolescents with such problems are at increased risk for severe depression and suicide.
  3. Learning disorders include mathematics disorder, disorder of written expression, and reading disorder (dyslexia).
  4. Developmental coordination disorder, marked by poor motor coordination, affects 6 percent of children between 5 and 11 years.
  5. Children with an expressive language disorder have difficulty expressing themselves in language because they have a limited or inaccurate vocabulary, or have trouble acquiring new words, or regularly shorten sentences, or omit critical parts of sentences, or do not order words in the usual way; between 3 and 10 percent of all children have such a disorder.
  6. Children with a mixed receptive/expressive language disorder have such difficulty comprehending and expressing language that it interferes with academic achievement or daily activities; up to 3 percent of schoolchildren have this problem.

7. About 1 percent of children (75 percent of them boys) stutter, or display a disturbance in the normal fluency and timing of their speech.
8. Researchers have linked these disorders to genetic defects, birth injuries, lead poisoning, inappropriate diet, sensory dysfunction, and poor teaching.
9. Perceptual deficit theory sees these disorders as products of problems in perceptual processing.
10 Academic instruction theory sees learning disorders as reflecting deficiencies in teaching.

H. Autistic disorder
 1. Autism was first identified by Lea Kanner in 1943.
 2. Autism, characterized by extreme unresponsiveness to others, poor communication skills, and bizarre responses to the environment, appears before age 3.
 3. DSM-IV groups autistic and several other disorders as pervasive developmental disorders, but it is common practice to refer to them all as "autism."
 4. Autism affects 2 to 5 of every 10,000 children—80 percent of them boys.
 5. Two in three remain severely impaired into adulthood; only one in six makes a fair adjustment.
 6. Autistic people with a higher IQ and better language skills tend to have a more promising future.
 7. Autistic children are typically aloof, unresponsive, and uninterested in other people.
 8. A common speech problem among these children is echolalia, or the exact echoing of phrases said by others, either immediately or hours or days later (delayed echolalia).
 9. Autistic children also display pronominal reversal: they say "you" instead of "I."
 10. They may use metaphorical language or neologisms.
 11. Some have difficulty naming objects (nominal aphasia).
 12. Incorrect speech inflections and improper facial expressions and gestures are common.
 13. These children have difficulty understanding speech and speaking spontaneously.
 14. They display ritualistic and repetitive behaviors and resistance to change (perseveration of sameness).
 15. Some autistic children engage in self-stimulatory and self-injurious behaviors.

16. Some perceptual-cognitive theorists consider these children to have primary perceptual or cognitive disturbances, such as a fundamental impairment of the ability to comprehend sounds.
17. Another such theory focuses on stimulus overselectivity, or attention to only one dimension of a stimulus, such as its color.
18. Examinations of the relatives of autistic children are consistent with the possibility of a genetic factor in this disorder.
19. Some studies link autism to prenatal difficulties or birth complications.
20. Other point to neurological dysfunction which may be due to disturbances in the brain stem, abnormalities in the reticular activating system or in the brain cortex, or neurotransmitter imbalances.
21. Research has failed to support the theory that autism can be traced to personality characteristics of the parents ("refrigerator parents").
22. Bruno Bettelheim's family interaction theory, which traced autism to negative parent interactions with the child, was influential for years but has received little empirical support.
23. Research has also failed to establish a connection between autism and unusual environmental stress.
24. The antipsychotic drug haloperidol is helpful in conjunction with behavioral approaches, and vitamin B6 and magnesium increase attention and language.
25. Psychodynamic-humanistic therapists have attempted to counter stressful environmental experiences by providing great warmth and acceptance, but their claims of success have not been supported by research.
26. Behavioral therapists teach speech, social, classroom, and self-help skills, and try to reduce dysfunctional behaviors.
27. Therapists who use modeling and operant conditioning techniques must shape the children's behavior.
28. Some therapists seek to eliminate injurious behaviors by ignoring them or by punishments.
29. Integrated education and peer-mediated interventions teach autistic children to socialize.
30. Sign language, simultaneous communication, augmentative communication systems, and facilitated communication have been used in efforts to help these children communicate.
31. Programs have been developed to teach autistic persons living and work skills and help integrate them into the community.

I. Mental retardation
   1. One in every 100 persons manifests significant subaverage general intellectual functioning (an IQ of 70 or below) and displays impairment in adaptive behavior before the age of 18, thus qualifying for a diagnosis of mental retardation.
   2. The validity of intelligence tests has been questioned on the basis of school and work performance, sociocultural bias, and language difficulties.
   3. People with IQ scores below 70 tend to be deficit in adaptive functioning—in the ability to be personally independent and socially responsible, to communicate, and to fulfill daily living requirements.
   4. Adaptive behavior is measured by the Vineland and AAMR adaptive behavior scales.
   5. Retarded people learn more slowly than nonretarded people and manifest deficits in attention, short-term memory, and language.
   6. DSM-IV distinguishes four levels of mental retardation: mild (IQ 50-70), moderate (IQ 35-49), severe (IQ 20-34), and profound (IQ below 20).
   7. The AAMR distinguishes four categories on the basis of the level of support the person needs: intermittent, limited, extensive, or pervasive.
   8. Some 85 percent of retarded persons are mildly retarded: they are capable of schoolwork at the sixth-grade level and of social and vocational skills adequate for self-support.
   9. Most mildly retarded people come from poor and deprived home environments, so their condition is called cultural, familial, or environmental retardation; but some genetic and biological factors, such as poor prenatal care, also seem to be at work.
   10. Adoption studies show that both heredity and environment play a role in intellectual functioning.
   11. Moderate drinking, drug use, and malnourishment during pregnancy may impair a child's intellectual potential.
   12. Mild mental retardation attributable to malnourishment during childhood is at least partially reversible.
   13. About 10 percent of retarded people are moderately retarded or can learn to care for themselves and to work in semiskilled or unskilled jobs.
   14. The roughly 4 percent who are severely retarded require supervision and can learn to perform only basic tasks.

15. The 1 percent who are profoundly retarded require a highly structured environment with close supervision.
16. The primary causes of moderate, severe, and profound retardation are chromosomal and metabolic disorders, prenatal conditions, birth complications, and postnatal diseases and injuries.
17. Down syndrome (formerly called mongolism) is the most common chromosomal disorder leading to mental retardation, appearing in 1 of every 800 live births (1 in 100 if the mother is over 35).
18. Amniocentesis can detect Down syndrome and other chromosomal abnormalities during pregnancy.
19. The three types of Down syndrome are trisomy 21, translocation, and mosaicism.
20. People with Down syndrome have a distinctive appearance, problems with articulation, and an IQ of 35-55.
21. Down syndrome and early dementia may co-occur because the genes that produce both disorders are located close to each other on chromosome 21.
22. Fragile X syndrome is the second most common genetic cause of mental retardation, accounting for about 7 percent of all cases of retardation among boys; a few girls are also affected by it.
23. The most common retardation-causing metabolic disorder, typically caused by the pairing of two recessive genes, is phenylketonuria (PKU); less common is Tay-Sachs disease, a fatal disorder that may be transmitted by 1 of every 900 Jewish couples, particularly those of Eastern European ancestry.
24. Prenatal problems that can lead to retardation include a low level of iodine, which can lead to cretinism, and alcohol abuse, which can cause fetal alcohol syndrome.
25. Mental retardation can be caused by maternal infections, such as rubella or syphilis, or by a birth complication, such as anoxia or extreme prematurity.
26. Some forms may have multiple biological causes, as with microencephaly and hydrocephalus.
27. At state schools retarded persons might function reasonably well under normalization programs or suffer neglect; today community programs provide supported living arrangement, community living families, and intermediate care facilities.
28. The 1975 Education for All Handicapped Children Act requires all states to provide mentally retarded children with "free appropriate public education in the least restrictive environment."

29. Some educators favor special classes; others support mainstreaming.
30. Token economy and other operant learning programs are regularly used.
31. Insight, group, and drug therapies are used to help retarded people cope with the emotional and behavioral problems to which their condition subjects them.
32. Retarded persons need opportunities for personal, social, and vocational growth.
33. Between a quarter and half of all mildly retarded persons eventually marry.
34. Involuntary sterilization has given way to training in family planning and in parenting.
35. Sheltered workshops provide job training and employment.

II. The State of the Field: Problems with Childhood and Adolescence

A. Once largely ignored, the problems of children and adolescents are now the focus of many studies, and numerous clinicians specialize in these populations.

B. The diagnosis and treatment of these problems have improved.

C. The government has moved to protect children's rights.

LEARNING OBJECTIVES

1. List and describe the eight crises in Erik Erikson's developmental scheme.
2. Describe the prevalence of mental disorders among children and adolescents.
3. Describe persistent childhood anxiety disorders.
4. Describe and explain childhood depression.
5. Compare and contrast oppositional defiant disorder and conduct disorder.
6. Describe the prevalence, symptoms, causes, and treatments of attention-deficit hyperactivity disorder.
7. Name and describe the elimination disorders and discuss possible treatments.
8. Describe the various disorders of learning, coordination, and communication.
9. Compare perceptual deficit theory and academic instruction theory.

10. Describe the symptoms of autistic disorder and discuss the various etiologies that have been proposed.
11. Describe various treatments of autism.
12. Know the prevalence of the various types of mental retardation.
13. Evaluate the usefulness of intelligence tests and measures of adaptive functioning.
14. Discuss the environmental, genetic, and biological factors that contribute to mental retardation.
15. Evaluate treatments for mental retardation, including normalization programs and behavioral techniques.

INSTRUCTION SUGGESTIONS

1. *Class discussion.* Generate a list of stereotypes of adolescence ("the best years of one's life," "the bridge between childhood and adulthood," and so forth). Discuss the opinions of various psychologists, such as G. Stanley Hall's concept of "storm and stress" (known today as "the generation gap") and David Elkind's "hurried child." Discuss how these various beliefs affect parent-child relationships and perceptions of mental disorders among the young.

2. *Class activity.* Devise an example of a child who has developed school phobia. Have the class (perhaps in small groups) design a treatment program that will get the child back into school, help the child to cope better with school situations, and build the child's self-esteem. What techniques are mentioned most?

3. *Class demonstration.* Bring in one or more authentic fairly tales (such as "Little Red Riding Hood," in which the wolf devours the grandmother, or "Cinderella," in which one of the stepsisters mutilates her foot to fit it into the glass slipper) and read the scariest portions to the class. Why are these tales for children? Do they build anxiety? Do they serve a necessary function?

4. *Class discussion.* Have a discussion about ways to help children deal with such family adjustments as divorce, financial changes, and death.

5. *Class discussion.* The text mentions that more than half of the juveniles arrested each year have been arrested before. Why do you

think this is the case? What changes should communities make in order to change this statistic? At what age do you hold individuals to be fully responsible for their actions? Would you ever hold parents responsible for their children's crimes? Can you think of creative punishments that might be more effective than incarceration?

6. *Minilecture: Improving Children's Diets*
Although the majority of professionals do not view diet choices as the primary cause of hyperactivity in children, better diet decisions can help alter undesirable behaviors in both hyperactive children and other children with lesser attention deficits. The following are some of the suggestions offered by William G. Crook, M.D., in his book Help for the Hyperactive Child.
*Avoid processed meats.
*Serve lots of fruits and vegetables.
*Serve whole-grain breads and muffins. For children sensitive to yeast, serve rice crackers and flat breads.
*Serve jellies and preserves that do not contain sugar.
*Serve aspartame and saccharin if the child has no adverse reactions to them.
*For dessert serve fresh fruits, a thin slice of cake without icing, or a yogurt pop.
*Serve low-fat milk products (for children over 2 years old).
*Serve nuts that are not processed with fats, sugar, and salt.
*Encourage the child to drink water to quench thirst and just to sip at other beverages.
*Limit or avoid caffeine-containing drinks and drinks loaded with sugar, food colorings, chemicals, and preservatives.

7. *Class demonstration.* Ask a special education teacher to explain to your class how teaching techniques are adapted for children with various developmental disorders. How does the teacher deal with student and educator biases? What are his or her thoughts about mainstreaming vs. special classes? You might ask your speaker to bring in some materials designed to help students with various specific developmental disorders.

8. *Class discussion.* Have students address ethical issues about counseling with children. How would they deal with confidentiality? What do they think a parent should have the right to know? How

would they explain the various aspects of confidentiality to an elementary school child? To an adolescent? How would they deal with the emotional response of a child who had told the counselor about physical or sexual abuse, then discovered that the counselor had to report it, and now a parent is in trouble? How do they feel about the use of aversive conditioning to eliminate self-destructive behaviors (as in autism)? What regulations would they recommend?

9. *Class demonstration.* Have a speaker from a group home for autistic or mentally retarded children come and tell about the home and the procedures they have devised to meet the needs of clients and staff. Even better, arrange for your class to visit a local group home.

10. *Class demonstration.* Show a couple of relevant excerpts from the television series Life Goes On, in which one of the family members has Down syndrome. One effective episode has Corky meet another Down syndrome individual who has not been mainstreamed and taught self-reliance. When this man's mother dies, he must learn to adjust to a group home.

11. *Class activity.* Ask students to visit libraries and bookstores to locate materials that are specifically designed to help children cope with problems, such as Prokop's *Divorce Happens to the Nicest Kids: A Self-Help Book for Kids (3-15) and Adults.* Have students look over some of the books and discuss their usefulness. You might also include books addressed to parents of troubled kids and others that are written for professionals who deal with kids.

12. *Class discussion.* Have students discuss the decision making of parents who choose to institutionalize children with serious defects or keep them at home. You might want to include some book excerpts to add specific situations for them to debate. For example, Fern Kupfer's book *Before and after Zachariah* deals with a family's decision to place a young child in a caring institution.

13. *Class demonstration.* Have a child protective worker or social worker who works with children and adolescents speak to the class on several issues, including mandatory reporting.

14. *Minilecture: The Diagnosis of Autism*

Henry Maudsley suggested that children could exhibit "insanity" back in 1887, and in the early 1900s Emil Kraepelin adopted his term for schizophrenia, "dementia praecox," to childhood and spoke of "dementia praecozissima." Mahler referred to childhood psychosis as "symbiotic psychosis." From these early postulations came the more enduring description of early infantile autism by Leo Kanner in 1943.

Kanner based his description of early infantile autism on his observation of eleven children who seemed to have an inherited inability to relate to other people while relating to some aspects of the nonliving environment. The symptoms he described included (1) insistence on sameness and resistance to change; (2) stereotyped mannerisms; (3) no language or unusual language with such features as echolalia, pronoun reversal, and extreme literalness. Modern descriptions of autism also include these features. Kanner described autism as a disturbance of affective contact, and social deviance remains one of its primary characteristics.

Some of Kanner's ideas about autism, however, have not held up so well. He did not believe, for example, that autism was associated with mental retardation or with other organic conditions. Today researchers find relationships with a variety of medical conditions, including congenital rubella and fragile X syndrome.

Kanner was also mistaken in his belief that autistic children were more likely to come from more educated families and that parental psychopathology was involved. Psychologists have now come to appreciate the contribution of the child to deviant parent-child interaction. It seems likely that deviant patterns in parent-child interaction stem primarily from the disturbance of the autistic child.

Kanner thought that when autism occurred, it was always present from birth, but it is more accurate to say that it is typically apparent in the first year of life, although occasionally, it first appears in the second year.

It is not surprising that Kanner described the syndrome more accurately than he assessed its associated risk factors and causes. This complex task requires the observations of many researchers.

15. *Minilecture: Pica*

Pica is a disorder characterized by the persistent ingestion of nonnutritive substances over a period of at least one month. Children have been known to eat paper, cloth, paint, plaster, insects, metal, needles, gravel, stones, feces, hair, ice, clay, and matches. Some substances have attracted so many children that the ingestion of them has acquired specific names: geophagia (clay, dirt, sand), pagophagia (ice), lithophagia (gravel, stones) coproghagia (feces), amylophagia (starch), and trichophagia (hair).

Possible complications include lead poisoning (from paint and plaster), trichobezoars (hairball tumors) and other intestinal obstructions, intestinal perforation, and toxoplasma (from ingestion of feces and dirt) and other infections, some of which can be fatal. There seems to be a connection between pica in early childhood and bulimia nervosa and adolescence.

Diverse explanations have been offered, including addictions, unmet oral needs, nutritional deficiencies, and cultural factors. Iron, calcium, and zinc deficiencies are associated with pica, but have been cited as both possible causes and possible results. Among cultural factors that have been mentioned are the custom of some southern blacks to feed clay to infants as a pacifier and the belief in some African cultures that well-being is magically promoted by the ingestion of soil.

20

PROBLEMS OF AGING

∎

Topic Overview

This chapter describes the developmental stages of adulthood and the field of geropsychology. It looks at the stress-and-coping model with its approaches of primary appraisal and secondary appraisal and its emotion-focused and problem-focused modes. Mental health concerns of the elderly, including depression, anxiety disorders, and dementia, are discussed with emphasis on Alzheimer's disease. Alcohol-related problems, abuse of prescription drugs, psychotic disorders, and other factors in the mental health of the elderly are considered.

Lecture Overview

I. Early and Middle Adulthood

A. Early adulthood (22 to 40 years) is characterized by high energy, abundance, contradiction, and stress.

B. In middle adulthood (45 to 60 years), when biological functioning is declining, work and family responsibilities may produce stress.

C. Periods of transition
    1. The early adult transition (17 to 22 years), when relationships change, is often marked by confusion and anxiety.

    2. The middle life transition (40 to 45 years), which brings significant life changes, can provoke a "midlife crisis."

II. Later life

    A. Geropsychology
        1. The study of the mental health of elderly people has developed only within the last twenty years.
        2. It investigates the influences of socioeconomic status, ethnicity, and history on the mental health of the aging as well as those of their physical challenges.

    B. Old age
        1. Clinicians consider people between the ages of 65 and 74 to be the young-old.
        2. The old-old are from 75 to 84 years.
        3. The oldest-old are 85 and above.

    C. Life expectancy
        1. Women who reach the age of 65 today can expect to live another 19 years, men another 15 years.
        2. Older men are more than twice as likely as older women to be married.
        3. Two-thirds of older adults live with their families.

    D. Biological vs. functional age
        1. Chronological age is the number of years since birth.
        2. Functional age reflects three interrelated aspects of aging—biological, social, and psychological.
        3. Biological age represents one's present position with respect to one's potential life span.
        4. Social age reflects a person's roles, habits, and behavior in comparison with those of other members of society.
        5. Psychological age represents a person's capacity to adapt behavior to the changing environment.

III. Successful Aging: A Stress-and-Coping Model

    A. Control over risk factors
        1. Older people who avoid smoking and control cholesterol and blood pressure can reduce the risk of heart disease.
        2. Psychological stresses can become opportunities for learning and growth.

B. Evaluation of stressful situations
1. Primary appraisal is a judgment of a situation as irrelevant, positive, or stressful.
2. Stressful situations receive secondary appraisal, or determination of what can be done.
3. Reappraisals are changes in perception of the situation in response to new information.
4. People who adopt problem-focused coping strategies think of several solutions, gather information, and then make a plan of action.
5. Those who adopt problem-focused coping strategies seek emotional support, distance themselves from the problem, avoid thinking about it, of blame themselves.
6. In general, problem-focused strategies are the most effective in coping with loss and other stressors.
7. Another coping strategy is to turn to religion and spirituality.
8. Many problems common to elderly people respond well to cognitive and behavioral therapies, and older people generally accept these therapies well.

IV. Common Clinical Problems in Later Life

A. Incidence
1. Depression is the most common mental health problem of older adults: up to 20 percent fit DSM-IV's criteria for clinical depression, and as many as 30 percent of those with cognitive impairment are also clinically depressed.
2. Depression is better assessed through a structured clinical interview than through a self-report questionnaire.
3. Nevertheless, the Geriatric Depression Scale and the Beck Depression Inventory are commonly used.
4. Dementia has a number of symptoms in common with depression, which may lead to a misdiagnosis.
5. Antidepressant medications can help, but drugs remain in the older person's system longer and can accumulate to toxic levels, and older people find their unpleasant effects difficult to tolerate.
6. Selective serotonin reuptake inhibitors (SSRIs), such as Prozac, produce fewer adverse effects than tricyclics.
7. Elderly persons whose depression is situational respond well to brief psychodynamic therapy.
8. Drugs in combination with cognitive therapy work well for older people with physiologically caused depression.

9. Longer-term cognitive-behavioral therapy is helpful for depressed people who also have a personality disorder.
10. Some depressed older people may benefit from family therapy and group therapy.
11. Very severe depression that has been unresponsive to other treatments may be treated with electroconvulsive therapy (ECT).
12. Suicidal older persons may need inpatient care followed by outpatient counseling.
13. Manic symptoms more commonly appear for the first time in the fifth or sixth decade than was previously thought.
14. Classes have been organized to help elderly people cope with depression and to help caregivers cope with the stresses of long-term care for an elderly family member.

C. Anxiety disorders
1. Generalized anxiety disorder affects 7 percent of elders, agoraphobia from 2 to 5 percent, specific phobias from 1 to 12 percent, panic disorders less than 1 percent, and obsessive compulsive disorders, 1 to 10 percent.
2. Anxiety disorders may be underreported by the elderly.
3. The assessor must determine whether the client's anxiety is appropriate to the circumstances.
4. Antianxiety medications must be used with caution to avoid cognitive impairment, fatigue, and loss of coordination.
5. Anxiety management techniques (AMT), a cognitive-behavioral approach, are effective in developing skills for controlling fear.

D. Dementia
1. Around age 65 the prevalence of dementia is 2 to 4 percent; by 75 it is 10 to 15 percent; for people over 80 it is about 30 percent.
2. Delirium, a clouding of consciousness that causes difficulty in concentrating and focusing attention, can be mistaken for dementia.
3. Both dementia and delirium are common among the elderly, but those with dementia are alert and do not display clouded consciousness.
4. Delirium may be caused by substance intoxication, stress, nutritional imbalance, fever, infection, a neurological disorder, or major surgery.

5. Up to 20 percent of persons with dementia can recover if the cause can be determined.
6. Most dementias are caused by neurological problems that are difficult or impossible to correct.
7. Alzheimer's disease is a gradually progressive degenerative process involving formation of neurofibrillary tangles and senile plaques in the brain.
8. The course of Alzheimer's disease ranges from two to fifteen years.
9. Alzheimer's symptoms progress from mild lapses of memory to inability to perform simple tasks to changes in personality and judgment, disorientation, and agitation.
10. Vascular or multi-infarct dementia, caused by a cerebrovascular accident (stroke), is more common among men than among women.
11. Its symptoms develop abruptly, and not all cognitive functions are affected.
12. Other dementias include Pick's disease, Jakob-Creutzfeldt disease, Huntington's chorea, and Parkinson's disease.
13. The neurotransmitters acetylcholine and L-glutamate are depleted in the brains of Alzheimer's patients.
14. Research evidence indicates a genetic basis for Alzheimer's disease.
15. Other evidence implicating an infectious agent, the presence of heavy metals in the brain, and metabolic problems encourage the view that many agents may work together to cause the structural, biochemical, and behavioral changes of Alzheimer's disease.
16. The first step in treatment is an accurate diagnosis.
17. Behavioral interventions may reduce some symptoms, and support groups address the concerns of caregivers.
18. Of special concern are our ignorance of the influence of ethnicity on the care of people with dementia, abuses in nursing homes, the dearth of appropriate support services, and the cost of long-term care.

E. Substance abuse
1. The prevalence of substance abuse declines after age 60.
2. From 3 to 5 percent of the older population have alcohol-related problems.
3. Early-onset drinkers have had problems for years; late-onset alcohol abusers may not have started the pattern until their 50s and 60s.

4. A major problem is the misuse of prescription drugs, usually unintentional.
5. Among persons who receive prescriptions, the average number of prescriptions is 7.5, but it is 14.2 for those over 60.
6. Physicians should ask older patients directly about their use of alcohol, other substances, and prescription drugs.
7. Elderly alcohol abusers are treated in the same ways as younger adults; group therapy is especially helpful.
8. Active collaboration among physicians, pharmacists, and patients can reduce the misuse of medications.

F. Psychotic disorders
1. Some schizophrenic people show much improvement in later life.
2. New symptoms rarely appear in old age.
3. Most older schizophrenic people need structured care.
4. Delusional disorder is rare among all adults, but increases slightly with age.

V. Other Factors in the Mental Health of the Elderly

A. Ethnicity
1. To be old and a member of a minority group is to be in "double jeopardy."
2. To be old, a member of a minority group, and female is to be in "triple jeopardy."
3. The language barrier and cultural beliefs keep many ethnic elders from seeking mental health services.

B. Long-term care
1. Extended care provided to older adults takes a variety of forms.
2. The quality of care provided by nursing homes varies widely.
3. About 5 percent of the elderly reside in nursing homes.
4. The costs of nursing home care can affect the mental health of older people significantly.

C. Health maintenance
1. Increasing longevity and the rising costs of health care should encourage younger adults to take a wellness or health-promotion approach to aging.
2. Mental health professionals should encourage lifelong participation in prevention programs.

VI. The State of the Field: Problems of Aging

    A. Elderly people have only recently received the attention of clinical researchers.

    B. Some problems common in all age groups—depression, anxiety, alcoholism—may emerge in old age because of the special stresses of later life.

    C. As the number and percentage of elderly people increase, caretaking pressures and awareness of the problems of old age are being felt by younger adults.

LEARNING OBJECTIVES

1. Summarize Levinson's developmental view of adulthood.
2. Define geropsychology.
3. Distinguish among the young-old, the old-old, and the oldest-old.
4. Describe changes in life expectancy during the twentieth century.
5. Distinguish among chronological age, functional age, biological age, social age, and psychological age.
6. Compare and contrast primary appraisal and secondary appraisal, and problem-focused coping and emotion-focused coping.
7. Discuss the incidence of mental health problems among the elderly.
8. Describe and explain depression among the elderly and discuss appropriate treatment.
9. Describe and explain anxiety disorders among the elderly and discuss appropriate treatment.
10. Distinguish between dementia and delirium.
11. Describe and explain Alzheimer's disease and discuss available treatment.
12. Compare and contrast multi-infarct dementia, Pick's disease, Huntington's chorea, and Parkinson's disease.
13. Discuss alcohol-related disorders among the elderly, and compare early-onset drinkers and late-onset drinkers.
14. Discuss psychotic disorders among the elderly.
15. Discuss the possible effects of ethnicity on the mental health of the elderly.
16. Evaluate long-term care for the elderly.
17. Discuss health maintenance issues for the elderly.
18. Summarize the state of the field concerning problems of aging.

INSTRUCTION SUGGESTIONS

1. *Class demonstration.* You can help your students absorb the ideas of Erikson (presented in Chapter 19) and Levinson in regard to development during adulthood by visually charting (on the chalkboard, with a transparency, in a handout) the two theories together so that timing and critical tasks can easily be compared. You can find such a comparison in several developmental books (e.g., D. B. Irwin and J. A. Simons, *Lifespan Developmental Psychology* [1994]). Have students discuss the similarities and differences in these two major theories.

2. *Class discussion.* Describe the empty-nest syndrome of middle age. Discuss how it used to be considered a source of depression and now is associated with an emotional uplift. Have students discuss why attitudes toward the empty-nest syndrome have changed since the 1950s. What does this change indicate about attitudes toward the family? Toward aging? Also, it used to be considered a female phenomenon and now is descriptive of both men and women. Why?

3. *Lecture additions.* Through the DSM-II classification systems, one possible diagnosis was *involutional melancholia*, a type of depression that did not occur until middle age and was seen primarily in women. Various explanations were offered for this overwhelmingly severe depression. Some psychologists and physicians thought it was caused by hormonal changes associated with menopause. If a man did experience involutional melancholia, it appeared later (in his 60s instead of his 50s) and its symptoms were less dramatic because the hormonal changes that come with age were more gradual in men. Other explanations centered on the empty-nest syndrome. Once women lost their roles as mothers, their lives lost meaning, and severe depression resulted. Changes in society and in the field of psychiatry led to the dismissal of involutional melancholia in DSM-III.

4. *Minilectue: Psychological Masquerading*
You have already learned about psychological disorders that masquerade as medical problems—conversion disorders, somatization, somatoform pain, and the like. There are also cases in which organic disorders are misdiagnosed as psychological problems because professionals miss the signs of an organic syndrome. This situation is referred to as psychological masquerading.

Symptoms of depression, agitation, memory impairment, hallucinations, and poor judgment can indeed be indicators of mental disorders, but they may also be indicators of some medical problem. One graduate student had all the symptoms of an anxiety disorder— sleep disorder, change in appetite, sweating, pounding heart, weight loss, and so forth. Her friends thought she had plenty of reasons to be anxious. She was both working on a massive research project and writing a major paper. In addition, she was a foreign student, and her family support system was a couple of thousand miles away. However, a medical doctor was able to pick out a couple of features that did not match a typical anxiety reaction. First, her eyes now seemed to bulge right out of her head, her hair had become thinner and more brittle, and her appetite was huge yet she was losing weight steadily. Finally, instead of the cold sweat typical of anxiety, she broke out in a warm sweat. This student's problem was hyperthyroidism rather than an anxiety disorder.

Another example of psychological masquerading is seen in the story of the composer George Gershwin. At the height of his career, Gershwin began to experience headaches, irritability, memory problems, and many symptoms that are typical responses to stress. His brother and friends thought that Gershwin was overwhelmed by fame, overwork, and efforts to adjust to a new personal relationship. Indeed, they called him a hypochondriac. His symptoms became worse; now they included sensitivity to light, numbness, and unrelenting headaches. Sometimes he fell. An acquaintance who was with him on one of those occasions remarked, "Oh, just let him lie there—he just wants the attention." Finally he was taken seriously and hospitalized. Within a few days he fell into a coma and an operation revealed a malignant brain tumor. He died the next day.

Sometimes drug-induced problems are misdiagnosed as schizophrenia or dementia. A young man was diagnosed as a schizophrenic, but an alert counselor noticed that his hallucinations were mainly visual. Visual hallucinations are more commonly produced by organic disorders; schizophrenic hallucinations are more commonly, though not exclusively, auditory. The counselor asked the man more questions and discovered that chronic abuse of amphetamines had caused the symptoms. A concerned daughter of a woman recovering from health problems in a nursing home found that the aged mother's apparent dementia was really due to the interactions of twenty-eight prescription medications that she was taking. When a professional readjusted her mother's medications, the disorientation, memory impairment, and poor judgment were alleviated.

Obviously, few counselors are expert at diagnosing medical problems. They do need to learn to observe symptoms that make them suspicious of psychological masquerading. They can do some simple neurological assessments and make appropriate referrals when physical problems are a possibility. Many individuals with organic disorders have trouble drawing simple three-dimensional figures, drawing the face of a clock, remembering three simple objects for even five minutes, and doing simple calculations (e.g., what is left when 7 is subtracted from 22? What is one-third of 12?).

5. *Class project.* Have students interview an older person, asking about the person's dreams, life views, fears, biggest accomplishments, worst problems faced, typical coping strategies, and so forth. You might have your students list questions to ask all persons. You might want to arrange permission for students to interview people at a nearby nursing home, a congregate meal site, or a community senior citizens' center. Either have students discuss the interviews or write a report on them.

6. *Lecture additions.* You might mention that many older adults alleviate stress and depression by having contact with pets or children and by doing volunteer work within their community.

7. *Class demonstration.* Bring to class copies of the Geriatric Depression Scale, the Beck Depression Inventory, or Folstein's Mini-Mental State Examination. Share some of the items and discuss why the author has suggested that these measures are appropriate for use with an elderly population.

8. *Class discussion.* Propose that there is a caregiver syndrome that is experienced by middle-aged people who are taking care of both their children and their aging parents. Have the class discuss what the main symptoms of CS would be, and have them develop an appropriate treatment package.

9. *Class discussion.* Discuss the reasons why elderly people receive more medications and ECT than psychotherapy. Can the practice be traced to professional bias? Beliefs of the elderly clients? What is your opinion of appropriate treatments for the aged?

10. *Class discussion.* Have the class discuss whether research on Alzheimer's disease should have higher priority for government funding. How about other diseases common among aged people? Should we put more money into Alzheimer's research or into AIDS research (assuming only one can be increased)?

11. *Lecture additions.* When you discuss Huntington's chorea, you can mention that the folk singer Woody Guthrie died of this disorder. You can also discuss the fact that genetic testing for this disease is available, yet most family members choose not to be tested.

12. *Class discussion.* A case that received wide coverage concerned a doctor who helped a woman with Alzheimer's disease to commit suicide. How do students feel about Alzheimer's patients who kill themselves in the early stages of the disease, before they have lost most of their physical and mental abilities?

13. *Class activity.* Draw a long line on the chalkboard. At the left end write "Conception," and at the other end write "Age at death." Have students copy this line in their notebooks. Tell them to put an X where they currently are on this line. Have them also jot down numbers in answer to the questions "How old do you think you will be when you die?" and "How old would you like to be when you die?" Discuss these answers, perhaps in small groups.

14. *Class demonstration.* Have an administrator of a nursing home speak to your class about the needs of the home's elderly residents. As an alternative, you can visit a nursing home or retirement community.

15. *Class discussion.* Have students discuss what it means to be an "adult child" vs. an "adult orphan."

21

LAW, SOCIETY, AND THE MENTAL HEALTH PROFESSION

■

TOPIC OVERVIEW

This chapter describes clinical influences on the criminal justice system, including the concepts of insanity and incompetence to stand trail, and legal influences on the mental health system, including civil commitment and protection of patients' rights. Other clinical-legal interactions discussed include malpractice suits, jury selection, and the scope of clinical practice. Ethical issues in the mental health field are examined, as well as its business and economic aspects. Finally, the chapter discusses psychology as a profession.

LECTURE OVERVIEW

I. Clinical Influences on the Criminal Justice System

   A. Assumptions of the courts
      1. Courts mete out punishments they consider appropriate on the assumption that individuals are responsible for their crimes.
      2. They assume also that accused persons are capable of defending themselves.

   B. Criminal commitment and insanity during commission of a crime
      1. When a defendant pleads not guilty by reason of insanity, some states require the prosecution to prove that the defendant was sane beyond a reasonable doubt, but most states now place the burden of proof on the defendant.
      2. Insanity is a legal concept, not a scientific one.

3. The M'Naghten rule, established in 1843, provided that persons who claim to have been insane when they committed a crime must prove that they did not know what they were doing, or if they did know it, that they did not know it was wrong.

4. The irresistible impulse test, first applied in 1834, emphasized inability to control one's actions, as when one commits a crime in a "fit of passion."

5. The Durham test, based on a 1954 Supreme Court decision, stated that individuals were not criminally responsible if the "unlawful act was the product of mental disease or mental defect."

6. The Durham test's criteria which could have encompassed alcoholism, drug dependence, and psychophysiological disorders, force courts to rely on the often contradictory interpretations of clinicians.

7. In 1955 the American Law Institute formulated a penal code that combined elements of all three tests.

8. The Insanity Defense Reform Act of 1984, which essentially returned to the M'Naghten standard, now applies to cases tried in the federal courts and about half of the state courts.

9. Idaho, Montana, and Utah recognize no insanity plea.

10. About two-thirds of defendants acquitted by reason of insanity qualify for a diagnosis of schizophrenia.

11. The law's assumptions seem to be incompatible with theories of human behavior.

12. Expert witnesses called to testify for the prosecution and for the defense do not agree on their diagnostic assessments.

13. The most widespread criticism of the insanity defense is that it systematically allows dangerous criminals to escape punishment.

14. Less than 1 percent of defendants plea insanity.

15. In Foucha v. Louisiana (1992) the Supreme Court ruled that the only basis for determining the release of persons found to be insane is whether or not they are still insane; they cannot be held simply because they are dangerous.

16. Some states now permit a verdict of "guilty but mentally ill," which assigns moral blame to the defendant.

17. The option of a verdict of "guilty with diminished capacity" permits jurors to find a defendant guilty of a lessor crime than the one charged.

18. Some states categorize persons repeatedly found guilty of sex crimes as "mentally disordered sex offenders."

C. Criminal commitment and incompetence to stand trial
1. Competence provisions ensure that defendants understand the charges and proceedings they are facing and are able to consult with counsel in preparing and conducting an adequate defense.
2. The Supreme Court specified the minimum standard of competence in Dusky v. United States (1960).
3. A defendant who is held to be mentally incompetent to stand trial is sent to a mental health facility until he or she is found to be competent.
4. In Jackson v. Indiana (1972) the Supreme Court ruled that after a reasonable time a criminally committed person must be either found competent and tried, set free, or committed to a mental health facility under civil procedures.

II. Legal Influences on the Mental Health System

A. Civil commitment
1. People can be forced to undergo mental health treatment if they are considered to be in need of treatment and dangerous to themselves or others.
2. Under the principle of *parens partriae* the state can make decisions to promote the individual's best interests.
3. The state's police power enables it to protect society from the harm that might be done by a violent person.
4. Parham v. J. R. (1979) established that a due process hearing is not required for commitment of a minor, only a demonstration that a mental health professional considers such commitment warranted.
5. In Addington v. Texas (1979) the Supreme Court established "clear and convincing evidence" of mental illness is not required for commitment of a minor, only a demonstration as the minimum standard of proof necessary for commitment.
6. In emergencies most states permit immediate commitment of persons who are suicidal, violent, or in need of round-the-clock supervision upon presentation of two-physician certificates (2 PCs), by which two physicians attest that the persons are dangerous to themselves or others.
7. About 90 percent of people with mental disorders are not violent or dangerous.
8. Studies have found a moderate relationship between severe mental disorders and violent behavior (e.g., 15 percent of hospitalized patients have assaulted another person prior to admission; 25 percent assault someone during hospitalization).

9. Professionals are not good at predicting violence, even violence against themselves; typically they overestimate the likelihood of violent behavior.
10. Research is needed on prediction of imminent violence.
11. Critics charge that since predictions of dangerousness are often wrong, they should not be used to deprive anyone of liberty.
12. Critics also argue that the legal definitions of mental illness and dangerousness are so vague that they can be applied to anyone.
13. Thomas Szasz and others have denied the therapeutic value of involuntary commitment.
14. Some researchers argue that commitment decisions should be based on risk assessment rather than on judgments of dangerousness.
15. The Supreme Court's ruling in Robinson v. California (1962) encouraged involuntary commitment to a mental health facility instead of imprisonment for individuals whose unacceptable behavior seemed to be caused by psychological dysfunctioning.
16. In the late 1960s and 1970s the states narrowed the standards for commitment and the courts expanded patients' rights.
17. Commitment standards now tend to require a demonstration of imminent dangerousness.

B. Protecting patients' rights
1. In 1972 a federal court ruled in Wyatt v. Stickney that the states must provide adequate treatment to persons committed involuntarily.
2. In 1975 the Supreme Court's ruling in O'Connor v. Donaldson required periodic reviews of patients' cases and ruled that a nondangerous patient who was capable of surviving safely in freedom alone or with the help of willing and responsible others cannot constitutionally be confined.
3. Youngberg v. Romeo (1982) provided support for the right to treatment while cautioning courts against becoming too involved in the exact methods of treatment.
4. In 1986 Congress passed the Protection and Advocacy for Mentally Ill Individuals Act, establishing protection and advocacy systems and authorizing advocates to investigate and legally pursue cases of abuse and neglect.
5. Many advocates are suing federal and state agencies for failure to provide adequate community services, thus forcing many mentally ill homeless persons into the criminal justice system.
6. The courts have established patients' right to refuse treatment, but most rulings have dealt with biological treatments.

7. The states vary in the degree to which they allow patients to refuse ECT.
8. Some states grant patients the right to refuse psychotropic medications, but their refusal may be overridden after a review process in which the patient is supported by an advocate.
9. A district court ruled in Sounder v. Brennan (1973) that patients who work in mental institutions must receive payment; in 1976 the Supreme Court ruled that this right applied to private mental institutions but not to state hospitals.
10. Court decisions in the 1970s established the right of deinstitutionalized patients to aftercare and an appropriate community residence.
11. In Dixon v. Weinberger (1975) a district court ruled that persons whose mental dysfunctions are not so severe that they must be confined in a mental institution have a right to treatment in less restrictive facilities.
12. Rights and needs can at times be contradictory, as when a patient refuses medication that could eliminate paranoid delusions or when the right of patients to a minimum wage disrupts an effective token economy program.
13. Physicians' failure to monitor themselves and their inability to predict outcomes make statutory regulations appropriate.

III. Other Clinical-Legal Interactions

A. Malpractice suits
   1. The number of lawsuits against therapists has risen sharply in recent years.
   2. About 16 percent have been sued for malpractice on charges stemming from such events as attempted suicide, sexual activity with the patient, negligent drug therapy, improper termination of treatment, and wrongful commitment.
   3. Malpractice suits have significant effects on clinical decisions and practice.

B. Jury selection
   1. Clinical "jury specialists" advise lawyers on which prospective jurors are likely to favor their side and which procedures and strategies to use.
   2. The validity of such advice has not been established, but lawyers think it is useful.

C. The scope of clinical practice
1. The legislative and judicial systems have given more authority to psychologists and blurred the line that once separated psychiatry from psychology.
2. In 1989 Congress permitted psychologists to receive payment from Medicare.
3. Several states permit psychologists to admit patients to hospitals.
4. The authorization of psychologists to prescribe drugs is being explored by the Army in a program called Cutting Edge.
5. The lobbying efforts of psychologists to increase their power and of psychiatrists to curb it demonstrate the intertwining of the mental health system with other social institutions.

IV. Self-Regulation: Ethics and the Mental Health Field

A. Obstacles to good practice
1. Patients' rights and proper care raise complex questions that have no clear or simple answers.
2. Many psychologists do not grasp the ramifications of their actions and lack the power to alter the system in which they work.
3. Some clinicians are self-serving and even immoral.

B. Regulatory efforts
1. Clinicians establish ethical guidelines and constantly revise them.
2. Many laws and court rulings merely give these guidelines the force of law.

C. The Ethical code of the American Psychological Association
1. Psychologists are urged to guard against "factors that might lead to misuse of their influence."
2. They are permitted to offer advice in self-help books, television and radio programs, and other media provided their advice is based on "appropriate psychological literature and practices."
3. They may not plagiarize the work of others or publish fabricated data or falsified results.
4. They "must acknowledge their limitations with regard to patients who differ from them in gender, ethnicity, disability, language, socioeconomic status, and sexual orientation."

5. Those who evaluate defendants "and testify in legal cases must base their assessments on sufficient information and substantiate their findings appropriately."

D. Sexual misconduct in therapy
   1. Psychologists are prohibited from engaging in sexual intimacies with a client for at least two years after the end of treatment (and even then only in "the most unusual circumstances"), and may not accept as clients those with whom they have previously been sexually intimate.
   2. The number of clients who have told state licensing boards of sexual misconduct by their therapists or sued their therapists for such misconduct has increased.
   3. A 1977 study found that 12.1 percent of male and 2.6 percent of female psychologists admitted to having sexual contact with patients; a 1987 study found 3.6 and 0.5 percent, respectively; a 1989 study found 0.9 and 0.2 percent, respectively.
   4. This decline may be due either to growing recognition of the inappropriateness of such behavior or to fear of legal consequences.
   5. 72 percent of therapists surveyed reported engaging in a sexual fantasy about a client, though most claimed that they had done so rarely.
   6. About 90 percent reported having been sexually attracted to a client; 63 percent felt guilty, anxious, or concerned about the attraction.

E. Confidentiality
   1. Confidentiality is one of the most important features of therapy, but it may be breached in some circumstances.
   2. Therapists in training need to discuss cases with a supervisor.
   3. A therapist may breach confidentiality to initiate procedures to commit an outpatient who is clearly dangerous.
   4. A California court ruled in Tarasoff v. Regents of the University of California (1974) that "the protective privilege ends where the public peril begins": a person whom a therapist's client has threatened to harm must be warned.
   5. The APA enjoins therapists to reveal confidential information when necessary "to protect the patient or client or others from harm."
   6. A California court ruled in Thompson v. County of Alameda (1987) that the duty to warn applies only when the intended victim is readily identifiable.

7. A California court also ruled that therapists are obligated to protect persons in close proximity to a client's intended victim (Hedlund v. Collson).
8. The California courts have also held that the duty to warn does not apply when a client intends violence to property rather than to a person.
9. Many states have followed California's lead and adopted a "Duty to Protect Bill" to clarify the standards for confidentiality.

V. Mental Health, Business, and Economics

  A. Business and mental health
    1. Psychological disorders are among the top ten work-related diseases and injuries.
    2. The number of stress-related worker's compensation claims has risen about 700 percent in the past decade.
    3. Employee assistance programs help employees in psychological trouble.
    4. The costs of providing insurance benefits for treatment of health problems and substance abuse grew from an average of $163 per employee in 1987 to $306 in 1991.
    5. Businesses organize stress-reduction and problem-solving seminars run by mental health professionals for executives as well as lower-level employees.

  B. Economic and mental health
    1. Governments' desire to reduce expenses has been a major factor in deinstitutionalization programs.
    2. Funding for mental health services has risen only modestly while the number of people seeking therapy has increased greatly.
    3. Only 56 percent of all mental health services are now government-supported.
    4. To reduce expenditures for insurance, many firms permit insurance companies to determine which therapists an employee may consult, how much they will pay for a session, and how many sessions they will pay for.
    5. Most such firms have a peer review system in which a panel of clinicians paid by the insurance company reviews a therapist's report of a client's treatment (thereby learning intimate details of the client's life) and may recommend termination of treatment.

VI. The Person Within the Profession

A. The actions of clinicians are closely tied to their personal needs and goals.

B. Their preferences influence their responses to clients' concern, their theoretical orientations, the clients with whom they choose to work, and their attitudes toward professional standards.

C. 71 percent of psychotherapists have been in therapy themselves and many were brought up in dysfunctional families.

D. All therapists have felt like impostors at least occasionally (18 percent frequently.)

VII. The State of the Field: Law, Society, and the Mental Health Profession

A. Clinical researchers and professionals no longer work in relative isolation.

B. Clinicians' activities are linked to the legislative, judicial, and economic systems.

C. The clinical field has achieved a remarkable level of acceptance in our society.

D. Its acceptance gives it influence over other institutions, which prompts other institutions to want to monitor and restrict its activities.

E. The field has acquired an impressive body of knowledge in the past several decades.

F. Nevertheless, what mental health professionals do not know and cannot do outweighs what they do know and can do.

LEARNING OBJECTIVES

1. Compare and contrast the M'Naghten test, the irresistible impulse test, and the Durham test.

2. Discuss the 1955 American Law Institute's formulation of a widely accepted legal test of insanity and how the verdict led to the Insanity Defense Reform Act of 1984.
3. Evaluate the insanity defense and summarize recent trends.
4. Discuss the ruling in Foucha v. Louisiana and the options of verdicts of "guilty but mentally ill" and "guilty with diminished capacity."
5. Describe and evaluate sex offender statutes.
6. Explain incompetence to stand trial and the importance of the Supreme Court's rulings in Dusky v. United States and Jackson v. Indiana.
7. Describe current civil commitment procedures, the reasons for them, and the protections afforded persons civilly committed.
8. Discuss the criticisms of civil commitment.
9. Summarize the court cases that have served to protect patients' rights.
10. Discuss the Protection and Advocacy for Mentally Ill Individuals Act of 1986.
11. Compare and contrast patients' right to receive treatment and their right to refuse treatment.
12. Discuss the effects of malpractice suits on clinical practice.
13. Explain what a jury specialist does.
14. Discuss the blurring of the fields of psychiatry and psychology.
15. Discuss the implications of the Army's Cutting Edge program.
16. List and explain the main features of the APA code of ethics.
17. Discuss ethical issues in regard to the sexual conduct of therapists.
18. Discuss the importance of confidentiality and the situations in which it must be breached.
19. Discuss how businesses have addressed employees' mental health needs.
20. Describe and evaluate the funding of mental health treatment by the federal and state governments and by insurance companies.
21. Discuss the influence of mental health professionals' personal needs and goals on their professional practice.
22. Summarize the state of the field with respect to the law and society.

INSTRUCTION SUGGESTIONS

1. *Class Activity.* Develop some scenarios of court cases in which mental disorders play a role. You can create your own scenarios or, over time, develop synopses of real cases. Have small groups wrestle with the issue of whether juries should take information about the defendant's mental state into account in their deliberations and how they think it should affect the verdict. You might see if there is a consensus across groups, the kinds of cases in which an insanity plea is successful (e.g.,

Lorena Bobbitt), and so forth. A few possibilities: a man who sexually abuses a childlike subpersonality of a person who he knows has a dissociative identity disorder; a veteran of the Gulf War who commits an assault on a hot day at the beach and attributes his actions to PTSD; a serial murderer who dismembers his victims and cannibalizes them; a kidnap victim who is confined and subjected to brainwashing techniques for fifty days, then willingly joins her captors in committing a crime; a battered spouse who finally kills the batterer and claims she feared for her life; and a teenager who attributes his crime to the mental disorder of cocaine abuse and requests treatment instead of detention.

2. *Class discussion.* Have your students generate a list of criteria that might be used to determine if a person is mentally competent; then turn the task around and have them generate a list of criteria that could be used to determine that a person is mentally competent. Which condition is more difficult to establish?

3. *Class discussion.* Have your students discuss the advantages and disadvantages of each of the three rules that have governed a finding of not guilty by reason of insanity. Which of the three is best? What features would they use to develop the best model of all?

4. *Class discussion.* Have the class debate the advisability of verdicts of "guilty but mentally ill" or "guilty with diminished responsibility" for persons accused of drug crimes (possession, intent to sell, public intoxication). How would such a verdict affect the defendants' sentences?

5. *Class discussion.* Generate a list of characteristics that might indicate incompetence to stand trial. How does this list compare with a list of characteristics that might indicate insanity? What are the circumstances under which a person should be committed?

6. *Class demonstration.* Have a legal or mental health professional who has been involved in civil commitments address your class. In addition to the actual procedures and examples of circumstances in which commitment is appropriate, ask the speaker to explain how he or she deals with the emotional aspects of making involuntary commitments.

7. *Class discussion.* Addington v. Texas (1979) established minimum standards of proof necessary for commitment. What are your students' ideas about what constitutes "clear and convincing" proof?

8. *Lecture additions.* In 1991 both the National Alliance for the Mentally Ill and the American Psychological Association stated that many mentally ill patients are being held indefinitely in jails rather than being committed to mental health facilities. In some cases, mentally ill individuals have been "lost" in the correctional system for months without a hearing, trial, or treatment.

9. *Lecture additions.* When you lecture about the current grounds for involuntary commitment, you might wish to discuss abuses before modern standards were established in the 1950s, for example, some parents committed their pregnant teenage daughters to mental hospitals because "our daughter is a good girl so she must be mentally ill to have gotten herself pregnant." The infants were adopted out of the hospital, and professionals neglected to release the young women for several years.

10. *Lecture additions.* When mental health advocates have questioned the high doses of medicines being given to some patients, some psychiatrists have simply switched to stronger medications, so that the dose appeared to be reduced when in fact it is not.

11. *Class demonstration.* Read a variety of examples from the APA Ethics Casebook and have the class speculate on the rulings in these cases.

12. *Class discussion.* What consequences should there be for therapists who seduce their clients? Should they lose their licenses? Should they be prosecuted for sexual abuse or rape? When would it be acceptable for a therapist to develop a relationship with a former client?

13. *Class demonstration.* Have a counselor in an employee assistance program address the class on the problems counselors encounter and the ways they deal with them.

Especially for New Teachers

The following suggestions may be useful to you as you develop, organize, and teach your abnormal psychology course.

1. Before you do anything else, think about your personal teaching philosophy and views on psychology. How much of yourself do you wish to incorporate into the structure of the course? How are you going to translate your own values and goals into teaching, grading, and interacting with students? Are there beliefs that you want to emphasize and others that you want to minimize?

2. Prepare your course well in advance of the starting date if at all possible. Two of the things to get done early are (1) ordering desirable media and (2) constructing a course syllabus.

3. Students like to be provided with copies of the syllabus on the first day of class. It is wise to run off several extra copies so that you can provide students with a second copy if they lose the original, have copies for students who enter your class late, and have an extra copy for an interested colleague.

4. Make your syllabus as detailed and as informative as possible. A syllabus is like a road map of the course—if you tell students where you are headed and the landmarks along the way, they are much more likely to reach the final destination with you. Things that you might include in the course syllabus: textbook assignments (including dates), test dates and the chapters the tests will cover (if you cannot be sure of the exact date of a test, remember that it is better to give a test later than the scheduled date than earlier), procedures for make-up tests and the consequences of missing project-due dates, written assignments (what they are, how to do them, when they are due, how much they count toward the final grade), the grading scale, course objectives, class attendance policy, possibilities for extra credit, a statement about plagiarism (define it) and other forms of cheating, office hours, test forms (multiple choice, essay). Read over your first draft as though you were a student and make any adjustments necessary to make your syllabus complete and its tone appropriate.

5. Decide whether you want to lecture during each class period or introduce discussions, exercises, media, and other special activities in addition to your lectures. If you want to have guest speakers, arrange for them well in advance.

6. What test format do you wish to use? Decide on the basis of goals (e.g., essay questions require more thought processing; multiple-choice and true-false questions can allow more immediate feedback and test a wider range of information) and practicalities (e.g., multiple-choice questions can be scored quickly even when classes are large).

7. Do you wish to try anything different with your testing and evaluation? You might try letting students have copies of an entire test bank (without answers); they learn a lot by trying to figure out the answers to the entire pool of items. Or with classes of thirty, you might grade students' multiple-choice tests as they finish, and then allow them to review their errors so that they can be better prepared for a retake exam or a comprehensive final exam.

8. Decide whether you want to inform students about what is likely to be on a test. You may wish to say nothing so that students must either learn everything or figure out on their own what you are likely to emphasize. Or you may tell them that specific material will definitely be on the test, so that they are certain to know something you consider very important, and that another matter will definitely not need to be memorized, so that studying does not become a massive rote-learning experience. You may give a general guideline, such as "Material covered in the textbook and in class will be most heavily tested, but you are responsible for other material in the book and in your lecture notes."

9. Are you going to rely on assignments in addition to tests to determine grades? You might wish to adopt the philosophy that all college courses should incorporate some writing. Or perhaps you believe it is important for students to receive practice in presenting material orally. Spend some time thinking about what kinds of projects this course lends itself to easily, what students learn from various kinds of projects, and what you are interested in kinds of projects, and what you are interested in evaluating. You can use fictional and nonfictional stories about people with mental disorders; you can assign self-help books and more scholarly books for students to critique; you can assign journals, term papers, oral presentations, and so forth.

10. Will you have all students do the same type of project, or will you give them options? How will you make the options equal (a book critique is not a term paper)? Will all students do the same number of projects (e.g., I have at times adopted the policy of requiring satisfactory completion of one project for a C, two for a B, and three for an A)? Students will ask if they can do another project for extra credit, so have your answer ready.

11. What is your make-up test policy? Remember that commuter campuses and schools that attract large numbers of nontraditional students who have jobs and family responsibilities mean a large number of valid excuses. Can you develop a policy that is fair to students and to yourself? My own favorite policy is to use the final exam period for make-ups of multiple-choice tests; students are given a chance to make up missed (or poorly done) tests, but those who have skipped the most tests end up punishing themselves with a "comprehensive final exam," whereas those who have been prepared throughout the semester are finished with the course right before the final exam period. (Before you take this approach, make certain it is consistent with administrative policy. Some colleges mandate a final exam.)

12. What are you going to do the first day of class? Consider using this time to go through the entire syllabus, explaining the "map of the course" and giving sound study tips (many college students have never been formally instructed in studying techniques). Or you might plan a dramatic, attention-grabbing introduction to the course material.

13. If you are new to the campus, check out its resources for counseling so you can make proper and appropriate referrals if students become distressed by such topics as incest, suicide, and substance abuse.

14. Also check out the campus library and see what materials (books, journals, magazines, tapes) are available for student use. Ask the librarian how you can most appropriately use the library's services. Ask about the policies for interlibrary loans and for reserving materials. Find out if you can influence future book purchases by the library and build the collection of materials appropriate for your course(s).

15. Decide on your office policy (coordinating it with any school or department policy). Will you be available only during certain hours, or can students drop by whenever you are in your office?

16. Above all, remember that you are teaching a course to which everybody can relate. Everyone has experienced depression, anxiety, and anger. Many students have dealt or are dealing with such issues as incest, suicide, and substance abuse. Your course has the potential to have a large influence in your students' lives. Some students may learn things that will help them resolve an existing problem or give them the courage to get needed treatment. Some may discover a new concern and seek a direction in which to turn. Others will gain in understanding of the problems of family members or friends. Still others will be moved toward a career in psychology or another helping profession. Enjoy your course, but remember to take it as seriously as some of your students will take it. Be challenged by the responsibility.

Book Resources for Instructors

General Reading Resources

Adams, B. N., & Klein, D. M. (Series Eds.). *Perspectives on Marriage and the Family.* New York: Guilford. Relevant topics include social stress, family development, and domestic violence.

Annual Review of Psychology. Palo Alto: Annual Reviews. Excellent current material in many areas of psychology.

Bellack, A. S., & Hersen, M. (Series Eds.). *Applied Clinical Psychology.* New York: Plenum. A source of material on treatment topics.

Blane, H. T., & Kosten, T. R. (Series Eds.). *The Guilford Substance Abuse Series.* New York: Guilford. Volumes deal with psychological theories of drinking and alcoholism, alcohol problems in women, children of alcoholics, and cocaine.

Chilman, C. S., Nunnally, E. W., & Cox, F. M. (Series Eds.). *Families in Trouble Series.* Newbury Parks, CA: Sage. Volumes cover chronic illness and disability, variant family forms, and troubled relationships.

Costa, P. T., Jr., Whitfield, J., & Stewart, D. (Eds.) (1989) *Alzheimer's disease: Abstractions of the psychological and behavioral literature.* Washington, D.C.: American Psychological Association. Contains abstracts from about 1300 journals.

Franks, V. (Series Ed.). *Springer Series: Focus on Women.* New York: Springer. A 12-volume series of major psychological and social issues on women's status and problems.

G. Stanley Hall Lecture Series. Washington, D.C.: American Psychological Association. Lectures presented at the APA convention, published annually. Several applicable topics.

Green, R. (Series Ed.). *Perspectives in sexuality: Behavior, research, and therapy.* New York: Plenum. A source of material on sexual disorders.

Jones, J. L., Kerby, J., & Landy, C. P. (Eds.) (1989). AIDS: *Abstracts of the psychological and behavioral literature, 1983-1989.* 2nd ed. Washington, D.C.: American Psychological Association. Over 650 abstracts of journal articles and 150 listings of books and chapters.

Kastenbaum, R. (Series Ed.). *Springer Series: Death and Suicide.* New York: Springer. Several volumes on death issues; those on suicide and grief are especially applicable to this course.

Kazdin, A. E. (Series Ed.). *Development Clinical Psychology and Psychiatry Series.* Newbury Parks, CA: Sage. Topics include adolescent delinquency, chronic childhood illness, attempted suicide among youth, infant psychiatry, and child abuse.

Master Lectures. Washington, D.C.: American Psychological Association. Includes volumes on psychology and health, clinical neuropsychology, and brain function.

Solnit, A. J. (Series Ed.). *The Psychoanalytic Study of the Child.* New Haven: Yale University Press. Over 40 volumes on a wide range of psychoanalytic topics.

Sonkin, D. J. (Series Ed.). *Springer Series: Focus on Men.* New York: Springer. A five-volume series of research and theoretical perspectives on topics of significance to men.

Weiner, I. B. (Series Ed.). *Wiley Series on Personality Processes.* New York: Wiley. Includes many volumes that are relevant to this course, such as those on heroin addiction, agoraphobia, hyperactivity, loneliness, depressive disorders, and acquaintance rape.

TEACHING MATERIALS AND TEACHING SKILLS

Benjamin, L. T., Jr. Daniel, R. S. & Brewer, C. L. (1985) *Handbook for teaching introductory psychology.* Hillsdale, NJ: Lawrence Erlbaum. Selections from the first ten years of *Teaching Psychology*, including several on abnormal psychology topics.

Benjamin, L. T., Jr. & Lowman, K. D. (Eds.) (1988). *Activities handbook for the teaching of psychology, vol. 1.* Washington, D.C.: American Psychology Association. Describes 44 classroom activities, demonstrations, and experiments, including some for abnormal psychology.

Bradley-Johnson, S., & Lesiak, J. L. (1989). *Problems in written expression: Assessment and remediation.* New York: Guilford. Sets forth the elements essential for effective written communication and explains how to evaluate and improve writing skills.

Bronstein, P., & Uina, K. (1988). *Teaching a psychology of people: Resources for gender and sociocultural awareness.* Washington, D.C.: American Psychological Association. Stresses awareness of minority and cultural issues and a variety of viewpoints.

Golub, S., & Freedman, R. J. (Eds.) (1987). *Psychology of women: Resources for a core curriculum.* New York: Garland. Provides discussion topics and demonstration projects that can help abnormal psychology instructors "mainstream" women's issues into their courses. Also a good source for film and book resources.

Makosky, V. P., Whitemore, L. G., & Rogers, A. M. (Eds.) (1987). *Activities handbook for the teaching of psychology, vol. 2.* Washington, D.C.: American Psychological Association. Describes about 90 activities.

McKeachie, W. J. (1990). *Teaching tips.* Lexington, MA: D. C. Heath, A good guide for the beginning teacher.

Network: The newsletter for psychology teachers at two-year colleges. Washington, D.C.: American Psychological Association. Includes resource ideas, teaching strategies, and film reviews.

Shapiro, E. S. (1989). *Academic skills problems: Direct assessment and intervention.* New York: Guilford. Detailed instructions for evaluating and improving academic skills.

Teaching of psychology. Washington, D.C.: American Psychological Association. A quarterly journal directed toward the improvement of teaching of psychology courses. Includes course descriptions, film and book reviews, demonstrations, and useful articles.

Young, R. E. (Editor-in-chief). *New directions for teaching and learning.* San Francisco: Jossey-Bass. Published quarterly for more than a decade, these volumes provide ideas and techniques for improving college teaching. Recent volumes have examined ways to develop critical thinking and problem-solving abilities, to improve teaching style, to teach large classes well, and to teach writing in all disciplines.

REFERENCES ON SPECIFIC TOPICS

Allison, J. A., & Wrightsman, L. S. (1993). *Rape: The misunderstood crime.* Newbury Park, CA: Sage. Provides up-to-date material on this violent crime.

Avis, H. (1992). *Drugs and life.* 2nd ed. Dubuque, IA: Wm. C. Brown. A source of current information on substance use and abuse.

Bagley, C., & King, K. (1989). *Child sexual abuse: The search for healing.* New York: Routledge. An overview of etiology, treatment, and prevention.

Barbach, L. (1993). *The pause: Positive approaches to menopause.* New York: Dutton. Examines the symptoms of menopause and ways to deal with them. Also discusses ways to prevent heart disease and osteoporosis.

Bass, E., & Davis, L. (1992). *The courage to heal: A guide for women survivors of child sexual abuse.* Red. ed. New York: HarperPerennial. In addition to providing information about sexual abuse, this volume presents the experiences of many adult victims of child sexual abuse.

Bass, E., & Thornton, L. (Eds.) (1988). *I never told anyone: A collection of writings by survivors of child sexual abuse.* New York: Harper & Row. A collection of poetry and recollections by survivors; many excerpts can usefully be incorporated in lectures.

Baumeister, R. F. (1991). *Escaping the self: Alcoholism, spirituality, masochism, and other flights from the burden of selfhood.* New York: Basic Books. Examines problems created by societies that overemphasize the self, and the means people burdened by the self use to escape (e.g., alcoholism and masochism).

Bemporad, J. R., & Herzog, D. B. (1989). *Psychoanalysis and eating disorders.* New York: Guilford. Examines Freud's early views on anorexia and then reinterprets this teaching in the light of new developments in psychoanalysis.

Berglas, S. (1986). *The success syndrome.* New York: Plenum. Examines how some successful people sabotage their own careers and lives.

Berglas, S., & Baumeister, R. F. (1993). *Your own worst enemy.* New York: Basic Books. Explores a wide range of self-defeating behaviors with examples that can be used in class.

Berry, G. L., & Asamen, J. K. (1993). *Children and television.* Newbury Park, CA: Sage. A good source of up-to-date material on the effects of television.

Blazer, D. (1990). *Emotional problems in later life: Intervention strategies for professional caregivers.* New York: Springer. Topics include memory loss, depression, suspiciousness and agitation, anxiety, hypochondriasis, sleeping problems, substance abuse, emotional problems associated with physical illness, bereavement, and family members of the elderly.

Bohmer, C., & Parrot, A. (1993). *Sexual assault on campus.* New York: Lexington. A source for an important lecture topic.

Bradburn, N. M., & Sudman, S. (1988). *Polls and surveys: Understanding what they tell us.* Contains material to help students understand popular polls, such as Gallup, Harris, and television election-night polls.

Braun, B. G. (1988). *The treatment of multiple personality disorder.* Washington, D.C.: American Psychiatric Press. Students will appreciate added lecture material on this intriguing disorder.

Bruch, H. (1989). *Conversations with anorexics.* New York: Basic Books. Provides material to adapt for your lectures.

Burns, D. (1980). *Feeling good.* New York: Avon. Traces the development of cognitive therapy and its approach to depression; presents the key elements of this therapy as it is applied to depression.

Calam, R. M., & Franchi, C. (1987). *Child abuse and its consequences: Observational approaches.* New York: Cambridge University Press. Examines long-term psychological effects of child abuse.

Campbell, A (1993). *Men, women, and aggression.* New York: Basic Books. Examines aspects of culture that affect gender's influence on aggression and violence in intimate situations, in gangs, and in fighting.

Colgrove, M., Bloomfield, H., & McWilliams, P. (1991). *How to survive the loss of a love.* Los Angeles: Prelude. A good book to recommend to students experiencing grief; excerpts make good additions to lecture material.

Crewdson, J. (1989). *By silence betrayed: Sexual abuse of children in America.* New York: Harper & Row. One of many topics discussed is whether pedophiles can be treated successfully.

Cromwell, R. L., & Snyder, C. R. (1993). *Schizophrenia.* New York: Oxford University Press. Provides a wide range of information useful in lectures on schizophrenia.

Curran, D. K. (1987). *Adolescent suicidal behavior.* New York: Hemisphere. Provides information on many aspects of adolescent suicidal behavior.

Curtiss, S. (1977). *Genie: A psycholinguistic study of a modern-day "wild child."* New York: Academic Press. A case study of a severely neglected child who grew up without being taught language.

David, H. P., Dytrych, Z., Matejcek, Z., & Schuller, V. (Eds.) (1988). *Born unwanted: Developmental effects of denied abortion.* New York: Springer. Examines the long-term adverse effects of being born to a mother who would have aborted the child if she could. Based on data from studies in Prague and some Scandinavian societies. Material from this book can spark a lively class discussion.

Davis, L. (1990). *The courage to heal workbook: For women and men survivors of child sexual abuse.* Useful to show in class because some students may want to buy it for personal healing.

Derogatis, L. R., & Wise, T. N. (1989). *Anxiety and depressive disorders in the medical patient.* Washington, D.C.: American Psychiatric Press. Basic and sound information about both anxiety and depressive disorders.

Diamant, L. (Ed.) (1987). *Male and female homosexuality: Psychological perspectives.* New York: Hemisphere. Includes historical approaches, ego-dystonic homosexuality, a theory of normal homosexuality, and a humanistic perspective.

Diamond, M. (1988). *Enriching heredity: The impact of the environment on the anatomy of the brain.* New York: Free Press. Covers three decades of research that provides evidence that at any stage of life an enriched environment can increase brain size. Useful in building lecture material on the biological aspects of mental disorders.

Doctor, R. F. (1988). *Transvestites and transsexuals: Toward a theory of cross-gender behavior.* New York: Plenum. Provides much material for a lecture on sexual disorders, from fetishism through primary transsexualism.

Emery, G. (1988). *Getting un-depressed.* New York: Touchstone. A cognitive approach to women's depression.

Feierman, J. R. (1990). *Pedophilia: Biosocial dimensions.* New York: Springer-Verlag. Important information on a topic of growing importance.

Figley, C. R. (1989). *Helping traumatized families.* San Francisco: Jossey-Bass. A comprehensive approach to assessing and treating families under stress as a result of criminal assaults, natural disorders, and terminal illness.

Fingarette, H. (1988). *Heavy drinking: The myth of alcoholism as a disease.* Berkeley: University of California Press. A controversial book that suggests an alternative to the approach of Alcoholics Anonymous.

Fossum, M. A., & Mason, M. J. (1989). *Facing shame: Families in recovery.* New York: Norton. Suggests that alcohol abuse, eating disorders, and child abuse may be related to an underlying process of shame.

Friedman, R. C. (1988). *Male homosexuality: A contemporary psychoanalytic perspective.* New Haven: Yale University Press. Attempts to integrate sexual orientation with psychoanalytic theory; explores the role of erotic fantasy in childhood, unconscious homosexuality, and bisexuality.

Garbino, J., Guttmann, E., & Seeley, J. W. (1986). *The psychologically battered child: Strategies for identification, assessment, and intervention.* San Francisco: Jossey-Bass. Guidelines for identifying, investigating, preventing, and treating child victims of psychological maltreatment.

Gay, P. (1988). *Freud: A life for our time.* New York: Norton. You can add material about Freud's thinking and life to the introductory chapter on theoretical perspectives.

Green, R. (1987). *The "sissy boy syndrome" and the development of homosexuality.* New Haven: Yale University Press. Traces the development of male homosexuality from the early years into adulthood.

Heaslip, J., Van Dyke, D., Hogenson, D., & Vedders, L. (1989). *Young people and drugs: Evaluation and treatment.* Center City, MN: Hazelden. Good for learning about the differences between evaluation and treatment of young people and of adults.

Hersen, M., & Turner, S. M. (Eds.) (1991). *Adult psychopathology & diagnosis.* 2nd ed. New York: Wiley. Chapters follow the DSM diagnostic system in explaining each syndrome, and material is provided on diagnostic criteria, etiology, and assessment.

Higgins, R. L., Snyder, C. R., and Berglas, S. (1990). *Self-handicapping: The paradox that isn't.* New York: Plenum. Explains how and why people increase the odds against their success to justify possible failure.

Hsu, L. K. G. (1990). *Eating Disorders.* New York: Guilford. A coherent review and synthesis of the current thinking and findings on eating disorders.

Kagan, R., & Schlosberg, S. (1989). *Families in perpetual crisis.* New York: Norton. Information about families with long histories of chronic and severe problems.

Kernberg, P. F., Chazan, S. E. (1991). *Children with conduct disorders: A psychotherapy manual.* New York: Basic Books. Examines aspects of the diagnosis applied to at least half of the children in therapy, focusing on the disruptive and oppositional behavior of children with conduct disorders.

Lerman, H. (1986). *A mote in Freud's eye: From psychoanalysis to the psychology of women.* New York: Springer. Examines Freud's attitude toward women and how it influenced his theory. Also traces Freud's influence on present-day psychoanalytic theories. Useful for enriching class discussions on psychoanalytic theory.

Lerner, H. (1990). *The dance of intimacy.* New York: HarperPerennial. How women can explore the nature of their family upbringing to find clues to current difficulties in relationships.

Levenkron, S. (1991). *Obsessive-compulsive disorders.* New York: Warner. Explains the disorder as an attempt to reduce anxiety due to a genetic tendency toward anxiety or painful childhood experiences; suggests ways to reduce symptoms and provides case studies.

Mace, N., & Rabins, P. (1991). *The 36-hour day.* Baltimore: Johns Hopkins University Press. Describe caring for older adults in the early and middle stages of Alzheimer's and related diseases.

Miller, N. (1990). *In search of gay America.* New York: Harper & Row. Information on homosexuality in years past and in contemporary society; good lecture material.

Moyers, B. (1993). *Healing and the mind.* New York: Doubleday. Based on Bill Moyers's popular show on PBS. Provides lots of good lecture material.

Offer, D., & Sabshin, M. (Eds.) (1992). *The diversity of normal behavior: Further contributions to normatology.* New York: Basic Books. Takes the approach that better understanding of normality furthers understanding of the complexities of psychopathology. Seeks to determine why some families adapt well in trying circumstances, and explores cultural aspects of mental health.

Orbach, I. (1988). *Children who don't want to live: Understanding and treating the suicidal child.* San Francisco: Jossey-Bass. Compares adult suicides with child suicides. Explore children's attempts, threats, and messages in the light of personality factors and life circumstances.

Peele, S., & Brodsky, A. (1991). *The truth about addiction and recovery.* New York: Simon & Schuster. Explores addictions to alcohol, drug, cigarettes, food, gambling, and love from a nondisease approach, and shows how values and goals can be used to produce change.

Pillari, V. (1991). *Scapegoating in families: Intergenerational patterns of physical and emotional abuse.* The experience of the scapegoat is described as learning not to live and not knowing how to change. Besides therapy and the healing process, the book covers the nature of scapegoating, and the family of the scapegoat, and the personality of the scapegoated person.

Rodin, J. (1992). *Body traps.* New York: Morrow. Focuses on the relation of a person's body to self-image, and the destructiveness of the standard society has established for women's perceptions of their bodies.

Rosenthal, D. (1963). *The Genain quadruplets.* New York: Basic Books. A source of lecture material on a set of quadruplets, all diagnosed as schizophrenic.

Schaef, A. W., & Fassel, D. (1988). *The addictive organization.* New York: Harper & Row. Applies the twelve-step approach to addictions to the workplace, suggesting that many employees work in dysfunctional workplaces.

Segal, Z. V., & Blatt, S. J. (Eds.) (1993). *The self in emotional distress: Cognitive and psychodynamic perspectives.* New York: Guilford. Examines how the self is involved in the development and treatment of post-traumatic stress disorder, depression, eating disorders, and borderline personality disorder.

Seligman, M. E. P. (1990). *Learned optimism: How to change your mind and your life.* New York: Pocket Books. Based on psychological research, this book gives specific strategies for optimistic thinking.

Simon, S. B., & Simon, S. (1991). *Forgiveness: How to make peace with your past and get on with your life.* How to examine self-blame, denial, anger, resentment, and guilt and how to use a six-stage program to work through pain and isolation. A good source of practical information.

Simons, J. A., Kalichman, S., & Santrock, J. W. (1994). *Human adjustment.* Madison, WI: Brown & Benchmark. In addition to chapters on stress, coping, and health psychology, this text provides detailed descriptions of the most popular and useful self-help books recommended by trained counseling professionals.

Sweeney, T. J. (1989). *Adlerian counseling: A practical approach for a new decade.* 3rd ed. Muncie: Accelerated Development. Focuses on major life tasks, the interrelation of early recollections and present behavior, and their usefulness in therapy. Many of Adler's concepts fit well into an undergraduate abnormal psychology course.

Weinrech, J. D. (1987). *Sexual landscapes: Why we are what we are, why we love whom we love.* New York: Scribner's. Explores the sociobiology of sex, core gender identity, and sexual orientation.

Westkott, M. (1986). *The feminist legacy of Karen Horney.* New Haven: Yale University Press. Examines Karen Horney's theory and its central theme of women's conflict between dependency and ambition. Can tie into many modern topics, including codependency and stress from the need to balance career, marriage, and parenthood.

White, G. L., & Mullen, P. E. (1989). *Jealousy: Theory, research, and clinical strategies.* New York: Guilford. Deals with both normal and pathological romantic jealousies.

Wilson, R. (1989). *Don't panic.* New York: HarperPerennial. Describes a self-help program for coping with panic attacks.

Windle, M., & Searles, J. S. (Eds.) (1990). *Children of alcoholics: Critical perspectives.* New York: Guilford. A wide range of topics and a critical evaluation of COA research.

Wolff, L. (1988). *Postcards from the end of the world: Child abuse in Freud's Vienna.* New York: Atheneum. Can be used to elaborate on the way Freud's zeitgeist influenced his theoretical ideas or to give a historical perspective to your lecture on child abuse.

Wyatt, G. E., & Powell, G. J. (1988). *Lasting effects of child sexual abuse.* Newbury Park, CA: Sage. The lasting effects of child sexual abuse on adult survivors and their families.

Zeanah, C. H., Jr. (Ed.) (1993). *Handbook of infant mental health.* New York: Guilford. Examines the developmental, clinical, and social aspects of infant mental health. Covers the risk factors of poverty, prematurity, adolescent parents, maternal substance abuse, prenatal mental illness, and maltreatment. Looks at several disorders of infancy, including autism, mental retardation, attachment disorders, failure to thrive, communication disorders, and sleep disorders.

General Resources: Media List

One of the first tasks you should attend to as you develop your abnormal psychology course is to decide which media to use and when. It is usually necessary to reserve your media choices even before the semester begins, especially if you want to use the media during a specific class period. You should first check with your college's media department/library to (1) learn its procedures for booking materials; (2) see if the college owns any media on abnormal psychology topics; (3) learn of any budget constraints on your choices; and (4) find out if a collection of media resource catalogs is available for you to peruse. If you want to begin a collection of media catalogs, you can request catalogs from the film distributors listed at the end of this section or by picking up catalogs from film distributors who exhibit their materials at regional or national APA conventions. The newest media materials are screened at these conventions, so that you can discover which items are most appropriate. Some media choices are provided here on some general and popular topics in psychology.

Chapter 2. Models of Psychological Abnormality
Being Abraham Maslow. FML. 30 min. Video. Maslow talks about his childhood, education, professional conflicts, and overall philosophy.
B. F. Skinner and Behavior Change: Research, Practice, and Promise. RP. 45 min. Video. Behavioral interventions in various settings, including fear of dental procedures, learning social skills at a youth center, controlling epilepsy in a hospital , and working with a developmentally disabled child at home.
C. G. Jung: A Matter of Heart. IM. 107 min. Video. Jung's biography.
Freud: The Hidden Nature of Man. IM. 29 min. Video ($149). Examines Freud's theories of psychoanalysis, the Oedipus complex, the unconscious, infantile sexuality, and the relationship of the id, ego, and superego.
Mysteries of the Mind. FHS. 58 min. Video ($179). This program explores neurochemical and genetic factors in manic-depressive and obsessive-compulsive disorders, alcoholism, and other mood disorders.
Psychological defenses. IM. Part I, 45 min; Part II, 45 min. Video (each $149). Part I explains repression, denial, and regression. Part II distinguishes healthy and unhealthy uses of defense mechanisms, including projection, rationalization, identification, displacement, reaction formation, and sublimation.

Chapter 5. Treatments for Abnormal Psychological Functioning
Approaches to Therapy. RMI. 30 min. Video ($90). Therapists explain the techniques they use and how one approach differs from another.
Behavior Modification. IM. 45 min. Video ($149). Investigates modern techniques of behavior modification and their use to help people break habits, overcome anxieties, and improve social skills.
Process Psychology. TA. 90 min. Video ($50). Describes a therapeutic approach that incorporates dreamwork, bodywork, family systems, and social concerns.
Psychotherapy Pro and Con. FHS. 28 min. Video ($149). Explores the advantages and disadvantages of counseling.
Rational Emotive Therapy. RP. 30 min. Video ($495). Illustrates the basic rational emotive therapy paradigm and shows how different therapists apply its concepts.

Therapy Choices. RMI. 30 min. Video ($90). Focuses on alternatives to traditional psychotherapy and evaluates various kinds of therapy.

Chapter 6. Anxiety Disorders and
Chapter 7. Treatments for Anxiety Disorders

Breathing Away Stress. FHS. 30 min. Video ($140). Deep-breathing exercises designed to manage stress and promote relaxation.

Burnout. MTI. 26 min. Video ($470). Reveals the danger signs of burnout and practical ways to deal with it.

Dealing with Stress. FHS. 39 min. Video ($149). How to deal with stress without hurting job productivity; how to change stress into motivation for positive achievement.

Fear Itself. FHS. 26 min. Video ($149). Focuses on agoraphobia and the use of drug therapy, individual therapy, and support groups in treatment.

Getting a Handle on Stress. FHS. 26 min. Video ($149). Examines risk for stress-related diseases, the effects of prolonged stress, and ways to handle it.

Male Stress Syndrome. FHS. 26 min. Video ($149). Distinguishes between the ways men and women experience stress; discusses causes and cures of male stress syndrome.

Managing Stress. FHS. 19 min. Video ($149). Distinguishes between positive stress, which can strengthen the immune system, and negative stress, which can increase the likelihood of illness; shows the effects of various types of stress, and how an individual can reduce stress.

Mysteries of the Mind. FHS. 58 min. Video ($179). Explores the neurochemical and genetic components of manic-depressive and obsessive-compulsive disorders, alcoholism, and other mood disorders.

Obsessive-Compulsive Disorder: The Boy Who Couldn't Stop Washing. FHS. 28 min. Video ($149). Examines obsessive-compulsive behavior designed to keep something terrible from happening.

Panic! FHS. 26 min. Video ($149). Examines agoraphobia, panic attacks, and fears of poisoning and flying.

Posttraumatic Stress Disorder. FHS. 28 min. Video ($149). Examines PTSD resulting from the Vietnam War and other traumas.

Progressive Relaxation Training: A Clinical Demonstration. RP. 20 min. Video ($365). Identifies the sixteen muscle groups involved in relaxation training and shows how the procedure is done.

The Psychobiology of Stress. IM. 10 min. Video ($129). Investigates how the brain controls the stress response through regulation of the nervous system and of hormonal activity.

The Relaxation Response. FHS. 30 min. Video ($149). Explains the relaxation response and guides students through some exercises designed to trigger it.

Stress. FHS. 26 min. Video ($149). Examines the many ways stress can affect people of all ages and demonstrates proven methods of coping with life pressures.

Stress to Your Advantage. MTI. 30 min. Video ($149). What is the secret to stress-resistant hardiness?

Understanding Psychological Trauma. Part I: Learning from Survivors. Part II: Healing and Recovery. BAX. 29 min., 32 min. Video ($595). Survivors of trauma recount their experiences and their journeys toward recovery, and professionals in the area of post-traumatic stress provide commentary.

Understanding Stress. IM. 12 min. Video ($129). Explains stress and describes the key elements of an effective stress response.

Women and Stress. FHS. 28 min. Video ($149). Examines typical ways women deal with stress.

Chapter 8. Mood Disorders and
Chapter 9. Treatments for Mood Disorders

Beating the Depression Blues. MTI. 30 min. Video ($80). Discusses the incidence of depression, its causes, and its treatment.

Depression. FHS. 19 min. Video ($149). Explains the differences between occasional mood changes and depression.

Depression. PBS. 60 min. Video ($60). Examines depression and bipolar disorders, suicide, and explanations of depression based on research.

Depression: Beyond the Darkness. IM. 50 min. Video ($89). Examines misconceptions about the nature of depression and explore various theories about its causation.

Depression: Biology of the Blues. FHS. 26 min. Video ($149). Focuses on the biological causes of depression, the difference between sadness and depression, the functions of drug therapies and electroconvulsive therapy, and the neurotransmitter imbalances involved.

Grief. FHS. 50 min. Video ($149). An in-depth look at paintings depicting grief by Giotto, Grunewald, El Greco, David, and Bacon.

Men, Depression, and Desperation. FHS. 28 min. Video ($149). Men can be overwhelmed by crisis—death, divorce, job loss—and often seek escape through isolation, drugs, or even suicide.

Mysteries of the Mind. FHS. 58 min. Video ($179). Explores the neurochemical and genetic components of manic-depressive and obsessive-compulsive disorders, alcoholism, and other mood disorders.

Chapter 10. Suicide

Childhood's End: A Look at Adolescent Suicide. FML. 28 min. Video. Explores the emotional and complex issues surrounding adolescent suicide.

Dead Serious. MTI. 24 min. Video. Examines the major factors that contribute to teenage suicide.

Depression and Suicide. PBS. 30 min. Video ($65). Focuses on two high schools at which a student has recently committed suicide.

Everything to Live For. FHS. 52 min. Video. Features two attempted suicides and two completed suicides among teens and their affects on survivors.

Gifted Adolescents and Suicide. FHS. 26 min. Video. Explains the suicide risks of superachieving teens.

Suicide: Teenage Crisis. CRM. 10 min. Film. Discusses the prevalence of suicide among teens and suggests possible solutions.

Chapter 11. Psychological Factors and Physical Disorders

AIDS: Changing the Rules. PBS. 30 min. Video ($40). A compelling educational documentary aimed at protecting adult heterosexuals against AIDS.

AIDS: Face to Face. FHS. 28 min. Video ($149). Donahue converses with AIDS patients about courage, fear, remorse, and resignation.

AIDS: Facts over Fears. MTI. 10 min. Video. ($200). Barbara Walters addresses the ways in which AIDS is contracted.

AIDS: No Sad Songs. FML. 30 min. Film, video. Focuses on the emotional and psychological effects of AIDS on victims, friends, and family.

AIDS: The Women Speak. FHS. 28 min. Video ($149). Deals with mothers who lose a child to AIDS, social workers who work with AIDS patients, foster mothers of HIV-positive babies, and women infected with AIDS.

Controlling Pain. FHS. 19 min. Video ($149). Examines risk for stress-related diseases, the effects of prolonged stress, and ways to handle it.

Headaches. MTI. 29 min. Video ($80). Distinguishes among the many kinds of headaches and examines a variety of treatments.

Headaches: When the Pain Won't Stop. FHS. 19 min. Video ($149). Distinguishes among tension, cluster, and migraine headaches; how to diagnose serious problems and how to treat headaches.

Hypertension: Your Blood Pressure is Showing and Stress: Is Your Lifestyle is Killing You? PBS. 60 min. Video ($70). The first half explores the causes and effects of high blood pressure; the second half deals with ways to control stress that affects one's health.

Imagery in Healing. TA. 90 min. Video ($50). Explores ways in which mental images mediate between our conscious intentions and our physiology, including the functioning of the immune system.

Insomnia. FHS. 19 min. Video ($149). Explains the characteristics of different types and levels of sleep/sleeplessness; explains circadian rhythm and the consequences of its disturbance, sleep apnea and treatments for it, REM behavior disorder, narcolepsy, and the effects of sleeping pills.

Managing Stress. FHS. 19 min. Video ($149). Distinguishes between positive stress, which can strengthen the immune system, and negative stress, which can increases the likelihood of illness; shows the effects of various types of stress, and how one can reduce stress.

Mind/Body Wellness. RMI. 30 min. Video ($90). Examines the relationships between our emotional and personal well-being and our health.

Techniques for Mind/Body Wellness. RMI. 30 min. Video ($90). Teaches methods to achieve emotional and physical well-being.

Multiple Sclerosis. FHS. 26 min. Video. Discusses the symptoms and nature of multiple sclerosis, showing how the disease has affected four individuals.

The Psychobiology of Stress. IM. 10 min. Video ($129). Investigates how the brain controls the stress response through regulation of the nervous system and of hormonal activity.

Stress and Immune Function. FHS. 26 min. Video ($149). Examines the relationship between stress and illness and the studies that link malfunctions of the immune system to stress.

Western Medicine Meets East. FHS. 26 min. Video ($149). Examines the use of acupuncture and other traditional Eastern medical techniques as anesthetics during surgery and as treatment for such ailments as arthritis and backache.

Will to Be Well. MTI. 30 min. Video ($80). Investigates the effects of attitude and hope on illness, the field of psycho-neuroimmunology, and exercises designed to relieve headache pain; interviews Norman Cousins.

Chapter 12. Eating Disorders

Anorexia and Bulimia. FHS. 19 min. Video ($149). Explains the addictive nature of anorexia and bulimia and their possible effects.

Bulimia. CRM. 12 min. Film. Describes bulimia and the motives of its victims.

Bulimia: The Binge-Purge Obsession. BAX. 25 min. Video ($385). Explores the causes and effects of bulimia; topics include the social uses of food, dieting hazards, the sociocultural drive toward thinness, and health risks.

The Diet Dilemma. FHS. 56 min. Video ($159). Compares various diet programs and report on diet scams, dieting tips, and diet food tastes through the experiences of five people.

Dying to Be Thin. BAX. 25 min. Video ($295). Examines the lives of several people who literally risked death in order to be thin.

Eating Disorders. FHS. 26 min. Video ($149). Covers the personality profiles of typical anorexia patients and discusses how the disorder develops and how they may more from anorexia to bulimia; indicates how friends and families can help and what treatment is like.

Eating Disorders: The Slender Trap. RP. 21 min. Video ($385). Shows how easy it is to fall into the trap of anorexia nervosa, bulimia, or compulsive overeating.

Heavy Load. BAX. 36 min. Video ($295). The story of a mother struggling with an overwhelming compulsion to each—her denial of the problem, procrastination, hiding and sneaking of food; looks at the effects of her disorder on her family and her experience in a support group.

Landscapes and Interiors. FHS. 26 min. Video ($149). Extraordinary close-up filming of the body's exterior and its interior. Useful in combination with a discussion of body image.

Less than Nothing: Anorexia. IM. Video. A case study of an adolescent girl with anorexia.

Looks: How They Affect Your Life. MTI. 51 min. Video ($199). The social and psychological effects of achieving and failing to achieve the American standard of beauty.

A Matter of Fat. FHS. 26 min. Video ($149). Examines the biochemical and genetic explanations for obesity, the seesaw relationship between dieting and regaining lost weight, and the set-point theory.

Psychomotor Therapy of Anorexia Nervosa Patients. FHS. 27 min. Video ($149). Follows an anorexic patient through her first week of psychomotor therapy as she evaluates her distorted perception of her body and sets goals to achieve a realistic body image, enjoyment of her body, awareness and control of hyperactivity, and improved social skills.

The Waist Land: Eating Disorders. MTI. 23 min. Video ($350). Examines both bulimia and anorexia.

The Waist Land: Why Diets Don't Work. MTI. 23 min. Video ($350). Looks at our obsession with slimness and the effects of rapid weight loss/rapid weight gain cycles.

Weight Control. FHS. 19 min. Video ($149). Explains the problems of losing weight and keeping it off; focuses on establishing healthy eating patterns and lifestyles early on; examines the role of heredity in obesity.

You Can Be Too Thin: Understanding Anorexia and Bulimia. IM. Video. A case study of one woman's eating disorder and treatment.

Chapter 13. Substance-Related Disorders

Addiction and the Family. FHS. 19 min. Video. The family's role in an addicted person's recovery.

Addictions. PBS. 60 min. Video ($60). Emphasizes the physiological aspects of substance addiction.

Adult Children of Alcoholics: A Family Secret. FHS. 52 min. Video ($159). Famous adult children of alcoholics (e.g., Suzanne Somers, Susan Sullivan, Louie Anderson) speak about the effects of growing up in homes organized around an adult's drinking pattern.

Alcohol Addiction. FHS. 28 min. Video ($149). Access and attitudes explain why people begin to drink, and genetic predispositions explain why some people cannot stop.

The Broken Cord with Louise Erdrich and Michael Dorris. PBS. 30 min. Video ($40). Discusses Native American traditions of spirit and memory, alcoholism, and fetal alcohol syndrome.

A Chemical Called Cocaine. MTI. 30 min. Video ($80). Explains the effects of cocaine on the brain and body, and examines new techniques to fight cocaine addiction.

Circle of Recovery. IM. 60 min. Video ($99). Focuses on seven African-American men who are overcoming alcohol and drug addiction.

Cocaine: The End of the Line. FHS. 58 min. Video ($159). Focuses on understanding, preventing, and overcoming cocaine addiction.

Crack. FHS. 28 min. Video. Examines signs of crack use, long-term consequences of its use, and treatment for the addicted person.

Crack Street, USA: First Person Experiences. IM. 29 min. Video. Former users explain the devastating effects of crack.

Crystal. FHS. 56 min. Video. A documentary about crystal and its effects on users.

Designer Drugs. FHS. 28 min. Video. Examines synthetic drugs and the permanent brain damage they may cause.

Drinking and Driving: The Toil, the Tears. PBS. 60 min. Video ($50). The true story of a television reporter whose driving while drunk resulted in a man's death.

Growing Up in Smoke. MTI. 15 min. Film. Messages to young people about cigarette use; contrasts the tobacco industry's and health officials' positions on the effects of smoking.

Kick the Habit. FHS. 19 min. Video ($149). Focuses on the effects of cigarette smoking and how to quit.

Kids Under the Influence. FHS. 58 min. Video ($159). Explores the neurochemical and genetic components of manic-depressive and obsessive-compulsive disorders, alcoholism, and other mood disorders.

No Butts. MTI. 30 min. Video ($80). Looks at the pleasures and hazards of smoking and the affects of "passive smoking." Includes the antismoking TV commercial filmed by Yul Brenner just before his death from lung cancer in 1985 and the "smoking fetus" commercial. Former three-pack-a-day smoker Mary Tyler Moore discusses how she quit only when she was threatened by complications of diabetes.

Over-the-Counter Medicines. FHS. 26 min. Video ($149). Explains the possible problems that can occur when nonprescription drugs are taken carelessly; focuses on special concerns of the elderly.

Shadow of Addiction. BAS. 25 min. Video ($250). A recovering heroin addict takes the viewer through the darkest sides of addiction, from a crack house to death row.

Smoking/Emphysema: A fight for Breath. CRM. 12 min. Film, video. Shows the difference in functioning between healthy and diseased lungs.

Smoking . . . Hazardous to Your Health and Smoking . . . Kicking the Habit. PBS. 60 min. Video ($70). The first half looks at the effects of smoking on our bodies; the second half explores ways to quit smoking.

Steroids and Sports. FHS. 19 min. Video. Examines the use of steroids to increase performance and the physical risks associated with them.

Chapter 14. Sexual Disorders and Gender Identity Disorders

The Battered Woman. PBS. 60 min. Video ($70). Seven abused women reveal their experiences; discusses causes of this problem and responses to it.

Boys Will Be . . . BAX. 33 min. Video ($250). Looks at domestic violence by focusing on the characteristics of a successful, middle-class, intelligent, friendly wife batterer.

Date Rape. FHS. 28 min. Video ($149). An adaptation of a Donahue Program on the subject of date rape.

Homosexuality: Nature vs. Nurture. FHS. 26 min. Video. Biological, genetic, psychological, and cultural explanations of sexual orientations.

Men Who Molest: Children Who Survive. FML. 52 min. Film, video. Examines four child molesters and their treatment; child victims, their families, and their treatment.

My Husband Is Going to Kill Me. PBS. 60 min. Video ($60). Looks at domestic violence and the death of one abused wife.

No More Secrets. FHS. 24 min. Video ($149). Deals with childhood sexual abuse and the possible long-term damage it inflicts.

Three Styles of Marital Conflict. RP. 14 min. Video ($25). Shows the styles of the Hidden Agenda, the Passive Partner, and the Underadequate/Overadequate.

Chapter 15. Schizophrenia and
Chapter 16. Treatments for Schizophrenia

Schizophrenia. FHS. 28 min. Video ($149). Dr. Fuller Torrey reviews the suspected causes and symptoms of schizophrenia and the prognosis and family support of people with the disorder.

Schizophrenia: Captor of the Mind. MTI. 29 min. Looks at schizophrenia and how medical science helps people who have the disorder.

Schizophrenia: The Voices Within/The Community Without. FHS. 19 in. Video ($149). Discusses symptoms of schizophrenia and describes the psychotropic medications used to control them; focuses on the effects of deinstitutionalization.

Chapter 17. Personality Disorders

Borderline Syndrome? Personality Disorder of Our Time. IM. 74 min. Video ($250). Examines the symptoms, causes, development, and treatment of borderline syndrome.
Personality Disorders. IM. 45 min. Video ($169). Dramatizes antisocial, paranoid, schizoid, avoidant, narcissistic, passive-aggressive, histrionic, and compulsive disorders.

Chapter 19. Problems of Childhood and Adolescence

Babies Are People Too. CDF. 27 min. Film. A film aimed at stopping the abuse of infants.
Battered Teens. FI. 16 min. Film. Examines the lives of battered and neglected adolescents.
Child Abuse: Breaking the Cycle. IM. Video. Three adults tell their stories about being abused or abusers.
Childhood Physical Abuse. FHS. 26 min. Video ($149). Covers a range of physical abuses to which children are subjected.
Children in Peril. IM. 22 min. Video. A tour of several agencies and hospitals where battered children are treated.
Children of Divorce. FHS. IM. 28 min. Video. Looks at the pain, confusion, guilt, and displacement children experience when their parents divorce.
Divorce: A Teenage Perspective. MTI. 15 in. Film. Three teenagers discuss their feelings of isolation when their parents divorce and their difficulties in coping with their alienated parents.
Do Children Also Divorce? FML. 30 min. Video. Shows the stress experienced by children of various ages when their parents divorce and the help they need to deal with their negative reactions.
Generations of Violence. FML. 55 min. Video. Shows how it happens that some abused children grow up to become abusive parents and suggests solutions to the problem.
Hidden Family Agendas. MTI. 30 min. Video ($80). Examines the causes and cures of dysfunctional families.
Incest, the Family Secret. FML. 57 min. Video. Women's stories of being traumatized in their youth by incestuous fathers and their mothers' failure to protect them; describe the treatment of one abusive youth.
Learning Disabilities. FHS. 19 min. Video. A case study of a 9-year-old, revealing the symptoms, diagnosis, and treatment of learning disabilities.
May's Miracle: A Retarded Youth with a Gift for Music. FML., 28 min. Focuses on a blind, retarded, cerebral-palsied idiot savant who is musically gifted.
The Unquiet Death of Eli Creekmore. FML. 55 min. Video. A documentary on a case of brutal child abuse in which a preschooler was beaten to death for crying at the dinner table.

Chapter 20. Problems of Aging

Elder Abuse. IM. 40 min. Video ($335). Explores the abuse of old people from the points of view of five victims.
Grandma Didn't Wave Back. FHS. 24 min. Video. A family deals with a grandmother who has Alzheimer's disease.

Special Video Recommendations

The video package, *Video Segments for Abnormal Psychology,* that accompanies the textbook, includes excerpts from many superb clinical documentaries. While segments are ideal for augmenting lectures, it is also often useful to make viewing a full documentary an assignment for the enitre class or for individual students in the library. The following videos are heartily recommended for such use.

GENERAL INTEREST
Madness by Johnathan Miller
Lionheart Television International, Inc.
630 Fifth Avenue, Suite 2220
New York, NY 100111
(212) 373-4100

GENERAL TREATMENT
Demonstrations of the Cognitive Therapy of Depression
Aaron T. Beck, M.D., Director
The Beck Institute for Cognitive Therapy and Research
GSB Building, Suite 700
1 Belmont Avenue
Bala Cynwyd, PA 19004-1610
(610) 664-3020

The Royal Road—Psychoanalytic Approaches to the Dream
Menninger Video
Box 829
Topeka, KS 66601-0829
(913) 273-7500

Clincial Choice Points
Arnold Lazarus
56 Herrontown Circle
Princeton, NJ 08540

APA Psychotherapy Videotape Series: Multimodal Therapy
American Psychological Association
750 First Street, NE
Washington, DC 20002

Behavioral Therapy Demonstrations
Penn State Audio-Visual Services
Universtiy Division of Media and Learning Resources, Special Services Bldg.
Penn State University
University Park, PA 16802
(800) 826-0132

ANXIETY DISORDERS & THEIR TREATMENTS
Phobias: Overcoming the Fear
Filmmakers Library, Inc.
122 E. 58th Street, Suite 703A
New York, NY 10022
(212) 889-3820

MOOD DISORDERS & THEIR TREATMENTS
The Mind: Depression
PBS Video
1320 Braddock Place
Alexandria, VA 22314-1698
(800) 344-3337

PSYCHOLOGICAL FACTORS & PHYSICAL DISORDERS
Mysteries of the Mind
National Geographic Society
1145 17th Street, NW
Washington DC 20036-4688
(800) 638-7337

The Keys of Paradise
Lionheart Television International, Inc.
630 Fifth Avenue, Suite 2220
New York, NY 100111
(212) 373-4100

EATING DISORDERS
The Waist Land: Eating Disorders in America
Coronet/MTI Film & Video
4350 Equity Drive
Columbus, OH 43228
(800) 777-8100

SCHIZOPHRENIA & TREATMENTS FOR SCHIZOPHENIA
The Brain: Madness

PBS Video	or	Annenberg/CPB Project
1320 Braddock Place		P.O. Box 2345
Alexandria, VA 22314-1698		South Burlington, VT 05407-2345
(800) 344-3337		1-800 LEARNER

PROBLEMS OF CHILDHOOD & ADOLESCENCE
Behavioral Treatment of Autistic Children
Focus International
1160 E. Jericho Turnpike
Huntington, NY 11743
(516 549-5320

PROBLEMS OF AGING
Alzheimer's: Coping with Catastrophic Reaction
Health Sciences Consortium
201 Silver Cedar Court
Chapel Hill, NC 27514-1517
(919) 942-8731

ADDRESSES OF MEDIA DISTRIBUTORS

BAX   Baxley Media Groups, 110 West Main St., Urbana, IL 61801-2700; 217-384-4838.

BCN   Beacon Films, P.O. Box 575, 1250 Washington St., Norwood, MA 02062.

BF   Benchmark Films, Inc., 145 Scarborough Rd., Briarcliff Manor, NY 10510.

CDF   Cambridge Documentary Films, P.O. Box 385, Cambridge, MA 02139

CM   Concept Media, P.O. Box 19542, Irvine, CA 92714.

CPB   The Annenberg/CPB Project, Intellimation. P.O. Box 1922 AH, Santa Barbara, CA 93116-1922.

CRM   CRM/McGraw-Hill Films, 110 15th St., Del Mar, CA 92014.

DAV   Davison Films, Inc., 231 E St., Davis, CA 95616; 916-753-9604.

FHS   Films for the Humanities and Sciences, P.O. Box 2053, Princeton, NJ 08543-2053; 609-452-1128.

FI   Films, Inc., 5547 Ravenswood Ave., Chicago, IL 60640.

FML   Filmmakers Library, Inc., 122 E. 58th St., Suite 703A, New York, NY 10022.

HRM   Human Relations Media, 10 E. 53rd St., New York. NY 10022.

IM   Insight Media, 121 West 85th St., New York, NY 10024; 212-721-6316.

MTI   Coronet/MTI Film & Video, 108 Wilmot Rd., Deerfield, IL 60015; 800-621-2131.

ND   New Day Films, 121 W. 27th St., Suite 902, New York, NY 10001; 212-645-8210.

PBS   Public Broadcasting System, 1320 Braddock Pl., Alexandria, VA 22313; 703-739-5000.

PER   Perennial Education, Inc., 1825 Willow Rd., Northfield, IL 60091.

RMI   RMI Media Productions, Inc., 2807 W. 47th St., Shawness Mission, KS 66205; 800-745-5480.

RP   Research Press, Dept. N, P.O. Box 9177, Champaign, IL 61826.

TA   Thinking Allowed, 2560 Ninth St., Suite 123, Berkeley, CA 94710; 510-548-4415.